OECD Insurance Statistics 2018

2010-2017

OECD
BETTER POLICIES FOR BETTER LIVES

Please cite this publication as:
OECD (2019), *OECD Insurance Statistics 2018*, OECD Publishing, Paris.
https://doi.org/10.1787/g2g9fad8-en

ISBN 978-92-64-09566-3 (print)
ISBN 978-92-64-31310-1 (pdf)

OECD Insurance Statistics
ISSN 2307-8421 (print)
ISSN 2307-843X (online)

The statistical data for Israel are supplied by and under the responsibility of the relevant Israeli authorities. The use of such data by the OECD is without prejudice to the status of the Golan Heights, East Jerusalem and Israeli settlements in the West Bank under the terms of international law.

Corrigenda to OECD publications may be found on line at: *www.oecd.org/about/publishing/corrigenda.htm*.

Table of contents

Conventional signs and abbreviations

Signs and abbreviations

c	Confidential data
..	Not available
.	Decimal point
|	Break in series

ISO country codes and abbreviations for currency

	ISO code	Currency	Abbreviation
Australia	AUS	dollar	AUD
Austria	AUT	euro	EUR
Belgium	BEL	euro	EUR
Canada	CAN	dollar	CAD
Chile	CHL	peso	CLP
Czech Republic	CZE	koruna	CZK
Denmark	DNK	krone	DKK
Estonia	EST	euro	EUR
Finland	FIN	euro	EUR
France	FRA	euro	EUR
Germany	DEU	euro	EUR
Greece	GRC	euro	EUR
Hungary	HUN	forint	HUF
Iceland	ISL	króna	ISK
Ireland	IRL	euro	EUR
Israel	ISR	sheqel	ILS
Italy	ITA	euro	EUR
Japan	JPN	yen	JPY
Korea	KOR	won	KRW
Latvia	LVA	euro	EUR
Lithuania	LTU	euro	EUR
Luxembourg	LUX	euro	EUR
Mexico	MEX	peso	MXN
Netherlands	NLD	euro	EUR
New Zealand	NZL	dollar	NZD
Norway	NOR	krone	NOK
Poland	POL	zloty	PLN
Portugal	PRT	euro	EUR
Slovak Republic	SVK	euro	EUR
Slovenia	SVN	euro	EUR
Spain	ESP	euro	EUR
Sweden	SWE	krona	SEK
Switzerland	CHE	franc	CHF
Turkey	TUR	lira	TRY
United Kingdom	GBR	pound	GBP
United States	USA	dollar	USD

Common definitions and notes

Notes on data sources

All the data in the statistical tables of each country have been reported by the relevant national insurance authorities. Regarding comparative tables of indicators, the data are mainly drawn from the tables by country. Data on exchange rates are taken from the IMF International Financial Statistics database. Data on population are taken from the IMF publication *World Economic Outlook*. Data on GDP come from the OECD Annual National Accounts database for OECD countries and from the IMF publication *World Economic Outlook* for all the other countries.

> To achieve greater clarity, the number of variables selected and displayed in this publication has been limited. Data have been extracted from the Global Insurance Statistics database. The complete database can be accessed online at the following link:
>
> OECD Insurance Statistics, *http://dx.doi.org/10.1787/ins-data-en.*

A significant effort has been made to achieve comparability among countries. Definitions, classifications, calculation methods, and units have been standardised as far as possible.

General notes

Life and non-life categories follow the definitions used in national law. However, the premiums for accident and sickness insurance underwritten by life companies should be included in non-life figures.

Up until 2008, the insurance business is broken down between life and non-life business. As of 2009, the insurance business is broken down between the business of pure life, pure non-life and composite undertakings. The insurance business of composite undertakings is further broken down between life and non-life components. Some countries do not allow for insurance undertakings to be active in both life and non-life insurance business and therefore composite insurance undertakings do not exist in these countries. In other countries (e.g., Austria, Hungary, Mexico, Spain) however, composite insurance undertakings account for more than 25% of all insurance undertakings operating in these countries. Therefore, to have comparable data across years for life business data (respectively non-life), one has to sum up the life (respectively non-life) business of pure life (respectively non-life) undertakings and the life (respectively non-life) business of composite undertakings as of 2009.

Figures provided for the number of companies and for insurance premiums should include all insurance companies licensed or authorised in the reporting country, *including* professional reinsurers, whether or not these are controlled, but *excluding* any statutory system of social security administered by the State.

Domestic companies means those companies incorporated under national law, together with those companies in the reporting country which are unincorporated, but excluding the branches and agencies of foreign companies.

Foreign-controlled companies means those domestic companies controlled by foreign interests, such "control" being defined according to national law (see the definition of foreign controlled companies in notes by country). The data of *foreign-controlled companies* are part of those of *Domestic companies*.

Foreign companies means companies incorporated outside the reporting country.

In 2016, a new supervisory framework for insurance and reinsurance companies was implemented in the European Union (EU) and the European Economic Area (EEA). This framework includes harmonised reporting requirements across EU/EEA countries. These requirements led to changes in national data collection, which may hamper the data comparability with the ones collected before 2016 for some countries which only collect data with the Solvency II framework.

International Comparisons:

Detailed metadata at: *http://metalinks.oecd.org/ins/20190221/0f8b*.

Country tables

In this part, the main insurance statistics are presented through separate tables for each OECD member country. Figures refer to the calendar year. The premiums and other amounts are described in millions of the national currency unit.

International comparisons

Table 1. Balance sheet and income, direct insurance (All insurance companies)

2017

Million US dollars

	Gross claims payments	Gross operating expenses	Commissions	Outstanding claims provision (changes)	Total assets	Gross technical provisions	Gross technical provisions unit-linked	Shareholders' equity	Net income
Argentina	8 225	3 611	2 197	-2 843	26 478	6 851	..	5 786	1 402
Australia	57 601	11 067	3 109	..	249 927	56 518	..	33 477	3 987
Austria	16 949	983	3 586	435	156 412	110 851	23 240	13 061	..
Belgium	30 447	3 527	3 754	488	341 098	294 059	42 907	15 458	2 553
Bolivia	259	248	45	..	1 010	485	..	1 496	27
Brazil	14 445	14 087	6 495	-20	303 854	209 531	176 660	26 373	5 422
Canada	..	..	..	..	..	..	..	..	..
Chile	8 250	1 902	1 007	2 709	71 249	61 709	6 148	7 039	954
Colombia	259	248	45	..	1 010	485	..	1 496	27
Costa Rica	635	260	197	38	3 975	1 517	0	1 656	125
Cuba	..	..	..	..	..	..	..	..	..
Czech Republic	3 881	1 794	341	99	22 844	5 790	4 377	3 452	468
Denmark	23 996	2 567	342	27 425	527 790	426 207	175 411	33 057	2 714
Ecuador	..	..	..	..	..	..	..	..	..
El Salvador	..	..	..	..	..	..	..	..	..
Estonia	447	194	..	..	2 246	1 263	567	510	81
Finland	8 353	1 396	364	-515	96 906	79 522	45 260	6 862	1 417
France	277 873	49 663	..	22 213	3 291 629	2 640 735	420 304	..	..
Germany	173 383	16 980	20 257	11 338	1 884 869	1 714 223	133 159	69 382	2 887
Greece	2 248	1 173	..	..	20 293	14 652	2 883	4 227	..
Guatemala	537	273	142	..	1 358	650	..	489	103
Honduras	203	..	..	..	..	..	..	..	..
Hong Kong, China	2 524	623	840	..	..	..	..	..	..
Hungary	2 165	883	543	63	10 161	8 527	4 587	1 025	236
India	57 694	13 276	5 608	19 629	584 522	..	..	13 006	1 072
Indonesia	10 805	3 495	1 586	108	43 672	34 661	12 851	11 482	1 923
Iceland	426	130	..	..	1 450	718	60	563	91
Ireland	29 179	1 125	2 853	..	367 530	322 768	255 952	29 364	..
Israel[1]	10 445	1 928	2 074	821	148 412	130 739	88 474	7 219	889
Italy	108 547	15 297	12 108	-1 602	1 017 708	874 824	166 225	80 107	6 722
Japan	304 173	71 236	11 949	19 301	3 888 262	3 057 704	..	141 278	20 366
Korea	..	..	..	..	..	..	..	..	..
Latvia	407	103	46	21	850	592	68	195	18
Lithuania	368	179	8	-24	1 760	1 295	600	348	34
Luxembourg	17 612	2 481	1 486	460	229 874	216 427	151 231	6 426	521
Malaysia	8 673	2 359	1 291	43	71 436	58 017	11 091	6 944	1 132
Mexico	13 321	1 691	3 738	6 222	74 381	56 873	..	10 655	2 606
Netherlands	86 799	9 180	..	-2 454	578 322	467 927	123 639	67 834	335
New Zealand	5 855	8 072	986	..	20 445	..	..	5 625	697
Nicaragua	99	..	..	..	..	..	..	..	..
Norway	12 966	2 322	460	-206	209 973	177 322	36 220	21 970	2 930
Panama	..	..	..	..	..	..	..	..	..
Paraguay	186	173	52	34	583	411	..	229	29
Peru	2 522	1 014	449	-5	13 934	10 260	..	2 185	257
Poland	10 542	4 108	469	578	56 478	43 002	16 976	10 468	1 507
Portugal	10 798	1 851	798	530	64 543	54 676	14 741	6 607	365
Puerto Rico	..	..	..	..	..	..	..	..	..
Russia	8 959	6 358	3 501	3 603	42 181	25 144	..	10 512	1 443
Singapore	14 823	1 921	2 078	..	175 986	138 047	..	23 123	2 570
Slovak Republic	..	..	..	..	9 698	6 048	1 753	..	..
Slovenia	1 613	511	117	13	8 608	6 291	1 444	1 734	141
South Africa	..	..	..	..	..	..	..	..	..
Spain	52 993	10 166	6 210	905	366 341	261 598	18 638	50 037	5 587
Sri Lanka	636	294	126	191	4 709	991	36	1 859	444
Sweden	16 730	3 405	1 086	32 825	570 748	219 968	136 424	139 560	18 068
Switzerland	52 032	4 543	5 441	1 594	487 087	360 861	..	49 461	6 429
Thailand	..	..	..	..	..	..	..	..	..
Tunisia	..	..	..	..	..	..	..	..	..
Turkey	5 951	2 450	1 912	1 252	39 410	14 594	..	5 143	993
United Kingdom	370 999	38 892	..	-25 013	3 249 364	2 750 314	1 730 845	234 820	..
United States	1 405 768	307 317	102 169	61 950	6 000 043	845 432	..	1 211 880	99 949
Uruguay	514	309	178	532	4 872	3 931	..	641	76

.. Not available

Note: Detailed metadata at: *http://metalinks.oecd.org/ins/20190221/11be*.

1. Information on data for Israel: *http://oe.cd/israel-disclaimer*.

Source: Balance sheet and income, OECD Insurance Statistics (database)

Table 2. Balance sheet and income, direct insurance (Life insurance companies)
2017

Million US dollars

	Gross claims payments	Gross operating expenses	Commissions	Outstanding claims provision (changes)	Total assets	Gross technical provisions	Gross technical provisions unit-linked	Shareholders' equity	Net income
Argentina	272	139	22	2	4 181	3 437	..	478	153
Australia	33 405	5 251	1 927	..	166 495	..	..	14 758	1 471
Austria	1 101	47	82	11	13 207	11 116	4 297	437	..
Belgium	587	57	63	-20	13 437	11 738	1 260	716	48
Bolivia	98	89	20	..	635	405	..	527	8
Brazil	531	1 736	370	-17	165 347	120 238	117 793	9 090	2 039
Canada	..	..	..	..	..	..	..	..	..
Chile	5 915	1 128	509	2 674	64 660	56 831	6 148	5 801	901
Colombia	98	89	20	..	635	405	..	527	8
Costa Rica	..	..	..	0	0	0	0	..	..
Cuba	..	..	..	..	..	..	..	..	..
Czech Republic	281	96	3	3	2 310	2 075	987	164	19
Denmark	17 113	753	54	26 907	499 210	410 445	175 411	24 482	1 357
Ecuador	..	..	..	..	..	..	..	..	..
El Salvador	..	..	..	..	..	..	..	..	..
Estonia	c	c	..	..	c	c	c	c	c
Finland	4 770	400	152	-82	74 848	66 833	45 260	2 701	669
France	164 049	18 169	..	19 731	653 783	565 593	89 874	..	..
Germany	77 838	4 403	5 488	307	1 273 862	1 193 802	133 101	19 450	652
Greece	254	43	..	..	3 499	2 887	151	474	..
Guatemala	..	..	..	..	..	..	..	..	..
Honduras	..	..	..	..	..	..	..	..	..
Hong Kong, China	..	..	..	..	..	..	..	..	..
Hungary	628	127	64	4	3 427	3 116	1 555	210	29
India	43 083	7 591	3 927	..	534 642	..	..	4 191	..
Indonesia	8 695	2 611	1 415	50	33 757	30 859	12 851	7 488	1 560
Iceland	16	16	..	..	178	74	60	60	21
Ireland	24 432	434	1 752	..	312 456	289 419	255 952	15 476	..
Israel[1]	c	c	c	c	c	c	c	c	c
Italy	23 944	1 093	699	-92	269 259	253 132	92 441	9 700	897
Japan	261 401	42 913	..	18 530	3 590 499	3 057 704	..	106 356	14 309
Korea	..	..	..	..	..	..	..	..	..
Latvia	0	0	0	0	0	0	0	..	..
Lithuania	33	18	0	0	334	293	256	37	13
Luxembourg	15 597	1 343	759	49	214 291	206 210	151 231	3 797	331
Malaysia	2 681	493	531	..	32 564	26 545	3 940	1 231	211
Mexico	858	85	70	77	15 850	14 155	..	1 471	305
Netherlands	28 306	2 254	..	-2 460	496 663	420 204	123 639	40 280	..
New Zealand	1 122	1 759	430	..	9 807	..	..	2 889	437
Nicaragua	..	..	..	..	..	..	..	..	..
Norway	6 613	910	95	..	181 448	163 224	36 220	12 422	1 026
Panama	..	..	..	..	..	..	..	..	..
Paraguay	..	..	..	..	0	23	..	..	..
Peru	363	135	25	-101	3 251	2 659	..	456	71
Poland	5 386	1 460	48	57	30 074	25 516	16 976	3 432	607
Portugal	4 440	336	116	31	35 971	32 515	14 420	2 189	149
Puerto Rico	..	..	..	..	..	..	..	..	..
Russia	784	1 429	1 129	28	12 720	10 500	..	1 321	475
Singapore	6 491	535	933	..	91 569	75 820	..	6 074	1 380
Slovak Republic	..	..	..	..	1 951	1 203	608	..	..
Slovenia	52	17	4	1	1 081	653	172	369	17
South Africa	..	..	..	..	..	..	..	..	..
Spain	4 153	513	305	22	35 031	26 927	4 319	3 376	369
Sri Lanka	168	123	59	18	2 269	435	36	880	339
Sweden	8 936	1 550	415	4 349	494 001	182 130	136 424	123 692	17 241
Switzerland	29 811	1 110	884	67	340 638	294 467	..	16 229	1 386
Thailand	..	..	..	..	..	..	..	..	..
Tunisia	..	..	..	..	..	..	..	..	..
Turkey	903	725	503	29	26 011	2 476	..	1 883	550
United Kingdom	274 228	4 195	..	-13 691	2 353 560	2 068 758	1 573 309	94 054	..
United States	370 318	73 300	52 126	42 880	4 310 973	18 412	..	443 756	46 802
Uruguay	0	0	0	0	0	0	..	..	..

.. Not available; c Confidential data

Note: Detailed metadata at: *http://metalinks.oecd.org/ins/20190221/11be*.

1. Information on data for Israel: *http://oe.cd/israel-disclaimer*.

Source: Balance sheet and income, OECD Insurance Statistics (database)

Table 3. Balance sheet and income, direct insurance (Non-life insurance companies)

2017

Million US dollars

	Gross claims payments	Gross operating expenses	Commissions	Outstanding claims provision (changes)	Total assets	Gross technical provisions	Gross technical provisions unit-linked	Shareholders' equity	Net income
Argentina	3 798	892	489	-1 529	8 351	544	..	1 581	300
Australia	24 196	5 816	1 182	..	83 432	56 518	..	18 719	2 516
Austria	2 130	151	809	154	16 871	4 736	0	5 014	..
Belgium	2 608	764	789	300	13 482	8 292	0	2 645	349
Bolivia	161	160	25	..	375	79	..	969	18
Brazil	2 835	1 679	843	-46	7 967	4 713	0	1 758	158
Canada	..	..	..	..	..	..	..	..	..
Chile	2 335	773	497	36	6 589	4 878	..	1 237	53
Colombia	161	160	25	..	375	79	..	969	18
Costa Rica	45	12	11	-9	80	45	0	24	2
Cuba	..	..	..	..	..	..	..	..	..
Czech Republic	168	153	29	10	693	325	..	228	6
Denmark	6 883	1 814	288	519	28 580	15 762	..	8 575	1 357
Ecuador	..	..	..	..	..	..	..	..	..
El Salvador	..	..	..	..	..	..	..	..	..
Estonia	304	154	..	..	896	405	0	401	48
Finland	3 582	996	212	-433	22 058	12 689	..	4 162	747
France	113 824	31 495	..	2 482	350 806	157 483	0	..	..
Germany	95 545	12 577	14 769	11 031	611 007	520 421	58	49 932	2 235
Greece	278	339	..	..	2 666	1 490	0	909	..
Guatemala	1	15	5	..	140	33	..	76	11
Honduras	..	..	..	..	..	..	..	..	..
Hong Kong, China	2 524	623	840	..	..	..	..	..	..
Hungary	118	78	49	20	385	167	0	145	25
India	14 611	5 684	1 682	19 629	49 880	..	..	8 815	1 072
Indonesia	2 110	885	171	59	9 915	3 803	..	3 994	363
Iceland	410	115	..	..	1 273	644	0	503	71
Ireland	4 746	691	1 101	..	55 074	33 349	0	13 888	..
Israel[1]	590	116	95	100	4 345	3 204	..	486	73
Italy	6 201	3 015	2 341	80	27 356	17 303	0	7 069	496
Japan	42 772	28 323	11 949	770	297 763	..	..	34 922	6 057
Korea	..	..	..	..	..	..	..	..	..
Latvia	305	98	46	21	613	386	0	166	17
Lithuania	266	137	7	-20	690	403	0	187	11
Luxembourg	2 015	1 138	727	411	15 583	10 216	0	2 629	190
Malaysia	1 973	660	273	70	7 483	3 834	..	3 517	349
Mexico	1 736	394	608	1 630	8 245	4 863	..	1 732	306
Netherlands	58 492	6 926	..	6	81 659	47 724	..	27 554	335
New Zealand	4 734	6 312	556	..	10 638	..	..	2 735	260
Nicaragua	..	..	..	..	..	..	..	..	..
Norway	6 353	1 413	365	-206	28 525	14 098	..	9 549	1 904
Panama	..	..	..	..	..	..	..	..	..
Paraguay	..	..	..	..	0	182	..	..	..
Peru	692	262	110	-87	1 193	536	..	312	43
Poland	5 156	2 648	421	521	26 404	17 486	0	7 036	901
Portugal	1 592	556	282	156	3 965	2 532	..	873	34
Puerto Rico	..	..	..	..	..	..	..	..	..
Russia	7 364	4 508	2 150	3 378	27 011	13 562	..	8 272	697
Singapore	2 183	758	176	..	14 558	4 621	..	7 481	455
Slovak Republic	..	..	..	..	170	78	..	..	..
Slovenia	439	57	9	3	320	99	0	177	1
South Africa	..	..	..	..	..	..	..	..	..
Spain	11 585	3 472	1 895	574	34 639	18 003	0	10 758	1 049
Sri Lanka	350	116	50	112	1 191	556	..	576	75
Sweden	7 795	1 856	671	28 476	76 747	37 839	..	15 868	826
Switzerland	22 220	3 433	4 558	1 527	146 449	66 394	..	33 232	5 043
Thailand	..	..	..	..	..	..	..	..	..
Tunisia	..	..	..	..	..	..	..	..	..
Turkey	5 048	1 725	1 410	1 223	13 400	12 118	..	3 260	444
United Kingdom	35 812	17 071	..	-640	151 444	90 830	0	39 012	..
United States	1 035 450	234 017	50 043	19 070	1 689 070	827 020	..	768 124	53 147
Uruguay	19	14	5	1	61	21	..	28	-1

.. Not available

Note: Detailed metadata at: *http://metalinks.oecd.org/ins/20190221/11be.*

1. Information on data for Israel: *http://oe.cd/israel-disclaimer.*

Source: Balance sheet and income, OECD Insurance Statistics (database)

Table 4. Portfolio allocation, direct insurance (All insurance companies)

2017

Million US dollars

	Cash and deposits	Land and buildings	Equity	Bills and bonds	Loans	Collective investment schemes	Private equity funds	Hedge funds	Structured products	Assets for unit-linked contracts	Total investments
Argentina	438	318	1 082	11 308	41	5 019	0	0	0	0	20 539
Australia	6 737	c	8 358	49 528	2 837	..	..	..	..	..	192 553
Austria	4 165	9 719	19 000	60 573	4 365	25 403	115	..	1 713	23 949	149 069
Belgium	9 279	10 323	18 940	234 647	33 600	15 925	913	..	2 599	42 617	369 662
Bolivia	28	84	10	301	19	0	44	0	0	0	638
Brazil	378	537	903	22 151	117	22 899	8 068	466	0	217 264	272 831
Canada	..	..	..	..	..	..	..	..	..	..	..
Chile	3	10	1	36	7	3	0	0	0	6	66
Colombia	28	84	10	301	19	0	44	0	0	0	638
Costa Rica	188	57	151	2 436	389	60	0	0	0	0	3 282
Cuba	..	..	..	..	..	..	..	..	..	..	..
Czech Republic	894	178	1 198	12 350	125	957	4	3	42	3 531	19 346
Denmark	15 459	1 769	141 011	119 187	5 900	25 720	..	..	..	182 737	527 790
Ecuador	..	..	..	..	..	..	..	..	..	..	..
El Salvador	..	..	..	..	..	..	..	..	..	..	..
Estonia	201	0	2	1 073	7	101	2	0	6	632	2 032
Finland	4 488	2 522	3 570	22 459	2 047	8 333	..	..	..	45 260	90 301
France	61 756	41 785	231 608	1 699 095	32 075	484 445	..	..	..	434 068	3 066 513
Germany	16 717	33 544	117 107	724 519	328 179	629 817	3 938	..	..	132 208	1 998 781
Greece	903	739	166	11 805	154	1 483	0	0	2	2 823	18 510
Guatemala	234	30	16	475	5	..	..	..	..	..	869
Honduras	..	..	..	..	..	..	..	..	..	..	..
Hong Kong, China	..	..	..	..	..	..	..	..	..	..	..
Hungary	278	96	47	4 562	15	445	..	..	..	4 632	10 295
India	..	1 901	66 169	375 021	17 423	2 594	..	..	..	58 145	523 798
Indonesia	5 088	865	3 197	7 853	13	6 992	..	..	..	17 819	42 228
Iceland	55	12	357	525	12	211	..	..	..	..	..
Ireland	8 546	1 340	3 822	44 540	3 382	4 561	..	..	1 394	259 843	328 432
Israel[1]	3 595	1 832	1 433	28 787	5 290	2 421	1 202	101	95	88 525	135 300
Italy	11 485	7 420	71 837	567 844	5 009	..	..	..	..	166 424	945 366
Japan	92 882	63 904	343 580	2 523 537	324 917	..	..	..	..	..	3 788 141
Korea	..	..	..	..	..	..	..	..	..	..	..
Latvia	138	18	8	420	3	73	0	3	0	69	735
Lithuania	80	7	14	676	8	105	0	0	7	597	1 514
Luxembourg	2 339	103	865	26 510	64	3 622	..	..	..	151 670	223 617
Malaysia	4 118	1 097	8 185	34 471	3 128	..	..	..	..	11 808	71 436
Mexico	390	824	887	44 506	1 578	6 504	77	..	..	..	58 674
Netherlands	..	7 902	11 901	214 918	109 778	..	..	..	..	..	392 783
New Zealand	..	..	..	3 439	..	..	..	..	..	..	6 176
Nicaragua	..	..	..	..	..	..	..	..	..	..	..
Norway	1 784	16 187	11 087	78 015	15 528	39 755	..	..	..	36 220	201 067
Panama	..	..	..	..	..	..	..	..	..	..	..
Paraguay	59	11	5	199	1	0	0	0	0	0	275
Peru	466	860	661	8 298	5	526	5	0	0	75	11 577
Poland	1 830	108	99	21 076	855	4 810	..	..	20	16 010	51 859
Portugal	1 943	613	3 823	34 107	23	2 625	88	4	243	14 763	58 331
Puerto Rico	..	..	..	..	..	..	..	..	..	..	..
Russia	13 500	150	2 455	17 062	269	225	..	..	..	..	47 891
Singapore	8 902	2 961	21 906	83 686	3 869	20 623	..	..	204	27 279	169 430
Slovak Republic	506	220	0	758	86	5	0	0	0	1 918	1 280
Slovenia	223	289	684	4 451	97	394	..	..	24	1 917	8 084
South Africa	..	..	..	..	..	..	..	..	..	..	..
Spain	27 211	12 968	18 326	249 116	2 587	14 152	473	456	5 420	21 366	345 597
Sri Lanka	..	..	..	..	..	..	..	..	..	..	..
Sweden	10 434	11 964	148 869	154 031	11 209	64 294	..	..	..	144 646	561 683
Switzerland	16 060	49 642	18 175	222 877	54 449	18 820	2 718	4 655	715	19 312	461 858
Thailand	..	..	..	..	..	..	..	..	..	..	..
Tunisia	..	..	..	..	..	..	..	..	..	..	..
Turkey	8 663	85	629	3 968	46	316	..	..	..	1 055	14 763
United Kingdom	11 577	5 887	19 096	209 205	10 861	28 994	..	..	24	..	287 090
United States	200 635	37 807	539 757	3 910 766	615 443	..	..	19 814	1 631	..	5 592 566
Uruguay	494	15	8	3 730	8	0	0	0	17	0	4 279

.. Not available; c Confidential data

Note: Detailed metadata at: *http://metalinks.oecd.org/ins/20190221/abe4*.

1. Information on data for Israel: *http://oe.cd/israel-disclaimer*.

Source: Outstanding investment by direct insurance companies, OECD Insurance Statistics (database)

Table 5. Portfolio allocation, direct insurance (Life insurance companies)
2017

Million US dollars

	Cash and deposits	Land and buildings	Equity	Bills and bonds	Loans	Collective investment schemes	Private equity funds	Hedge funds	Structured products	Assets for unit-linked contracts	Total investments
Argentina	39	38	37	2 892	1	767	0	0	0	0	4 003
Australia	2 427	c	7 114	20 049	720	..	..	..	..	112 492	146 458
Austria	122	10	64	3 398	177	4 792	10	..	85	4 336	12 996
Belgium	881	292	463	6 225	2 149	1 934	9	..	791	1 266	14 189
Bolivia	21	67	5	245	19	0	35	0	0	0	472
Brazil	79	21	307	5 217	77	6 304	5 266	176	0	145 050	162 503
Canada	..	..	..	..	..	..	..	..	..	..	..
Chile	2	10	1	34	7	3	0	0	0	6	64
Colombia	21	67	5	245	19	0	35	0	0	0	472
Costa Rica	..	..	..	..	..	..	..	..	..	..	..
Cuba	..	..	..	..	..	..	..	..	..	..	..
Czech Republic	c	c	c	c	c	c	c	c	c	c	c
Denmark	11 821	1 525	137 694	101 564	5 437	23 363	..	..	..	182 737	499 210
Ecuador	..	..	..	..	..	..	..	..	..	..	..
El Salvador	..	..	..	..	..	..	..	..	..	..	..
Estonia	c	c	c	c	c	c	c	c	c	c	c
Finland	3 267	1 505	1 879	13 992	1 184	4 383	..	..	..	45 260	71 734
France	8 983	11 308	40 752	371 653	5 563	79 590	..	..	..	92 514	625 760
Germany	7 353	22 701	50 452	471 019	233 325	437 594	2 349	..	..	132 150	1 365 819
Greece	112	2	55	3 030	0	7	0	0	0	150	3 426
Guatemala	..	..	..	..	..	..	..	..	..	..	..
Honduras	..	..	..	..	..	..	..	..	..	..	..
Hong Kong, China	..	..	..	..	..	..	..	..	..	..	..
Hungary	96	6	2	1 713	5	170	..	..	..	1 555	3 566
India	..	1 862	61 469	347 372	17 377	2 022	..	..	..	58 145	490 332
Indonesia	2 965	813	2 436	6 525	10	5 917	..	..	..	17 819	36 829
Iceland	10	0	6	70	0	12	..	..	..	60	158
Ireland	3 976	156	2 962	24 544	553	2 232	..	..	91	259 843	295 284
Israel[1]	c	c	c	c	c	c	c	c	c	c	c
Italy	3 268	333	4 692	139 228	113	..	..	..	..	92 508	257 945
Japan	75 615	55 769	273 160	2 449 406	310 511	..	..	..	..	..	3 515 446
Korea	..	..	..	..	..	..	..	..	..	..	..
Latvia	0	0	0	0	0	0	0	0	0	0	0
Lithuania	15	0	0	57	0	2	0	0	0	256	330
Luxembourg	1 444	9	567	21 677	64	3 165	..	..	..	151 670	212 792
Malaysia	1 165	478	5 492	16 059	1 862	..	..	..	..	4 268	32 564
Mexico	17	15	5	14 607	180	4	0	..	..	..	15 598
Netherlands	..	7 600	8 829	183 859	106 162	..	..	..	..	..	338 235
New Zealand	..	..	..	2 189	..	..	..	..	..	..	4 655
Nicaragua	..	..	..	..	..	..	..	..	..	..	..
Norway	971	15 602	9 284	66 620	15 265	35 673	..	..	..	36 220	181 838
Panama	..	..	..	..	..	..	..	..	..	..	..
Paraguay	..	..	..	..	..	..	..	..	..	..	..
Peru	156	226	120	2 409	3	72	0	0	0	2	3 015
Poland	831	39	20	9 540	207	2 211	..	..	6	16 010	29 107
Portugal	579	117	276	15 521	13	1 308	33	0	83	14 477	32 407
Puerto Rico	..	..	..	..	..	..	..	..	..	..	..
Russia	3 717	150	219	9 362	5	34	..	..	..	..	14 543
Singapore	3 994	1 293	10 744	37 832	1 540	16 139	..	..	121	17 803	89 465
Slovak Republic	243	1	0	718	6	0	0	0	0	650	960
Slovenia	38	0	143	558	..	163	..	..	2	171	1 075
South Africa	..	..	..	..	..	..	..	..	..	..	..
Spain	1 363	290	473	23 878	349	789	102	29	1 215	4 323	32 852
Sri Lanka	..	..	..	..	..	..	..	..	..	..	..
Sweden	8 212	9 266	129 898	128 981	7 981	54 188	..	..	..	141 495	493 983
Switzerland	6 606	42 031	12 613	178 251	43 135	9 156	1 878	3 278	651	19 301	330 615
Thailand	..	..	..	..	..	..	..	..	..	..	..
Tunisia	..	..	..	..	..	..	..	..	..	..	..
Turkey	2 379	40	64	1 293	46	45	..	..	..	1 055	4 922
United Kingdom	1 009	2 485	2 893	60 604	6 132	7 445	..	..	5	..	81 416
United States	99 503	23 744	159 996	3 031 195	608 803	..	..	19 838	1 754	..	4 150 149
Uruguay	..	..	..	..	..	..	..	..	..	..	..

.. Not available; c Confidential data

Note: Detailed metadata at: *http://metalinks.oecd.org/ins/20190221/abe4.*

1. Information on data for Israel: *http://oe.cd/israel-disclaimer.*

Source: Outstanding investment by direct insurance companies, OECD Insurance Statistics (database)

Table 6. Portfolio allocation, direct insurance (Non-life insurance companies)

2017

Million US dollars

	Cash and deposits	Land and buildings	Equity	Bills and bonds	Loans	Collective investment schemes	Private equity funds	Hedge funds	Structured products	Assets for unit-linked contracts	Total investments
Argentina	124	86	119	3 551	6	1 858	0	0	0	0	6 909
Australia	4 310	83	1 243	29 479	2 117	8 490	..	..	..	..	46 095
Austria	1 521	739	9 044	1 616	160	2 476	0	..	4	0	15 560
Belgium	939	341	766	6 364	279	1 658	2	..	78	..	10 462
Bolivia	8	17	4	57	0	0	10	0	0	0	166
Brazil	54	2	13	2 108	0	1 561	2	16	0	0	3 756
Canada	..	..	..	..	..	..	..	..	..	..	..
Chile	0	0	0	1	0	0	0	0	0	0	2
Colombia	8	17	4	57	0	0	10	0	0	0	166
Costa Rica	13	0	0	30	17	0	0	0	0	0	60
Cuba	..	..	..	..	..	..	..	..	..	..	..
Czech Republic	100	24	3	162	4	10	0	0	0	0	303
Denmark	3 638	244	3 317	17 623	463	2 357	..	..	..	..	28 580
Ecuador	..	..	..	..	..	..	..	..	..	..	..
El Salvador	..	..	..	..	..	..	..	..	..	..	..
Estonia	142	0	1	596	2	42	0	0	6	0	795
Finland	1 221	1 017	1 691	8 467	863	3 949	..	..	..	..	18 568
France	15 721	7 400	77 282	127 579	6 842	53 976	..	..	..	0	292 395
Germany	9 365	10 844	66 655	253 500	94 853	192 222	1 589	..	..	58	632 961
Greece	308	187	34	1 346	47	374	0	0	0	0	2 344
Guatemala	47	4	0	47	3	..	..	..	..	..	108
Honduras	..	..	..	..	..	..	..	..	..	..	..
Hong Kong, China	..	..	..	..	..	..	..	..	..	..	..
Hungary	44	3	0	274	0	9	..	..	..	0	342
India	..	38	4 699	27 649	46	572	..	..	..	..	33 466
Indonesia	2 124	52	761	1 328	3	1 075	..	..	..	0	5 399
Iceland	45	12	351	455	12	199	..	..	..	0	1 075
Ireland	4 571	1 184	860	19 996	2 829	2 329	..	..	1 302	0	33 147
Israel[1]	412	54	75	1 727	176	927	35	6	5	0	3 441
Italy	1 106	719	2 482	14 226	31	..	..	..	..	0	20 577
Japan	17 267	8 134	70 419	74 131	14 406	..	..	..	..	..	272 695
Korea	..	..	..	..	..	..	..	..	..	..	..
Latvia	125	18	8	329	3	14	0	0	0	0	499
Lithuania	38	7	5	339	1	63	0	0	0	0	472
Luxembourg	895	95	298	4 833	0	457	..	..	..	0	10 825
Malaysia	1 749	106	177	2 012	12	..	..	..	..	..	7 483
Mexico	111	185	113	2 877	50	206	4	..	..	..	3 754
Netherlands	..	302	3 071	31 059	3 616	..	..	..	..	..	54 548
New Zealand	..	..	..	1 250	..	..	..	..	..	..	1 521
Nicaragua	..	..	..	..	..	..	..	..	..	..	..
Norway	812	584	1 803	11 395	263	4 082	..	..	..	..	19 229
Panama	..	..	..	..	..	..	..	..	..	..	..
Paraguay	..	..	..	..	..	..	..	..	..	..	..
Peru	56	66	111	195	0	23	0	0	0	0	593
Poland	998	69	79	11 536	648	2 599	..	..	14	0	22 752
Portugal	170	172	57	2 184	4	181	0	4	22	0	2 795
Puerto Rico	..	..	..	..	..	..	..	..	..	..	..
Russia	9 039	..	1 700	5 670	202	71	..	..	..	..	28 449
Singapore	3 712	405	1 432	4 555	1 300	219	..	..	2	0	11 625
Slovak Republic	57	0	0	8	3	2	0	0	0	0	72
Slovenia	38	21	1	186	..	7	..	..	..	0	252
South Africa	..	..	..	..	..	..	..	..	..	..	..
Spain	4 373	2 347	3 275	10 434	557	3 286	174	244	111	0	24 977
Sri Lanka	..	..	..	..	..	..	..	..	..	..	..
Sweden	2 222	2 698	18 971	25 050	3 227	10 106	..	..	..	3 151	67 700
Switzerland	9 454	7 611	5 562	44 626	11 313	9 664	840	1 377	64	11	131 243
Thailand	..	..	..	..	..	..	..	..	..	..	..
Tunisia	..	..	..	..	..	..	..	..	..	..	..
Turkey	6 284	45	565	2 675	0	271	..	..	..	1	9 841
United Kingdom	3 023	1 451	2 558	24 603	567	4 203	..	..	0	..	36 469
United States	101 132	14 063	379 761	879 571	6 641	..	..	-24	-123	..	1 442 417
Uruguay	11	0	0	23	0	0	0	0	0	0	33

.. Not available

Note: Detailed metadata at: *http://metalinks.oecd.org/ins/20190221/abe4.*

1. Information on data for Israel: *http://oe.cd/israel-disclaimer.*

Source: Outstanding investment by direct insurance companies, OECD Insurance Statistics (database)

Table 7. Total gross premiums (Life and Non-life)

Million US dollars

	2010	2011	2012	2013	2014	2015	2016	2017
Argentina	..	..	13 983	16 643	18 622	19 376	19 749	18 519
Australia	70 793	84 541	85 880	87 591	97 011	78 796	74 145	72 339
Austria	..	..	..	25 077	25 069	21 082	20 633	20 435
Belgium	39 170	40 818	41 938	37 510	38 294	30 734	30 411	30 763
Bolivia	..	..	316	..	..	..	468	499
Brazil	..	..	..	..	69 867	55 519	58 914	66 431
Canada	85 752	93 998	97 037	98 545	93 075	83 591	..	..
Chile	8 309	9 699	11 298	11 776	10 976	11 413	12 401	12 860
Colombia	..	..	316	..	..	..	468	499
Costa Rica	718	793	927	1 036	1 157	1 049	1 211	1 319
Cuba	..	..	..	..	..	..	..	..
Czech Republic	8 167	8 764	7 846	7 998	7 608	6 173	6 002	6 402
Denmark	..	33 844	32 745	225 775	37 098	31 997	33 498	37 549
Ecuador	..	..	..	..	..	2 316	2 135	..
El Salvador	..	478	503	546	572	609	619	..
Estonia	565	560	617	774	838	764	815	922
Finland	11 615	10 119	9 353	13 057	14 106	11 912	10 005	10 059
France	297 035	288 704	258 656	275 671	293 642	250 772	314 037	313 543
Germany	240 817	255 374	302 757	333 618	338 313	292 969	294 460	310 439
Greece	6 948	6 884	5 781	5 405	5 049	3 963	3 906	4 202
Guatemala	..	..	611	683	749	804	856	953
Honduras	..	..	..	368	379	398	..	..
Hong Kong, China	26 903	29 268	33 191	37 856	43 121	47 901	59 301	64 310
Hungary	4 053	4 054	3 377	3 582	3 584	2 991	3 146	3 484
India	..	71 625	..	..	..	70 878	..	100 841
Indonesia	..	..	16 249	15 782	14 325	14 629	17 290	19 483
Iceland	382	415	404	419	444	420	487	611
Ireland	45 269	44 533	45 589	45 301	52 487	48 782	54 145	45 392
Israel[1]	11 234	12 665	12 471	13 941	14 366	14 117	15 142	17 427
Italy	169 745	156 776	138 240	161 115	193 198	165 787	151 321	150 359
Japan	518 775	590 342	475 139	349 905	347 080	313 822	434 737	390 096
Korea	120 803	137 828	163 065	169 186	187 068	183 642	185 646	..
Latvia	434	555	574	625	686	589	589	728
Lithuania	596	685	665	753	797	715	785	893
Luxembourg	27 438	19 151	25 169	24 698	28 907	21 270	20 275	24 254
Malaysia	13 242	14 878	16 338	16 974	17 588	15 346	15 100	15 156
Mexico	19 548	22 683	23 596	27 184	27 349	24 929	24 150	26 569
Netherlands	52 399	58 577	51 270	51 127	48 539	37 384	77 306	80 266
New Zealand	3 372	..	4 590	5 139	5 359	4 657	4 753	5 144
Nicaragua	..	..	138	157	178	191	204	..
Norway	20 570	23 794	25 748	25 536	26 461	20 647	20 210	20 407
Panama	..	..	1 159	1 316	..	..	..	..
Paraguay	..	..	224	367	..	428	368	390
Peru	..	2 660	3 041	3 392	3 602	3 709	3 354	3 500
Poland	17 963	19 289	19 231	18 307	17 412	14 539	14 213	16 499
Portugal	21 046	15 622	13 560	16 998	18 642	13 939	12 071	12 909
Puerto Rico	..	..	..	9 610	9 108	11 145	13 470	..
Russia	..	23 718	..	..	26 658	17 299	18 218	22 517
Singapore	20 231	23 470	24 947	27 186	30 379	30 331	33 160	36 830
Slovak Republic	2 813	2 994	2 772	2 958	2 982	2 399	..	5 035
Slovenia	2 885	3 035	2 816	2 807	2 779	2 385	2 414	2 590
South Africa	50 272	56 005	51 452	54 268	51 527	47 054	42 473	..
Spain	76 313	86 265	72 884	77 155	76 502	65 488	73 605	74 058
Sri Lanka	..	..	..	..	746	931	..	1 128
Sweden	25 624	28 062	24 669	27 203	49 890	40 254	39 107	44 382
Switzerland	61 637	71 482	70 214	74 264	74 480	70 367	67 483	67 772
Thailand	13 528	15 644	..	..	..	..	..	..
Tunisia	..	..	..	..	..	..	864	909
Turkey	9 971	10 247	11 399	13 212	12 314	11 775	13 718	13 074
United Kingdom	325 141	339 365	368 525	340 385	365 688	336 743	403 794	394 100
United States	2 035 562	2 154 851	2 279 817	2 289 921	2 431 323	2 621 083	2 703 793	2 836 293
Uruguay	..	..	1 062	1 208	1 303	1 277	..	1 576
OECD Total	4 342 743	4 636 577	4 689 690	4 864 517	4 949 417	4 842 891	5 123 203	5 051 855

.. Not available

Note: Detailed metadata at: *http://metalinks.oecd.org/ins/20190221/0f8b*.

1. Information on data for Israel: *http://oe.cd/israel-disclaimer*.

Source: Insurance activity indicators, OECD Insurance Statistics (database)

INTERNATIONAL COMPARISONS

Table 8. Total gross premiums (Life)

Million US dollars

	2010	2011	2012	2013	2014	2015	2016	2017
Argentina	..	..	2 891	2 969	3 076	2 966	3 158	2 724
Australia	40 318	47 949	46 069	48 122	59 315	46 633	41 066	37 668
Austria	..	..	..	8 554	8 890	7 437	6 696	6 477
Belgium	25 465	25 795	27 142	21 645	21 635	17 038	16 549	16 506
Bolivia	..	..	69	..	..	..	157	202
Brazil	..	..	..	..	42 061	34 819	38 935	44 172
Canada	30 491	32 005	31 148	32 390	26 679	23 996	..	..
Chile	5 484	6 067	7 400	7 830	7 224	7 795	8 726	8 930
Colombia	..	..	69	..	..	..	157	202
Costa Rica	63	84	110	139	142	133	186	194
Cuba	..	..	..	..	..	..	..	..
Czech Republic	3 757	4 069	3 680	3 657	3 429	2 537	2 435	2 451
Denmark	..	23 069	22 489	215 331	25 124	22 055	23 001	25 945
Ecuador	..	..	..	..	..	453	471	..
El Salvador	..	99	114	146	147	156	153	..
Estonia	229	223	209	227	254	238	245	251
Finland	6 914	5 179	4 786	7 421	8 097	6 941	5 060	5 103
France	51 003	184 360	160 628	172 138	188 383	160 881	182 290	173 177
Germany	115 270	116 636	107 431	120 258	121 584	99 588	97 584	99 523
Greece	3 005	3 008	2 497	2 237	2 497	1 999	1 844	2 120
Guatemala	..	..	124	136	156	156	170	196
Honduras	..	..	..	114	134	145	..	..
Hong Kong, China	22 867	24 808	28 123	32 425	37 459	41 972	53 421	58 134
Hungary	2 155	2 212	1 790	1 951	1 965	1 529	1 559	1 679
India	..	61 214	..	..	..	55 415	..	71 312
Indonesia	..	..	11 465	10 720	9 490	10 093	12 560	14 530
Iceland	29	30	29	33	36	35	43	54
Ireland	36 342	35 275	36 586	36 514	43 164	38 837	37 101	37 438
Israel[1]	5 792	6 682	6 602	7 374	7 426	7 568	7 986	9 368
Italy	121 811	105 179	91 863	115 115	148 447	129 025	114 701	112 705
Japan	415 985	476 138	475 139	349 905	347 080	313 822	328 210	293 005
Korea	71 964	79 314	96 195	100 261	106 188	104 801	104 560	..
Latvia	100	102	101	118	141	127	137	163
Lithuania	207	226	213	241	285	262	273	261
Luxembourg	25 870	17 309	23 499	22 705	27 130	19 633	18 556	22 262
Malaysia	8 090	8 976	9 907	10 200	10 594	9 306	9 317	9 603
Mexico	9 016	10 143	10 900	12 523	12 812	11 530	11 266	11 421
Netherlands	26 774	30 133	24 393	24 256	23 171	16 300	15 187	14 618
New Zealand	..	..	..	..	..	..	..	..
Nicaragua	..	..	22	27	32	33	38	..
Norway	11 017	12 771	14 051	13 838	14 629	11 383	11 202	11 313
Panama	..	..	447	523	..	..	..	..
Paraguay	..	..	..	45	..	57	1	54
Peru	..	1 276	1 435	1 587	1 768	1 794	1 519	1 644
Poland	10 421	10 749	11 170	9 892	9 087	7 302	6 051	6 499
Portugal	15 703	10 030	8 582	11 981	13 599	9 407	7 195	7 562
Puerto Rico	..	..	..	411	570	542	1 279	..
Russia	..	1 777	..	..	3 353	2 408	3 721	6 171
Singapore	13 828	15 723	16 402	18 449	20 808	21 033	23 739	27 593
Slovak Republic	1 492	1 592	1 493	1 641	1 619	1 229	..	3 703
Slovenia	645	669	623	629	636	552	544	581
South Africa	39 453	43 695	40 746	42 679	41 476	37 576	33 870	..
Spain	36 291	40 499	33 822	34 387	33 567	28 520	34 672	33 180
Sri Lanka	..	..	..	..	265	395	..	467
Sweden	12 510	13 923	13 311	14 190	34 734	29 507	29 302	33 761
Switzerland	29 210	34 589	33 598	35 791	36 140	34 407	31 672	30 486
Thailand	9 349	10 794	..	..	..	..	..	..
Tunisia	..	..	..	..	..	..	175	179
Turkey	1 743	1 880	1 758	2 072	1 510	1 390	2 048	2 268
United Kingdom	239 465	249 303	277 966	246 475	268 267	246 702	277 703	269 258
United States	799 066	864 830	919 547	881 541	880 040	973 634	970 503	1 009 291
Uruguay	..	..	280	347	384	427	..	665
OECD Total	2 155 544	2 451 935	2 496 711	2 563 243	2 484 787	2 384 642	2 395 966	2 289 028

.. Not available

Note: Detailed metadata at: *http://metalinks.oecd.org/ins/20190221/0f8b*.

1. Information on data for Israel: *http://oe.cd/israel-disclaimer*.

Source: Insurance activity indicators, OECD Insurance Statistics (database)

Table 9. Total gross premiums (Non-life)

Million US dollars

	2010	2011	2012	2013	2014	2015	2016	2017
Argentina	..	..	11 092	13 673	15 546	16 410	16 591	15 795
Australia	30 475	36 592	39 812	39 469	37 695	32 163	33 079	34 671
Austria	..	..	..	16 523	16 179	13 645	13 937	13 957
Belgium	13 705	15 023	14 797	15 865	16 658	13 696	13 862	14 257
Bolivia	..	..	248	..	..	..	312	297
Brazil	..	..	..	..	27 806	20 699	19 979	22 258
Canada	55 261	61 993	65 889	66 155	66 396	59 596	..	..
Chile	2 825	3 633	3 898	3 946	3 751	3 619	3 676	3 930
Colombia	..	..	248	..	..	..	312	297
Costa Rica	655	709	816	897	1 014	916	1 024	1 125
Cuba	..	..	..	..	..	..	..	..
Czech Republic	4 410	4 695	4 165	4 341	4 179	3 636	3 566	3 951
Denmark	..	10 775	10 256	10 445	11 974	9 943	10 497	11 604
Ecuador	..	..	..	..	..	1 864	1 665	..
El Salvador	..	379	389	400	412	437	446	..
Estonia	336	337	408	547	584	526	570	671
Finland	4 701	4 941	4 567	5 636	6 009	4 972	4 946	4 956
France	94 470	104 344	98 028	103 533	105 258	89 891	131 747	140 366
Germany	125 547	138 738	195 326	213 359	216 729	193 381	196 876	210 917
Greece	3 943	3 876	3 284	3 168	2 552	1 963	2 062	2 083
Guatemala	..	..	487	547	593	648	685	757
Honduras	..	..	..	254	246	253	..	..
Hong Kong, China	4 037	4 460	5 068	5 431	5 661	5 929	5 880	6 177
Hungary	1 898	1 842	1 587	1 631	1 619	1 462	1 588	1 804
India	..	10 411	..	..	..	15 463	..	29 529
Indonesia	..	..	4 784	5 062	4 835	4 537	4 730	4 954
Iceland	353	385	374	385	408	384	444	556
Ireland	8 927	9 258	9 003	8 787	9 323	9 945	17 044	7 955
Israel[1]	5 442	5 983	5 868	6 567	6 940	6 548	7 156	8 059
Italy	47 934	51 598	46 377	46 000	44 751	36 762	36 620	37 654
Japan	102 790	114 204	..	..	..	..	106 527	97 090
Korea	48 839	58 515	66 870	68 925	80 880	78 841	81 086	..
Latvia	334	452	473	507	545	462	452	564
Lithuania	389	459	452	512	512	454	513	633
Luxembourg	1 568	1 842	1 671	1 993	1 777	1 637	1 719	1 991
Malaysia	5 152	5 902	6 431	6 773	6 994	6 041	5 782	5 553
Mexico	10 532	12 540	12 696	14 661	14 536	13 399	12 884	15 148
Netherlands	25 625	28 445	26 877	26 871	25 367	21 084	62 118	64 658
New Zealand	3 372	..	4 590	5 139	5 359	4 657	4 753	5 144
Nicaragua	..	..	116	130	146	158	166	..
Norway	9 553	11 023	11 697	11 697	11 833	9 264	9 008	9 094
Panama	..	..	713	793	..	..	..	..
Paraguay	..	..	159	322	..	371	367	335
Peru	..	1 384	1 605	1 805	1 834	1 916	1 835	1 856
Poland	7 542	8 540	8 061	8 416	8 325	7 237	8 162	10 000
Portugal	5 342	5 592	4 977	5 017	5 044	4 532	4 876	5 347
Puerto Rico	..	..	..	9 199	8 538	10 603	12 191	..
Russia	..	20 193	..	..	16 937	14 891	14 497	16 346
Singapore	6 403	7 748	8 544	8 737	9 571	9 298	9 421	9 238
Slovak Republic	1 321	1 403	1 279	1 317	1 364	1 170	..	1 332
Slovenia	2 240	2 367	2 193	2 178	2 143	1 833	1 870	2 009
South Africa	10 819	12 310	10 706	11 589	10 051	9 478	8 602	..
Spain	40 023	45 766	39 062	42 767	42 935	36 967	38 933	40 878
Sri Lanka	..	..	..	..	481	535	..	661
Sweden	13 114	14 140	11 357	13 013	15 156	10 746	9 805	10 621
Switzerland	32 428	36 893	36 616	38 474	38 340	35 959	35 811	37 287
Thailand	4 179	4 850	..	..	..	..	..	..
Tunisia	..	..	..	..	..	..	689	730
Turkey	8 228	8 367	9 641	11 140	10 804	10 386	11 670	10 806
United Kingdom	85 677	90 062	90 559	93 910	97 421	90 041	126 091	124 843
United States	1 236 495	1 290 021	1 360 270	1 408 380	1 551 283	1 647 449	1 733 290	1 827 002
Uruguay	..	..	782	862	918	850	..	911
OECD Total	2 035 637	2 184 643	2 192 979	2 301 274	2 464 630	2 458 249	2 727 238	2 761 836

.. Not available

Note: Detailed metadata at: *http://metalinks.oecd.org/ins/20190221/0f8b.*

1. Information on data for Israel: *http://oe.cd/israel-disclaimer.*

Source: Insurance activity indicators, OECD Insurance Statistics (database)

Table 10. Market share in OECD (Life and Non-life)

Per cent

	2010	2011	2012	2013	2014	2015	2016	2017
Australia	1.6	1.8	1.8	1.8	2.0	1.6	1.4	1.4
Austria	..	..	..	0.5	0.5	0.4	0.4	0.4
Belgium	0.9	0.9	0.9	0.8	0.8	0.6	0.6	0.6
Canada	2.0	2.0	2.1	2.0	1.9	1.7	..	..
Chile	0.2	0.2	0.2	0.2	0.2	0.2	0.2	0.3
Czech Republic	0.2	0.2	0.2	0.2	0.2	0.1	0.1	0.1
Denmark	..	0.7	0.7	4.6	0.8	0.7	0.7	0.7
Estonia	0.0	0.0	0.0	0.0	0.0	0.0	0.0	0.0
Finland	0.3	0.2	0.2	0.3	0.3	0.2	0.2	0.2
France	6.8	6.2	5.5	5.7	5.9	5.2	6.1	6.2
Germany	5.5	5.5	6.5	6.9	6.8	6.0	5.7	6.1
Greece	0.2	0.1	0.1	0.1	0.1	0.1	0.1	0.1
Hungary	0.1	0.1	0.1	0.1	0.1	0.1	0.1	0.1
Iceland	0.0	0.0	0.0	0.0	0.0	0.0	0.0	0.0
Ireland	1.0	1.0	1.0	0.9	1.1	1.0	1.1	0.9
Israel	0.3	0.3	0.3	0.3	0.3	0.3	0.3	0.3
Italy	3.9	3.4	2.9	3.3	3.9	3.4	3.0	3.0
Japan	11.9	12.7	10.1	7.2	7.0	6.5	8.5	7.7
Korea	2.8	3.0	3.5	3.5	3.8	3.8	3.6	..
Latvia	0.0	0.0	0.0	0.0	0.0	0.0	0.0	0.0
Lithuania	0.0	0.0	0.0	0.0	0.0	0.0	0.0	0.0
Luxembourg	0.6	0.4	0.5	0.5	0.6	0.4	0.4	0.5
Mexico	0.5	0.5	0.5	0.6	0.6	0.5	0.5	0.5
Netherlands	1.2	1.3	1.1	1.1	1.0	0.8	1.5	1.6
New Zealand	0.1	..	0.1	0.1	0.1	0.1	0.1	0.1
Norway	0.5	0.5	0.5	0.5	0.5	0.4	0.4	0.4
Poland	0.4	0.4	0.4	0.4	0.4	0.3	0.3	0.3
Portugal	0.5	0.3	0.3	0.3	0.4	0.3	0.2	0.3
Slovak Republic	0.1	0.1	0.1	0.1	0.1	0.1	..	0.1
Slovenia	0.1	0.1	0.1	0.1	0.1	0.0	0.0	0.1
Spain	1.8	1.9	1.6	1.6	1.5	1.4	1.4	1.5
Sweden	0.6	0.6	0.5	0.6	1.0	0.8	0.8	0.9
Switzerland	1.4	1.5	1.5	1.5	1.5	1.5	1.3	1.3
Turkey	0.2	0.2	0.2	0.3	0.2	0.2	0.3	0.3
United Kingdom	7.5	7.3	7.9	7.0	7.4	7.0	7.9	7.8
United States	46.9	46.5	48.6	47.1	49.1	54.1	52.8	56.1
OECD Total	100.0	100.0	100.0	100.0	100.0	100.0	100.0	100.0

.. Not available

Note: Detailed metadata at: *http://metalinks.oecd.org/ins/20190221/0f8b*.

Source: Insurance activity indicators, OECD Insurance Statistics (database)

Table 11. Market share in OECD (Life)

Per cent

	2010	2011	2012	2013	2014	2015	2016	2017
Australia	1.9	2.0	1.8	1.9	2.4	2.0	1.7	1.6
Austria	..	..	..	0.3	0.4	0.3	0.3	0.3
Belgium	1.2	1.1	1.1	0.8	0.9	0.7	0.7	0.7
Canada	1.4	1.3	1.2	1.3	1.1	1.0	..	..
Chile	0.3	0.2	0.3	0.3	0.3	0.3	0.4	0.4
Czech Republic	0.2	0.2	0.1	0.1	0.1	0.1	0.1	0.1
Denmark	..	0.9	0.9	8.4	1.0	0.9	1.0	1.1
Estonia	0.0	0.0	0.0	0.0	0.0	0.0	0.0	0.0
Finland	0.3	0.2	0.2	0.3	0.3	0.3	0.2	0.2
France	2.4	7.5	6.4	6.7	7.6	6.7	7.6	7.6
Germany	5.3	4.8	4.3	4.7	4.9	4.2	4.1	4.3
Greece	0.1	0.1	0.1	0.1	0.1	0.1	0.1	0.1
Hungary	0.1	0.1	0.1	0.1	0.1	0.1	0.1	0.1
Iceland	0.0	0.0	0.0	0.0	0.0	0.0	0.0	0.0
Ireland	1.7	1.4	1.5	1.4	1.7	1.6	1.5	1.6
Israel	0.3	0.3	0.3	0.3	0.3	0.3	0.3	0.4
Italy	5.7	4.3	3.7	4.5	6.0	5.4	4.8	4.9
Japan	19.3	19.4	19.0	13.7	14.0	13.2	13.7	12.8
Korea	3.3	3.2	3.9	3.9	4.3	4.4	4.4	..
Latvia	0.0	0.0	0.0	0.0	0.0	0.0	0.0	0.0
Lithuania	0.0	0.0	0.0	0.0	0.0	0.0	0.0	0.0
Luxembourg	1.2	0.7	0.9	0.9	1.1	0.8	0.8	1.0
Mexico	0.4	0.4	0.4	0.5	0.5	0.5	0.5	0.5
Netherlands	1.2	1.2	1.0	0.9	0.9	0.7	0.6	0.6
New Zealand	..	..	..	..	..	..	..	..
Norway	0.5	0.5	0.6	0.5	0.6	0.5	0.5	0.5
Poland	0.5	0.4	0.4	0.4	0.4	0.3	0.3	0.3
Portugal	0.7	0.4	0.3	0.5	0.5	0.4	0.3	0.3
Slovak Republic	0.1	0.1	0.1	0.1	0.1	0.1	..	0.2
Slovenia	0.0	0.0	0.0	0.0	0.0	0.0	0.0	0.0
Spain	1.7	1.7	1.4	1.3	1.4	1.2	1.4	1.5
Sweden	0.6	0.6	0.5	0.6	1.4	1.2	1.2	1.5
Switzerland	1.4	1.4	1.3	1.4	1.5	1.4	1.3	1.3
Turkey	0.1	0.1	0.1	0.1	0.1	0.1	0.1	0.1
United Kingdom	11.1	10.2	11.1	9.6	10.8	10.3	11.6	11.8
United States	37.1	35.3	36.8	34.4	35.4	40.8	40.5	44.1
OECD Total	100.0	100.0	100.0	100.0	100.0	100.0	100.0	100.0

.. Not available

Note: Detailed metadata at: *http://metalinks.oecd.org/ins/20190221/0f8b*.

Source: Insurance activity indicators, OECD Insurance Statistics (database)

Table 12. Market share in OECD (Non-life)

Per cent

	2010	2011	2012	2013	2014	2015	2016	2017
Australia	1.5	1.7	1.8	1.7	1.5	1.3	1.2	1.3
Austria	..	..	..	0.7	0.7	0.6	0.5	0.5
Belgium	0.7	0.7	0.7	0.7	0.7	0.6	0.5	0.5
Canada	2.7	2.8	3.0	2.9	2.7	2.4	..	..
Chile	0.1	0.2	0.2	0.2	0.2	0.1	0.1	0.1
Czech Republic	0.2	0.2	0.2	0.2	0.2	0.1	0.1	0.1
Denmark	..	0.5	0.5	0.5	0.5	0.4	0.4	0.4
Estonia	0.0	0.0	0.0	0.0	0.0	0.0	0.0	0.0
Finland	0.2	0.2	0.2	0.2	0.2	0.2	0.2	0.2
France	4.6	4.8	4.5	4.5	4.3	3.7	4.8	5.1
Germany	6.2	6.4	8.9	9.3	8.8	7.9	7.2	7.6
Greece	0.2	0.2	0.2	0.1	0.1	0.1	0.1	0.1
Hungary	0.1	0.1	0.1	0.1	0.1	0.1	0.1	0.1
Iceland	0.0	0.0	0.0	0.0	0.0	0.0	0.0	0.0
Ireland	0.4	0.4	0.4	0.4	0.4	0.4	0.6	0.3
Israel	0.3	0.3	0.3	0.3	0.3	0.3	0.3	0.3
Italy	2.4	2.4	2.1	2.0	1.8	1.5	1.3	1.4
Japan	5.1	5.2	..	..	..	..	3.9	3.5
Korea	2.4	2.7	3.0	3.0	3.3	3.2	3.0	..
Latvia	0.0	0.0	0.0	0.0	0.0	0.0	0.0	0.0
Lithuania	0.0	0.0	0.0	0.0	0.0	0.0	0.0	0.0
Luxembourg	0.1	0.1	0.1	0.1	0.1	0.1	0.1	0.1
Mexico	0.5	0.6	0.6	0.6	0.6	0.5	0.5	0.5
Netherlands	1.3	1.3	1.2	1.2	1.0	0.9	2.3	2.3
New Zealand	0.2	..	0.2	0.2	0.2	0.2	0.2	0.2
Norway	0.5	0.5	0.5	0.5	0.5	0.4	0.3	0.3
Poland	0.4	0.4	0.4	0.4	0.3	0.3	0.3	0.4
Portugal	0.3	0.3	0.2	0.2	0.2	0.2	0.2	0.2
Slovak Republic	0.1	0.1	0.1	0.1	0.1	0.0	..	0.0
Slovenia	0.1	0.1	0.1	0.1	0.1	0.1	0.1	0.1
Spain	2.0	2.1	1.8	1.9	1.7	1.5	1.4	1.5
Sweden	0.6	0.6	0.5	0.6	0.6	0.4	0.4	0.4
Switzerland	1.6	1.7	1.7	1.7	1.6	1.5	1.3	1.4
Turkey	0.4	0.4	0.4	0.5	0.4	0.4	0.4	0.4
United Kingdom	4.2	4.1	4.1	4.1	4.0	3.7	4.6	4.5
United States	60.7	59.1	62.0	61.2	62.9	67.0	63.6	66.2
OECD Total	100.0	100.0	100.0	100.0	100.0	100.0	100.0	100.0

.. Not available

Note: Detailed metadata at: *http://metalinks.oecd.org/ins/20190221/0f8b*.

Source: Insurance activity indicators, OECD Insurance Statistics (database)

INTERNATIONAL COMPARISONS

Table 13. Density (Life and Non-life)

US dollar per inhabitant

	2010	2011	2012	2013	2014	2015	2016	2017
Argentina	..	..	333	393	405	418	422	393
Australia	2 901	3 377	3 326	3 347	3 683	2 922	2 660	2 541
Austria	2 638	2 740	2 492	2 602	2 653	2 226	2 141	2 171
Belgium	3 510	3 596	3 684	3 259	3 304	2 652	2 612	2 647
Bolivia	..	..	31	..	..	..	43	43
Brazil	..	318	333	335	344	271	286	320
Canada	2 331	2 516	2 560	2 534	2 160	1 923	..	..
Chile	486	560	645	664	612	629	674	693
Colombia	..	..	31	..	..	..	43	43
Costa Rica	158	173	199	219	241	216	246	265
Cuba	..	..	35	..	..	..	..	..
Czech Republic	770	822	733	747	712	574	555	590
Denmark	..	6 069	5 823	6 079	6 543	5 610	5 699	6 315
Ecuador	..	..	..	..	..	139	127	..
El Salvador	..	..	..	..	..	..	..	..
Estonia	424	421	466	586	636	582	621	704
Finland	2 139	1 847	1 699	2 370	2 552	2 149	1 796	1 798
France	4 310	4 181	3 645	3 892	4 105	3 552	4 099	4 225
Germany	..	..	2 890	3 111	3 127	2 596	2 600	2 829
Greece	618	608	511	480	457	361	359	387
Guatemala	..	41	39	43	46	48	50	55
Honduras	..	..	46	47	48	49	..	..
Hong Kong, China	3 648	3 917	4 403	5 003	5 658	6 259	7 652	8 270
Hungary	402	403	336	357	360	300	317	350
India	..	58	..	..	..	55	63	72
Indonesia	..	60	63	60	55	56	65	73
Iceland	1 190	1 273	1 224	1 254	1 316	1 230	1 423	1 772
Ireland	9 791	9 572	9 721	9 649	11 145	10 278	11 267	9 532
Israel[1]	1 474	1 631	1 577	1 731	1 749	1 685	1 772	2 001
Italy	2 783	2 550	2 239	2 600	3 121	2 677	2 443	2 431
Japan	3 895	4 416	3 355	2 545	2 580	2 370	3 201	2 893
Korea	2 290	2 612	3 090	3 182	3 502	3 417	3 436	..
Latvia	203	263	277	309	343	297	299	373
Lithuania	192	226	222	254	272	246	274	316
Luxembourg	54 276	36 701	47 317	45 556	51 926	37 491	35 079	41 011
Malaysia	433	478	514	520	530	454	441	439
Mexico	168	192	198	226	224	203	194	211
Netherlands	2 930	3 483	3 019	2 997	2 836	2 171	4 516	4 615
New Zealand	759	..	1 024	1 141	1 169	964	983	1 006
Nicaragua	..	21	24	26	30	31	33	35
Norway	4 191	4 785	5 111	5 011	5 132	3 967	3 972	3 858
Panama	..	278	286	321	..	..	..	..
Paraguay	..	..	45	55	..	63	53	56
Peru	..	88	100	110	116	118	106	109
Poland	467	502	500	475	453	372	361	420
Portugal	1 936	1 425	1 237	1 569	1 732	1 293	1 109	1 186
Puerto Rico	..	..	..	2 661	2 552	3 182	3 927	..
Russia	..	159	..	..	179	117	123	152
Singapore	2 989	3 391	3 728	4 047	4 489	4 400	4 631	5 411
Slovak Republic	519	550	508	542	543	434	..	925
Slovenia	1 239	1 303	1 202	1 209	1 196	1 011	1 028	1 102
South Africa	989	1 086	..	998	934	840	742	..
Spain	1 605	1 735	1 518	1 529	1 519	1 295	1 457	1 470
Sri Lanka	..	..	..	..	35	44	..	51
Sweden	2 525	2 781	2 376	2 644	4 908	3 961	3 796	4 248
Switzerland	6 755	7 969	7 634	7 898	7 892	7 456	7 025	6 904
Thailand	197	227	..	..	..	..	..	..
Tunisia	..	..	..	..	..	..	75	75
Turkey	130	133	146	168	151	145	162	152
United Kingdom	4 885	4 937	5 316	4 793	5 098	4 598	3 950	5 112
United States	5 228	5 492	5 750	5 683	5 965	6 299	6 493	6 706
Uruguay	..	268	310	351	377	368	..	451
OECD Total	3 115	3 296	3 197	3 131	3 292	3 155	3 352	3 457

.. Not available

Note: Detailed metadata at: *http://metalinks.oecd.org/ins/20190221/0f8b*.

1. Information on data for Israel: *http://oe.cd/israel-disclaimer*.

Source: Insurance activity indicators, OECD Insurance Statistics (database)

Table 14. Density (Life)

US dollar per inhabitant

	2010	2011	2012	2013	2014	2015	2016	2017
Argentina	..	..	68	70	70	67	70	60
Australia	1 713	1 993	1 854	1 896	2 318	1 779	1 521	1 335
Austria	1 178	1 143	981	1 007	1 038	860	765	733
Belgium	2 339	2 334	2 445	1 936	1 928	1 511	1 457	1 450
Bolivia	..	..	7	..	..	..	14	18
Brazil	..	189	209	203	207	170	189	213
Canada	836	856	819	833	627	553	..	..
Chile	321	351	424	444	405	431	475	482
Colombia	..	..	7	..	..	..	14	18
Costa Rica	14	18	24	30	30	27	38	39
Cuba	..	..	..	..	..	..	..	..
Czech Republic	359	388	350	348	326	241	229	230
Denmark	..	4 147	4 005	4 236	4 443	3 878	4 006	4 495
Ecuador	..	..	..	..	..	28	28	..
El Salvador	..	..	..	..	..	..	..	..
Estonia	172	168	158	172	193	181	186	192
Finland	1 291	962	885	1 365	1 483	1 268	922	927
France	715	2 758	2 305	2 485	2 680	2 343	2 386	2 437
Germany	..	..	1 326	1 444	1 454	1 179	1 147	1 194
Greece	269	267	225	203	228	184	171	197
Guatemala	..	8	8	9	10	9	10	11
Honduras	..	..	22	23	17	18	..	..
Hong Kong, China	3 208	3 454	3 882	4 446	5 082	5 644	7 041	7 645
Hungary	215	221	180	197	199	155	159	171
India	..	50	..	..	..	43	48	54
Indonesia	..	44	47	43	38	40	49	55
Iceland	90	94	91	102	110	106	127	160
Ireland	7 883	7 635	7 867	7 838	9 235	8 240	7 841	7 906
Israel[1]	760	861	835	915	904	903	935	1 076
Italy	1 998	1 712	1 487	1 865	2 410	2 095	1 863	1 832
Japan	3 200	3 651	3 355	2 545	2 580	2 370	2 496	2 252
Korea	1 413	1 566	1 894	1 966	2 069	2 031	2 015	..
Latvia	47	49	49	59	71	64	69	84
Lithuania	67	75	71	81	97	90	95	92
Luxembourg	51 162	33 174	44 176	41 856	48 703	34 590	32 101	37 644
Malaysia	280	305	332	333	340	294	290	295
Mexico	78	87	93	105	106	95	92	92
Netherlands	1 431	1 804	1 455	1 444	1 374	962	892	855
New Zealand	..	..	..	..	..	..	..	..
Nicaragua	..	3	4	5	5	5	6	7
Norway	2 245	2 568	2 789	2 715	2 837	2 187	2 133	2 139
Panama	..	18	112	128	..	..	..	..
Paraguay	..	..	..	7	..	8	0	8
Peru	..	42	47	51	57	57	48	52
Poland	273	282	293	260	239	192	159	171
Portugal	1 483	950	816	1 146	1 307	908	697	734
Puerto Rico	..	..	..	114	161	156	373	..
Russia	..	12	..	..	23	17	26	43
Singapore	2 390	2 723	2 725	3 045	3 392	3 404	3 611	4 374
Slovak Republic	277	295	276	303	299	227	..	682
Slovenia	315	326	303	305	309	268	264	281
South Africa	776	847	..	804	769	686	609	..
Spain	778	857	722	729	711	605	736	706
Sri Lanka	..	..	..	..	13	19	..	22
Sweden	1 325	1 466	1 362	1 469	3 562	2 994	2 931	3 335
Switzerland	3 715	4 372	4 177	4 385	4 378	4 113	3 739	3 573
Thailand	139	159	..	..	..	..	..	..
Tunisia	..	..	..	..	..	..	15	15
Turkey	23	25	23	26	19	17	25	27
United Kingdom	3 687	3 670	4 054	3 488	3 781	3 411	2 508	3 651
United States	2 364	2 517	2 640	2 471	2 473	2 573	2 584	2 636
Uruguay	..	65	82	101	111	123	..	190
OECD Total	1 687	1 905	1 849	1 737	1 823	1 701	1 685	1 725

.. Not available

Note: Detailed metadata at: *http://metalinks.oecd.org/ins/20190221/0f8b*.

1. Information on data for Israel: *http://oe.cd/israel-disclaimer*.

Source: Insurance activity indicators, OECD Insurance Statistics (database)

Table 15. Density (Non-life)

US dollar per inhabitant

	2010	2011	2012	2013	2014	2015	2016	2017
Argentina	..	..	265	323	335	351	352	333
Australia	1 188	1 385	1 472	1 451	1 365	1 143	1 140	1 206
Austria	1 460	1 597	1 511	1 595	1 615	1 366	1 377	1 438
Belgium	1 171	1 263	1 239	1 323	1 376	1 141	1 155	1 197
Bolivia	..	..	24	..	..	..	28	26
Brazil	..	129	123	132	137	101	97	107
Canada	1 495	1 660	1 741	1 701	1 533	1 370	..	..
Chile	165	209	221	221	207	198	199	212
Colombia	..	..	24	..	..	..	28	26
Costa Rica	144	154	175	190	211	188	208	226
Cuba	..	..	35	..	..	..	..	..
Czech Republic	411	434	383	399	386	333	325	360
Denmark	..	1 923	1 818	1 843	2 101	1 732	1 692	1 820
Ecuador	..	..	..	..	..	112	98	..
El Salvador	..	..	..	..	..	..	..	..
Estonia	252	253	308	414	444	401	434	512
Finland	848	885	814	1 005	1 069	881	874	871
France	1 307	1 422	1 340	1 407	1 425	1 209	1 713	1 788
Germany	..	..	1 564	1 667	1 672	1 416	1 453	1 635
Greece	348	341	286	277	228	177	188	190
Guatemala	..	33	31	34	36	39	40	43
Honduras	..	..	24	24	31	31	..	..
Hong Kong, China	440	463	521	557	577	615	611	624
Hungary	187	182	156	160	161	145	158	179
India	..	8	..	..	..	12	15	18
Indonesia	..	16	17	17	18	17	17	18
Iceland	1 100	1 178	1 133	1 152	1 206	1 124	1 296	1 612
Ireland	1 908	1 938	1 854	1 811	1 910	2 038	3 427	1 626
Israel[1]	714	771	742	815	845	782	838	925
Italy	786	838	752	734	711	582	580	598
Japan	695	765	..	..	..	..	705	641
Korea	877	1 046	1 196	1 215	1 433	1 386	1 421	..
Latvia	156	214	228	250	272	232	230	289
Lithuania	125	151	151	173	175	156	179	224
Luxembourg	3 114	3 526	3 141	3 699	3 223	2 901	2 978	3 367
Malaysia	153	173	182	187	190	160	150	144
Mexico	90	105	105	121	118	108	103	119
Netherlands	1 499	1 679	1 564	1 553	1 462	1 209	3 624	3 759
New Zealand	759	..	1 024	1 141	1 169	964	983	1 006
Nicaragua	..	18	20	22	24	26	27	29
Norway	1 946	2 217	2 322	2 295	2 295	1 780	1 840	1 719
Panama	..	..	174	192	..	..	..	..
Paraguay	..	..	26	48	..	54	53	48
Peru	..	46	53	59	59	61	58	58
Poland	194	220	207	216	214	180	202	249
Portugal	453	475	421	423	425	385	412	452
Puerto Rico	..	..	..	2 546	2 391	3 026	3 554	..
Russia	..	135	..	..	112	100	97	109
Singapore	599	668	1 004	1 001	1 098	996	1 021	1 037
Slovak Republic	242	255	232	238	244	207	..	243
Slovenia	924	977	899	904	888	744	764	821
South Africa	213	239	..	195	165	154	133	..
Spain	827	878	796	800	808	689	721	764
Sri Lanka	..	..	..	..	22	25	..	30
Sweden	1 200	1 315	1 015	1 175	1 346	967	865	913
Switzerland	3 040	3 597	3 458	3 513	3 514	3 343	3 286	3 331
Thailand	59	68	..	..	..	..	..	..
Tunisia	..	..	..	..	..	..	60	59
Turkey	107	108	123	141	131	128	137	125
United Kingdom	1 198	1 267	1 262	1 306	1 317	1 188	1 441	1 461
United States	2 864	2 975	3 110	3 212	3 492	3 726	3 908	4 069
Uruguay	..	203	228	250	266	245	..	261
OECD Total	1 303	1 391	1 348	1 394	1 470	1 455	1 667	1 732

.. Not available

Note: Detailed metadata at: *http://metalinks.oecd.org/ins/20190221/0f8b.*

1. Information on data for Israel: *http://oe.cd/israel-disclaimer.*

Source: Insurance activity indicators, OECD Insurance Statistics (database)

Table 16. Penetration (Life and Non-life)

Per cent

	2010	2011	2012	2013	2014	2015	2016	2017
Argentina	..	..	2.3	2.4	2.4	2.6	2.6	2.6
Australia	5.0	4.9	4.8	5.1	6.0	5.6	4.9	4.4
Austria	5.6	5.3	5.1	5.1	5.1	5.0	4.7	4.6
Belgium	7.9	7.5	8.2	7.0	7.0	6.5	6.3	6.1
Bolivia	..	..	1.2	..	..	..	1.4	1.3
Brazil	..	2.4	2.7	2.7	2.8	3.1	3.3	3.2
Canada	4.9	4.8	4.9	4.8	4.3	4.4	..	..
Chile	3.8	3.8	4.2	4.2	4.2	4.6	4.9	4.6
Colombia	..	..	1.2	..	..	..	1.4	1.3
Costa Rica	1.9	1.9	2.0	2.1	2.3	1.9	2.1	2.3
Cuba	..	..	..	..	..	..	..	..
Czech Republic	3.9	3.8	3.7	3.8	3.6	3.2	3.0	2.9
Denmark	..	9.8	9.9	9.9	10.4	10.5	10.4	11.0
Ecuador	..	..	..	..	..	2.3	2.1	..
El Salvador	..	..	..	..	..	..	..	..
Estonia	2.9	2.4	2.7	3.1	3.1	3.3	3.4	3.5
Finland	4.6	3.6	3.6	4.8	5.1	5.1	4.1	3.9
France	10.2	9.2	8.6	8.8	9.2	9.4	10.7	10.6
Germany	..	..	6.6	6.7	6.5	6.3	6.1	6.3
Greece	2.3	2.4	2.3	2.2	2.1	2.0	2.0	2.1
Guatemala	..	1.3	1.2	1.2	1.2	1.2	1.2	1.2
Honduras	..	..	1.9	2.0	1.9	1.9	..	..
Hong Kong, China	11.3	11.2	12.0	13.1	14.1	14.8	17.6	17.9
Hungary	3.1	2.9	2.6	2.6	2.5	2.4	2.5	2.5
India	..	3.8	..	..	..	3.4	3.6	3.6
Indonesia	..	1.6	1.7	1.6	1.6	1.7	1.8	1.9
Iceland	2.8	2.7	2.7	2.6	2.4	2.4	2.3	2.5
Ireland	20.1	18.4	19.8	18.6	19.9	16.4	17.5	13.6
Israel[1]	4.8	4.8	4.8	4.8	4.6	4.7	4.7	4.9
Italy	7.8	6.7	6.5	7.4	8.8	8.9	7.9	7.6
Japan	8.4	8.8	6.8	6.4	6.8	6.8	7.7	7.4
Korea	10.4	10.8	12.7	12.3	12.6	12.6	12.4	..
Latvia	1.8	1.9	2.0	2.1	2.2	2.2	2.1	2.4
Lithuania	1.6	1.6	1.6	1.6	1.6	1.7	1.8	1.9
Luxembourg	51.2	31.3	43.8	39.6	43.2	36.9	34.3	38.8
Malaysia	4.9	4.7	4.8	4.9	4.8	4.8	4.7	4.5
Mexico	1.8	1.9	1.9	2.1	2.0	2.1	2.2	2.3
Netherlands	5.8	6.4	6.0	5.7	5.4	4.8	9.8	9.5
New Zealand	2.3	..	2.6	2.7	2.7	2.5	2.5	2.4
Nicaragua	..	1.3	1.3	1.4	1.5	1.5	1.5	1.6
Norway	4.8	4.8	5.0	4.9	5.3	5.3	5.6	5.1
Panama	..	2.9	2.6	2.6	..	..	..	..
Paraguay	..	..	1.2	1.2	..	1.4	1.4	1.3
Peru	..	1.6	1.6	1.7	1.8	1.9	1.7	1.6
Poland	3.7	3.6	3.8	3.5	3.2	3.0	2.9	3.0
Portugal	8.6	6.1	6.0	7.3	7.8	6.7	5.6	5.6
Puerto Rico	..	..	..	9.3	8.8	10.7	12.8	..
Russia	..	1.1	..	..	1.2	1.2	1.4	1.4
Singapore	6.4	6.4	6.8	7.2	7.9	8.0	8.4	9.4
Slovak Republic	3.1	3.0	2.9	3.0	2.9	2.7	..	5.3
Slovenia	5.3	5.2	5.3	5.2	4.9	4.8	4.7	4.7
South Africa	13.4	13.4	..	14.5	14.4	14.5	13.9	..
Spain	5.2	5.5	5.3	5.2	5.1	5.0	5.5	5.2
Sri Lanka	..	..	..	..	0.9	1.1	..	1.3
Sweden	4.9	4.7	4.2	4.4	8.3	7.8	7.4	8.0
Switzerland	9.0	9.0	9.1	9.2	9.1	9.0	8.7	8.6
Thailand	3.9	4.1	..	..	..	..	..	..
Tunisia	..	..	..	..	..	..	2.0	2.1
Turkey	1.2	1.2	1.3	1.4	1.3	1.3	1.5	1.4
United Kingdom	12.5	11.9	12.7	11.2	10.9	10.3	9.8	12.8
United States	10.8	11.0	11.2	10.7	10.9	11.1	11.2	11.2
Uruguay	..	1.9	2.1	2.1	2.3	2.4	..	2.6
OECD Total	8.7	8.6	8.3	8.2	8.4	8.6	9.0	8.9

.. Not available

Note: Detailed metadata at: *http://metalinks.oecd.org/ins/20190221/0f8b*.

1. Information on data for Israel: *http://oe.cd/israel-disclaimer*.

Source: Insurance activity indicators, OECD Insurance Statistics (database)

Table 17. Penetration (Life)

Per cent

	2010	2011	2012	2013	2014	2015	2016	2017
Argentina	..	..	0.5	0.4	0.4	0.4	0.4	0.4
Australia	2.9	2.9	2.7	2.9	3.7	3.4	2.8	2.3
Austria	2.5	2.2	2.0	2.0	2.0	1.9	1.7	1.6
Belgium	5.2	4.9	5.4	4.1	4.1	3.7	3.5	3.3
Bolivia	..	..	0.3	..	..	..	0.5	0.5
Brazil	..	1.4	1.7	1.7	1.7	1.9	2.2	2.2
Canada	1.8	1.6	1.6	1.6	1.2	1.3	..	..
Chile	2.5	2.4	2.8	2.8	2.8	3.2	3.5	3.2
Colombia	..	..	0.3	..	..	..	0.5	0.5
Costa Rica	0.2	0.2	0.2	0.3	0.3	0.2	0.3	0.3
Cuba	..	..	..	..	..	..	..	..
Czech Republic	1.8	1.8	1.8	1.7	1.7	1.4	1.2	1.1
Denmark	..	6.7	6.8	6.9	7.1	7.3	7.3	7.8
Ecuador	..	..	..	..	..	0.5	0.5	..
El Salvador	..	..	..	..	..	..	..	..
Estonia	1.2	1.0	0.9	0.9	1.0	1.0	1.0	0.9
Finland	2.8	1.9	1.9	2.7	3.0	3.0	2.1	2.0
France	1.7	6.1	5.4	5.6	6.0	6.2	6.2	6.1
Germany	..	..	3.0	3.1	3.0	2.8	2.7	2.7
Greece	1.0	1.0	1.0	0.9	1.1	1.0	0.9	1.0
Guatemala	..	0.2	0.2	0.3	0.3	0.2	0.2	0.3
Honduras	..	..	0.9	1.0	0.7	0.7	..	..
Hong Kong, China	9.9	9.9	10.6	11.6	12.6	13.3	16.2	16.6
Hungary	1.6	1.6	1.4	1.4	1.4	1.2	1.2	1.2
India	..	3.3	..	..	..	2.7	2.7	2.7
Indonesia	..	1.2	1.2	1.2	1.1	1.2	1.3	1.4
Iceland	0.2	0.2	0.2	0.2	0.2	0.2	0.2	0.2
Ireland	16.2	14.7	16.1	15.1	16.5	13.2	12.2	11.3
Israel[1]	2.5	2.6	2.6	2.5	2.4	2.5	2.5	2.7
Italy	5.6	4.5	4.3	5.3	6.8	7.0	6.0	5.7
Japan	6.9	7.3	6.8	6.4	6.8	6.8	6.0	5.8
Korea	6.4	6.5	7.8	7.6	7.4	7.5	7.3	..
Latvia	0.4	0.4	0.4	0.4	0.5	0.5	0.5	0.5
Lithuania	0.6	0.5	0.5	0.5	0.6	0.6	0.6	0.5
Luxembourg	48.3	28.3	40.9	36.4	40.5	34.0	31.4	35.6
Malaysia	3.1	3.0	3.1	3.1	3.1	3.1	3.1	3.0
Mexico	0.8	0.9	0.9	1.0	1.0	1.0	1.0	1.0
Netherlands	2.8	3.3	2.9	2.8	2.6	2.1	1.9	1.8
New Zealand	..	..	..	..	..	..	..	..
Nicaragua	..	0.2	0.2	0.2	0.3	0.3	0.3	0.3
Norway	2.6	2.6	2.8	2.6	2.9	2.9	3.0	2.8
Panama	..	0.2	1.0	1.1	..	..	..	..
Paraguay	..	..	..	0.2	..	0.2	0.0	0.2
Peru	..	0.7	0.7	0.8	0.9	0.9	0.8	0.8
Poland	2.2	2.0	2.2	1.9	1.7	1.5	1.3	1.2
Portugal	6.6	4.1	4.0	5.3	5.9	4.7	3.5	3.4
Puerto Rico	..	..	..	0.4	0.6	0.5	1.2	..
Russia	..	0.1	..	..	0.2	0.2	0.3	0.4
Singapore	5.1	5.1	5.0	5.4	6.0	6.2	6.5	7.6
Slovak Republic	1.7	1.6	1.6	1.7	1.6	1.4	..	3.9
Slovenia	1.3	1.3	1.3	1.3	1.3	1.3	1.2	1.2
South Africa	10.5	10.5	..	11.6	11.8	11.8	11.5	..
Spain	2.5	2.7	2.5	2.5	2.4	2.3	2.8	2.5
Sri Lanka	..	..	..	..	0.3	0.5	..	0.5
Sweden	2.6	2.5	2.4	2.4	6.0	5.9	5.7	6.3
Switzerland	5.0	4.9	5.0	5.1	5.0	5.0	4.6	4.4
Thailand	2.7	2.9	..	..	..	..	..	..
Tunisia	..	..	..	..	..	..	0.4	0.4
Turkey	0.2	0.2	0.2	0.2	0.2	0.2	0.2	0.3
United Kingdom	9.4	8.8	9.6	8.1	8.0	7.7	6.2	9.1
United States	4.9	5.1	5.1	4.7	4.5	4.5	4.5	4.4
Uruguay	..	0.5	0.5	0.6	0.7	0.8	..	1.1
OECD Total	4.7	5.0	4.8	4.5	4.7	4.7	4.5	4.5

.. Not available

Note: Detailed metadata at: *http://metalinks.oecd.org/ins/20190221/0f8b*.

1. Information on data for Israel: *http://oe.cd/israel-disclaimer*.

Source: Insurance activity indicators, OECD Insurance Statistics (database)

Table 18. Penetration (Non-life)

Per cent

	2010	2011	2012	2013	2014	2015	2016	2017
Argentina	..	..	1.8	2.0	2.0	2.2	2.1	2.2
Australia	2.0	2.0	2.1	2.2	2.2	2.2	2.1	2.1
Austria	3.1	3.1	3.1	3.1	3.1	3.1	3.1	3.0
Belgium	2.6	2.6	2.8	2.8	2.9	2.8	2.8	2.7
Bolivia	..	..	0.9	..	..	..	0.9	0.8
Brazil	..	1.0	1.0	1.1	1.1	1.1	1.1	1.1
Canada	3.1	3.2	3.3	3.2	3.0	3.2	..	..
Chile	1.3	1.4	1.4	1.4	1.4	1.5	1.5	1.4
Colombia	..	..	0.9	..	..	..	0.9	0.8
Costa Rica	1.8	1.7	1.8	1.8	2.0	1.7	1.8	1.9
Cuba	..	..	..	..	..	..	..	..
Czech Republic	2.1	2.0	1.9	2.0	2.0	1.9	1.8	1.8
Denmark	..	3.1	3.1	3.0	3.3	3.2	3.1	3.2
Ecuador	..	..	..	..	..	1.8	1.7	..
El Salvador	..	..	..	..	..	..	..	..
Estonia	1.7	1.5	1.8	2.2	2.2	2.3	2.4	2.5
Finland	1.8	1.7	1.7	2.0	2.1	2.1	2.0	1.9
France	3.1	3.1	3.2	3.2	3.2	3.2	4.5	4.5
Germany	..	..	3.6	3.6	3.5	3.4	3.4	3.7
Greece	1.3	1.3	1.3	1.3	1.1	1.0	1.0	1.0
Guatemala	..	1.0	0.9	1.0	1.0	1.0	1.0	1.0
Honduras	..	..	1.0	1.0	1.2	1.2	..	..
Hong Kong, China	1.4	1.3	1.4	1.5	1.4	1.5	1.4	1.4
Hungary	1.4	1.3	1.2	1.2	1.1	1.2	1.2	1.3
India	..	0.5	..	..	..	0.7	0.9	0.9
Indonesia	..	0.4	0.4	0.5	0.5	0.5	0.5	0.5
Iceland	2.6	2.5	2.5	2.3	2.2	2.2	2.1	2.2
Ireland	3.9	3.7	3.8	3.5	3.4	3.3	5.3	2.3
Israel[1]	2.3	2.3	2.3	2.2	2.2	2.2	2.2	2.3
Italy	2.2	2.2	2.2	2.1	2.0	1.9	1.9	1.9
Japan	1.5	1.5	..	..	..	..	1.7	1.6
Korea	4.0	4.3	4.9	4.7	5.2	5.1	5.1	..
Latvia	1.4	1.6	1.7	1.7	1.7	1.7	1.6	1.9
Lithuania	1.0	1.1	1.1	1.1	1.1	1.1	1.2	1.3
Luxembourg	2.9	3.0	2.9	3.2	2.7	2.9	2.9	3.2
Malaysia	1.7	1.7	1.7	1.7	1.7	1.7	1.6	1.5
Mexico	1.0	1.0	1.0	1.1	1.1	1.1	1.2	1.3
Netherlands	2.9	3.1	3.1	3.0	2.8	2.7	7.9	7.7
New Zealand	2.3	..	2.6	2.7	2.7	2.5	2.5	2.4
Nicaragua	..	1.1	1.1	1.2	1.2	1.2	1.3	1.3
Norway	2.2	2.2	2.3	2.2	2.4	2.4	2.6	2.3
Panama	..	..	1.6	1.6	..	..	..	..
Paraguay	..	..	0.7	1.1	..	1.2	1.4	1.2
Peru	..	0.8	0.8	0.9	0.9	1.0	0.9	0.9
Poland	1.5	1.6	1.6	1.6	1.5	1.4	1.6	1.8
Portugal	2.0	2.0	2.0	2.0	1.9	2.0	2.1	2.1
Puerto Rico	..	..	..	8.9	8.3	10.2	11.5	..
Russia	..	0.9	..	..	0.8	1.1	1.1	1.0
Singapore	1.3	1.3	1.8	1.8	1.9	1.8	1.8	1.8
Slovak Republic	1.5	1.4	1.3	1.3	1.3	1.3	..	1.4
Slovenia	3.9	3.9	4.0	3.9	3.7	3.6	3.5	3.5
South Africa	2.9	3.0	..	2.8	2.5	2.7	2.5	..
Spain	2.7	2.8	2.8	2.7	2.7	2.7	2.7	2.7
Sri Lanka	..	..	..	..	0.6	0.6	..	0.7
Sweden	2.3	2.2	1.8	2.0	2.3	1.9	1.7	1.7
Switzerland	4.1	4.0	4.1	4.1	4.0	4.1	4.1	4.1
Thailand	1.2	1.2	..	..	..	..	..	..
Tunisia	..	..	..	..	..	..	1.6	1.7
Turkey	1.0	1.0	1.1	1.1	1.1	1.2	1.3	1.2
United Kingdom	3.1	3.0	3.0	3.0	2.8	2.7	3.6	3.7
United States	5.9	6.0	6.0	6.1	6.4	6.6	6.8	6.8
Uruguay	..	1.4	1.5	1.5	1.6	1.6	..	1.5
OECD Total	3.6	3.6	4.1	4.1	4.2	4.4	4.5	4.5

.. Not available

Note: Detailed metadata at: *http://metalinks.oecd.org/ins/20190221/0f8b*.

1. Information on data for Israel: *http://oe.cd/israel-disclaimer*.

Source: Insurance activity indicators, OECD Insurance Statistics (database)

Table 19. Life insurance share

Percentage of total insurance

Per cent

	2010	2011	2012	2013	2014	2015	2016	2017
Argentina	..	..	20.7	17.8	16.5	15.3	16.0	14.7
Australia	57.0	56.7	53.6	54.9	61.1	59.2	55.4	52.1
Austria	..	..	..	34.1	35.5	35.3	32.5	31.7
Belgium	65.0	63.2	64.7	57.7	56.5	55.4	54.4	53.7
Bolivia	..	..	21.8	..	..	..	33.5	40.4
Brazil	..	..	..	..	60.2	62.7	66.1	66.5
Canada	35.6	34.0	32.1	32.9	28.7	28.7	..	..
Chile	66.0	62.5	65.5	66.5	65.8	68.3	70.4	69.4
Colombia	..	..	21.8	..	..	..	33.5	40.4
Costa Rica	8.8	10.6	11.9	13.4	12.3	12.7	15.4	14.7
Cuba	..	..	..	..	..	..	..	..
Czech Republic	46.0	46.4	46.9	45.7	45.1	41.1	40.6	38.3
Denmark	..	68.2	68.7	95.4	67.7	68.9	68.7	69.1
Ecuador	..	..	..	..	..	19.5	22.0	..
El Salvador	..	20.7	22.7	26.7	25.7	25.6	24.7	..
Estonia	40.6	39.8	33.9	29.3	30.3	31.2	30.0	27.3
Finland	59.5	51.2	51.2	56.8	57.4	58.3	50.6	50.7
France	17.2	63.9	62.1	62.4	64.2	64.2	58.0	55.2
Germany	47.9	45.7	35.5	36.0	35.9	34.0	33.1	32.1
Greece	43.3	43.7	43.2	41.4	49.5	50.5	47.2	50.4
Guatemala	..	..	20.3	19.9	20.8	19.4	19.9	20.5
Honduras	..	..	..	30.9	35.3	36.4	..	..
Hong Kong, China	85.0	84.8	84.7	85.7	86.9	87.6	90.1	90.4
Hungary	53.2	54.6	53.0	54.5	54.8	51.1	49.5	48.2
India	..	85.5	..	..	..	78.2	..	70.7
Indonesia	..	..	70.6	67.9	66.2	69.0	72.6	74.6
Iceland	7.5	7.3	7.3	7.9	8.2	8.4	8.8	8.9
Ireland	80.3	79.2	80.3	80.6	82.2	79.6	68.5	82.5
Israel[1]	51.6	52.8	52.9	52.9	51.7	53.6	52.7	53.8
Italy	71.8	67.1	66.5	71.4	76.8	77.8	75.8	75.0
Japan	80.2	80.7	100.0	100.0	100.0	100.0	75.5	75.1
Korea	59.6	57.5	59.0	59.3	56.8	57.1	56.3	..
Latvia	23.0	18.4	17.6	18.9	20.6	21.6	23.2	22.5
Lithuania	34.7	33.0	32.0	32.0	35.8	36.6	34.7	29.2
Luxembourg	94.3	90.4	93.4	91.9	93.9	92.3	91.5	91.8
Malaysia	61.1	60.3	60.6	60.1	60.2	60.6	61.7	63.4
Mexico	46.1	44.7	46.2	46.1	46.8	46.3	46.7	43.0
Netherlands	51.1	51.4	47.6	47.4	47.7	43.6	19.6	18.2
New Zealand	..	..	..	..	..	..	..	..
Nicaragua	..	..	15.8	17.2	17.8	17.4	18.6	..
Norway	53.6	53.7	54.6	54.2	55.3	55.1	55.4	55.4
Panama	..	..	38.5	39.7	..	..	..	..
Paraguay	..	..	..	12.2	..	13.3	0.2	13.9
Peru	..	48.0	47.2	46.8	49.1	48.4	45.3	47.0
Poland	58.0	55.7	58.1	54.0	52.2	50.2	42.6	39.4
Portugal	74.6	64.2	63.3	70.5	72.9	67.5	59.6	58.6
Puerto Rico	..	..	..	4.3	6.3	4.9	9.5	..
Russia	..	7.5	..	..	12.6	13.9	20.4	27.4
Singapore	68.4	67.0	65.8	67.9	68.5	69.3	71.6	74.9
Slovak Republic	53.0	53.2	53.9	55.5	54.3	51.2	..	73.6
Slovenia	22.4	22.0	22.1	22.4	22.9	23.1	22.5	22.4
South Africa	78.5	78.0	79.2	78.6	80.5	79.9	79.7	..
Spain	47.6	46.9	46.4	44.6	43.9	43.6	47.1	44.8
Sri Lanka	..	..	..	..	35.5	42.5	..	41.4
Sweden	48.8	49.6	54.0	52.2	69.6	73.3	74.9	76.1
Switzerland	47.4	48.4	47.9	48.2	48.5	48.9	46.9	45.0
Thailand	69.1	69.0	..	..	..	..	..	..
Tunisia	..	..	..	..	..	..	20.3	19.7
Turkey	17.5	18.3	15.4	15.7	12.3	11.8	14.9	17.3
United Kingdom	73.6	73.5	75.4	72.4	73.4	73.3	68.8	68.3
United States	39.3	40.1	40.3	38.5	36.2	37.1	35.9	35.6
Uruguay	..	..	26.4	28.7	29.5	33.4	..	42.2
OECD Total	49.6	52.9	53.2	52.7	50.2	49.2	46.8	45.3

.. Not available

Note: Detailed metadata at: *http://metalinks.oecd.org/ins/20190221/0f8b.*

1. Information on data for Israel: *http://oe.cd/israel-disclaimer.*

Source: Insurance activity indicators, OECD Insurance Statistics (database)

INTERNATIONAL COMPARISONS

Table 20. Direct total gross premiums per insurance company employee

US dollars

	2010	2011	2012	2013	2014	2015	2016	2017
Argentina	..	..	..	289 071	296 157	290 581	..	264 715
Australia	..	..	..	..	..	..	..	..
Austria	794 659	830 770	765 436	795 141	815 630	688 309	660 435	674 513
Belgium	907 893	..	..	..	..	..	..	..
Bolivia	..	..	..	..	..	..	112 942	99 464
Brazil	..	..	..	..	..	..	..	..
Canada	..	..	..	..	..	..	..	..
Chile	406 570	448 189	486 192	493 638	454 677	495 261	510 666	519 672
Colombia	..	..	..	..	..	..	112 942	99 464
Costa Rica	..	..	..	..	..	..	..	..
Cuba	..	..	..	..	..	..	..	..
Czech Republic	..	..	..	..	..	..	..	..
Denmark	..	2 092 465	2 052 306	2 215 121	2 158 639	1 927 585	2 018 459	2 661 767
Ecuador	..	..	..	..	..	2 202 989	292 344	..
El Salvador	..	..	..	..	..	..	..	..
Estonia	..	208 774	224 249	200 167	221 703	200 336	..	..
Finland	1 198 102	1 027 920	949 685	1 363 348	1 512 846	1 310 951	1 087 714	1 234 435
France	..	..	..	..	..	..	..	..
Germany	..	..	1 508 982	1 607 329	1 646 967	1 370 540	1 366 726	1 516 822
Greece	..	..	..	..	..	..	..	..
Guatemala	..	..	137 904	..	159 900	..	181 604	186 479
Honduras	..	..	..	267 721	183 148	217 165	..	..
Hong Kong, China	..	..	..	..	..	..	..	617 084
Hungary	145 931	151 723	143 598	157 425	161 509	147 122	169 626	168 073
India	..	..	..	..	..	..	..	32 479
Indonesia	..	..	23 320	..	..	..	..	..
Iceland	613 285	624 626	..	665 881	731 603	703 782	..	..
Ireland	..	4 521 646	5 146 079	5 004 239	..	..	..	..
Israel[1]	..	..	..	..	..	..	..	..
Italy	632 728	572 450	516 329	588 438	728 137	622 467	584 701	..
Japan	..	..	..	129 385	130 139	144 659	..	1 060 963
Korea	347 369	387 679	442 588	466 477	580 301	590 964	611 062	..
Latvia	104 420	134 363	144 568	198 707	237 130	301 704	..	..
Lithuania	118 376	131 547	116 324	128 811	136 338	120 793	129 952	147 340
Luxembourg	1 972 257	1 408 398	1 776 286	1 555 995	4 322 564	2 996 082	2 884 045	3 012 514
Malaysia	482 196	492 814	567 984	651 774	650 745	461 454	465 847	435 343
Mexico	397 414	447 668	457 259	436 528	403 458	330 532	410 335	423 179
Netherlands	..	..	..	..	..	..	..	..
New Zealand	343 870	..	425 805	473 708	..	..	..	..
Nicaragua	..	..	..	1 704 849	119 312	2 050 664	..	..
Norway	2 109 103	..	..	..	..	..	..	..
Panama	..	..	347 935	392 524	..	..	..	..
Paraguay	..	..	103 065	386 727	..	124 344	..	..
Peru	..	257 668	251 417	285 142	301 442	290 594	..	..
Poland	181 086	181 339	198 127	169 341	183 458	167 678	..	..
Portugal	561 280	414 091	389 160	490 832	550 771	416 110	371 730	412 331
Puerto Rico	..	..	..	780 437	704 962	856 812	1 042 984	..
Russia	..	51 053	..	..	73 609	..	61 185	121 961
Singapore	..	..	..	..	..	..	..	..
Slovak Republic	389 851	417 623	378 475	..	403 073	..	..	..
Slovenia	..	..	..	..	..	..	..	..
South Africa	..	..	..	..	..	..	..	..
Spain	1 462 199	..	..	424 580	402 914	..	..	..
Sri Lanka	..	..	..	..	24 436	26 631	..	17 383
Sweden	1 131 069	1 264 886	1 073 328	1 210 867	2 042 276	1 771 433	..	1 686 900
Switzerland	..	..	..	..	..	..	..	..
Thailand	..	..	..	..	..	..	..	..
Tunisia	..	..	..	..	..	..	173 680	..
Turkey	301 983	369 673	322 731	379 315	335 385	298 749	233 812	204 510
United Kingdom	..	..	..	..	..	..	..	..
United States	..	..	..	..	..	..	..	..
Uruguay	..	..	..	..	..	..	..	..
OECD Total	554 719	531 111	665 158	318 505	332 855	333 479	719 113	1 019 108

.. Not available

Note: Detailed metadata at: *http://metalinks.oecd.org/ins/20190221/0f8b*.

1. Information on data for Israel: *http://oe.cd/israel-disclaimer*.

Source: Insurance activity indicators, OECD Insurance Statistics (database)

Table 21. Retention ratio (Life and Non-life)

Per cent

	2010	2011	2012	2013	2014	2015	2016	2017
Argentina	..	..	88.9	90.6	86.5	87.5	88.4	88.7
Australia	85.2	84.5	84.1	84.5	86.0	83.8	80.4	77.1
Austria	..	..	..	81.3	83.6	84.2	81.1	82.7
Belgium	94.0	95.1	92.6	91.2	88.7	88.5	87.2	87.5
Bolivia	..	..	50.3	..	..	..	49.8	51.5
Brazil	..	..	..	..	95.2	95.4	95.8	95.7
Canada	78.9	75.2	73.3	73.1	73.5	71.4	..	..
Chile	..	80.6	83.1	84.4	84.0	84.8	84.4	83.4
Colombia	..	..	50.3	..	..	..	49.8	51.5
Costa Rica	79.4	81.1	80.9	78.6	80.2	77.9	78.9	79.4
Cuba	..	..	..	..	..	..	..	..
Czech Republic	82.4	81.5	81.3	80.6	80.3	79.3	78.9	78.7
Denmark	..	95.8	96.3	99.4	97.2	97.1	96.9	96.7
Ecuador	..	..	..	..	..	72.4	72.3	..
El Salvador	..	61.0	62.0	66.6	66.6	66.5	64.2	..
Estonia	95.2	95.1	..	..	..	..	..	..
Finland	97.2	96.7	96.7	97.4	97.6	97.7	97.3	97.4
France	91.4	89.9	89.2	89.3	91.0	88.6	84.8	88.0
Germany	..	..	90.2	89.7	89.0	87.7	87.9	87.5
Greece	88.2	83.3	88.1	79.8	87.6	87.2	88.8	89.2
Guatemala	..	..	68.0	66.3	64.2	64.9	67.8	67.2
Honduras	..	..	..	55.7	54.4	53.0	..	..
Hong Kong, China	89.0	86.0	87.6	87.0	87.7	88.3	90.4	90.4
Hungary	84.0	83.9	83.3	86.1	86.1	86.1	86.7	87.4
India	..	95.5	..	..	..	95.2	..	91.8
Indonesia	..	..	86.2	85.5	83.8	84.8	86.0	87.3
Iceland	92.2	92.9	93.3	93.9	94.4	94.8	95.4	96.0
Ireland	89.0	86.7	88.4	87.8	89.2	88.0	79.6	..
Israel[1]	86.0	85.6	85.7	87.3	88.5	88.4	84.9	86.5
Italy	95.9	95.5	95.1	96.2	97.1	97.2	96.4	96.3
Japan	94.1	93.3	94.1	94.9	94.3	94.6	89.5	89.8
Korea	93.8	94.6	95.0	94.7	94.7	94.7	94.7	..
Latvia	93.1	94.0	94.2	96.3	96.3	95.9	95.3	93.2
Lithuania	..	..	..	..	95.2	95.1	95.0	91.5
Luxembourg	73.9	78.4	68.6	74.9	71.8	84.1	82.2	85.8
Malaysia	87.1	86.5	86.9	87.8	87.8	87.9	88.3	88.6
Mexico	85.4	82.3	83.8	82.6	83.9	83.0	84.4	81.4
Netherlands	91.3	86.2	92.0	92.3	89.4	91.7	98.3	97.6
New Zealand	..	..	..	..	..	..	..	..
Nicaragua	..	..	62.0	63.8	63.3	65.7	66.7	..
Norway	..	..	93.0	92.9	93.1	92.2	92.7	93.0
Panama	..	..	57.4	55.6	..	..	..	..
Paraguay	..	..	..	79.1	..	79.6	78.0	77.4
Peru	..	78.0	76.7	76.7	75.5	74.5	73.3	75.0
Poland	93.7	93.3	92.7	92.7	92.4	90.5	87.9	88.4
Portugal	93.5	91.1	89.6	91.1	92.0	90.5	88.9	88.6
Puerto Rico	..	..	..	99.6	98.6	92.9	93.9	..
Russia	..	97.7	..	..	86.9	88.6	88.9	91.7
Singapore	87.3	86.9	85.5	85.9	86.8	79.2	77.6	77.0
Slovak Republic	86.9	85.5	85.6	85.8	85.3	84.5	..	92.2
Slovenia	87.3	87.2	87.1	87.8	86.9	88.1	87.7	86.5
South Africa	..	85.1	90.9	87.6	88.2	89.7	88.9	..
Spain	92.4	93.0	92.5	90.0	91.3	91.3	91.0	90.6
Sri Lanka	..	..	..	..	87.0	86.6	..	85.6
Sweden	92.6	92.9	92.2	92.7	95.6	97.0	97.3	97.2
Switzerland	91.8	93.0	92.5	92.6	92.9	93.1	93.7	92.6
Thailand	90.4	90.2	..	..	..	..	..	..
Tunisia	..	..	..	..	..	..	80.9	100.0
Turkey	76.9	74.9	77.9	75.6	75.0	74.8	76.1	72.0
United Kingdom	89.6	88.4	87.7	87.4	84.8	89.0	77.0	87.9
United States	73.9	74.0	73.6	71.3	74.9	72.8	72.5	71.4
Uruguay	..	..	91.0	91.2	90.8	91.5	..	92.9
OECD Total	82.6	82.3	82.1	81.5	82.5	80.7	79.5	79.1

.. Not available

Note: Detailed metadata at: *http://metalinks.oecd.org/ins/20190221/0f8b.*

1. Information on data for Israel: *http://oe.cd/israel-disclaimer.*

Source: Insurance activity indicators, OECD Insurance Statistics (database)

INTERNATIONAL COMPARISONS

Table 22. Retention ratio (Life)

Per cent

	2010	2011	2012	2013	2014	2015	2016	2017
Argentina	..	..	92.7	96.6	97.1	97.2	96.7	96.8
Australia	91.8	91.9	92.1	92.3	92.5	91.3	89.3	82.5
Austria	..	..	..	96.7	97.4	97.6	97.4	97.8
Belgium	97.8	97.6	97.7	97.0	97.6	97.9	96.7	98.0
Bolivia	..	..	79.5	..	..	..	64.6	63.7
Brazil	..	..	..	..	99.6	99.5	99.6	99.5
Canada	78.5	75.6	73.9	75.2	69.5	67.6	..	..
Chile	..	96.3	97.4	98.0	97.7	97.5	95.0	92.6
Colombia	..	..	79.5	..	..	..	64.6	63.7
Costa Rica	93.0	93.3	90.8	84.7	87.4	81.4	82.8	81.4
Cuba	..	..	..	..	..	..	..	..
Czech Republic	97.8	96.1	95.0	93.9	93.0	92.4	92.3	91.7
Denmark	..	99.7	99.7	100.0	99.8	99.8	99.8	99.8
Ecuador	..	..	..	..	..	81.6	99.2	..
El Salvador	..	78.4	81.1	95.0	87.3	81.6	80.8	..
Estonia	99.1	98.9	..	..	..	..	..	..
Finland	99.3	99.0	99.0	99.4	99.5	99.5	99.3	99.4
France	89.2	93.1	92.9	92.5	94.1	90.7	86.5	93.2
Germany	..	..	96.9	96.8	97.0	97.0	96.6	97.0
Greece	94.8	84.8	95.1	94.8	95.6	95.9	96.2	95.0
Guatemala	..	..	76.6	75.3	76.6	76.9	80.9	79.9
Honduras	..	..	..	61.1	45.4	56.1	..	..
Hong Kong, China	92.4	89.2	91.0	90.0	90.5	91.0	92.8	92.7
Hungary	92.8	93.1	93.6	95.0	96.3	96.8	97.3	98.7
India	..	99.8	..	..	..	99.6	..	99.5
Indonesia	..	..	97.3	97.2	96.7	96.8	97.3	97.4
Iceland	84.2	82.0	82.5	83.9	82.3	83.7	85.2	85.9
Ireland	93.5	91.3	94.4	93.7	94.0	94.1	94.9	..
Israel[1]	95.0	95.0	95.2	95.3	95.2	95.5	95.1	95.2
Italy	98.4	98.2	98.3	98.8	99.0	99.1	99.1	99.1
Japan	97.2	96.4	94.1	94.9	94.3	94.6	93.1	93.6
Korea	97.2	98.5	98.8	98.8	98.8	98.7	98.6	..
Latvia	99.3	99.7	99.7	99.8	99.8	99.8	99.8	99.8
Lithuania	..	..	..	..	98.5	98.0	98.5	98.3
Luxembourg	74.1	80.0	68.9	76.4	72.1	85.3	83.6	87.4
Malaysia	96.8	96.8	96.7	97.3	96.9	96.7	96.6	95.9
Mexico	97.4	94.6	94.8	95.3	96.6	96.4	96.2	95.4
Netherlands	95.8	94.6	94.9	95.4	89.6	94.0	97.2	96.4
New Zealand	..	..	..	..	..	..	..	..
Nicaragua	..	..	63.7	60.3	55.3	59.2	58.2	..
Norway	..	..	98.6	98.8	98.9	98.7	98.9	98.9
Panama	..	..	80.4	77.7	..	..	..	..
Paraguay	..	..	..	80.7	..	81.7	41.0	83.0
Peru	..	90.8	88.8	89.5	84.4	84.7	82.4	83.7
Poland	98.2	99.1	97.6	98.6	98.5	98.2	98.3	99.4
Portugal	98.5	97.9	96.4	97.0	97.7	97.2	96.5	96.5
Puerto Rico	..	..	..	103.3	100.0	56.0	78.0	..
Russia	..	..	..	..	98.4	98.6	98.8	99.2
Singapore	95.3	96.3	96.6	95.1	96.1	88.4	84.3	82.3
Slovak Republic	99.2	98.3	98.4	98.4	98.2	97.9	..	99.0
Slovenia	98.1	97.6	97.5	97.2	96.9	96.7	96.3	96.4
South Africa	..	89.4	94.9	92.5	93.2	95.2	94.6	..
Spain	98.1	98.0	94.7	93.9	96.4	96.8	97.3	96.2
Sri Lanka	..	..	..	..	96.3	96.3	..	96.0
Sweden	98.0	98.0	99.1	98.7	99.6	99.8	99.9	99.7
Switzerland	99.3	99.3	99.4	99.3	99.4	99.4	99.3	99.3
Thailand	98.4	98.4	..	..	..	..	..	..
Tunisia	..	..	..	..	..	..	90.4	100.0
Turkey	89.3	90.5	95.1	95.7	94.8	95.1	95.8	96.2
United Kingdom	92.7	90.4	89.0	88.9	85.4	91.2	80.3	95.3
United States	84.7	84.3	83.5	77.4	88.3	80.4	80.0	77.8
Uruguay	..	..	97.0	97.5	97.6	97.6	..	97.4
OECD Total	90.9	90.7	89.8	88.7	91.6	88.6	86.8	87.3

.. Not available

Note: Detailed metadata at: *http://metalinks.oecd.org/ins/20190221/0f8b*.

1. Information on data for Israel: *http://oe.cd/israel-disclaimer*.

Source: Insurance activity indicators, OECD Insurance Statistics (database)

Table 23. Retention ratio (Non-life)

Per cent

	2010	2011	2012	2013	2014	2015	2016	2017
Argentina	..	..	87.9	89.3	84.4	85.7	86.8	87.3
Australia	76.6	74.9	74.9	75.0	75.7	73.0	69.3	71.3
Austria	..	..	..	73.2	76.0	77.0	73.3	75.8
Belgium	83.2	87.0	83.2	83.4	77.2	76.8	75.8	75.4
Bolivia	..	..	42.2	..	..	..	42.4	43.1
Brazil	..	..	..	..	88.5	88.5	88.4	88.3
Canada	79.1	75.0	73.0	72.1	75.2	72.9	..	..
Chile	..	54.4	55.9	57.6	57.7	57.4	59.1	62.7
Colombia	..	..	42.2	..	..	..	42.4	43.1
Costa Rica	78.1	79.7	79.5	77.6	79.2	77.3	78.2	79.0
Cuba	..	..	..	..	..	..	..	..
Czech Republic	69.2	68.8	69.2	69.4	69.8	70.2	69.8	70.6
Denmark	..	87.3	88.9	88.1	91.7	91.1	90.6	89.9
Ecuador	..	..	..	..	..	70.1	64.7	..
El Salvador	..	56.4	56.3	56.2	58.4	60.1	57.1	..
Estonia	92.6	92.5	..	..	..	..	..	..
Finland	94.2	94.3	94.3	94.7	95.0	95.2	95.3	95.4
France	84.9	84.2	83.2	84.1	85.3	84.8	82.4	81.7
Germany	..	..	86.5	85.7	84.6	82.9	83.7	83.0
Greece	83.2	82.2	82.9	69.1	79.8	78.3	82.2	83.3
Guatemala	..	..	65.9	64.0	61.0	62.0	64.5	63.9
Honduras	..	..	..	53.3	59.3	51.3	..	..
Hong Kong, China	69.9	68.5	68.7	69.3	69.0	69.8	68.9	68.7
Hungary	74.1	72.9	71.6	75.3	73.6	75.0	76.2	76.9
India	..	70.4	..	..	..	79.5	..	73.1
Indonesia	..	..	59.4	60.8	58.4	58.3	55.7	57.6
Iceland	92.9	93.7	94.2	94.7	95.5	95.8	96.3	97.0
Ireland	70.9	69.3	64.1	63.1	67.1	64.1	46.3	..
Israel[1]	76.4	75.1	75.0	78.2	81.2	80.2	73.6	76.4
Italy	89.4	90.0	89.0	89.9	90.5	90.6	87.9	87.8
Japan	81.4	80.2	..	..	..	..	78.4	78.2
Korea	88.8	89.4	89.5	88.6	89.5	89.4	89.8	..
Latvia	91.3	92.7	93.0	95.5	95.4	94.8	93.9	91.3
Lithuania	..	..	..	..	93.3	93.4	93.0	88.6
Luxembourg	70.7	64.1	64.3	58.5	65.9	68.9	66.7	67.7
Malaysia	71.8	70.9	71.8	73.6	74.0	74.4	74.9	76.0
Mexico	75.1	72.5	74.4	71.7	72.8	71.5	74.0	70.8
Netherlands	86.6	77.2	89.4	89.5	89.2	89.9	98.5	98.1
New Zealand	87.0	..	78.7	77.5	80.0	80.5	73.8	74.4
Nicaragua	..	..	61.7	64.6	65.0	67.0	68.7	..
Norway	..	..	86.2	85.9	85.9	84.3	85.0	85.5
Panama	..	..	43.0	41.0	..	..	..	..
Paraguay	..	..	71.2	78.9	..	79.3	78.0	76.5
Peru	..	66.1	65.8	65.5	67.0	65.0	65.7	67.3
Poland	87.6	85.9	85.9	85.8	85.8	82.8	80.2	81.3
Portugal	78.6	78.8	77.9	76.9	76.8	76.6	77.7	77.4
Puerto Rico	..	..	..	99.5	98.5	94.8	95.5	..
Russia	..	84.3	..	..	82.0	87.0	86.4	88.9
Singapore	70.0	67.9	64.2	66.5	66.5	58.4	60.9	61.0
Slovak Republic	73.0	71.0	70.7	70.1	69.9	70.4	..	73.3
Slovenia	84.2	84.3	84.2	85.1	84.0	85.5	85.2	83.6
South Africa	..	69.5	75.7	69.8	67.7	68.0	66.8	..
Spain	87.3	88.5	90.5	86.8	87.3	87.0	85.3	86.0
Sri Lanka	..	..	..	..	81.9	79.4	..	78.3
Sweden	87.4	87.9	84.0	86.1	86.5	89.3	89.5	89.1
Switzerland	85.2	87.0	86.1	86.4	86.7	87.0	88.8	87.1
Thailand	72.5	72.1	..	..	..	..	..	..
Tunisia	..	..	..	..	..	..	78.6	100.0
Turkey	74.3	71.4	74.8	71.9	72.2	72.1	72.7	66.9
United Kingdom	81.0	82.8	83.8	83.4	83.2	82.8	69.5	72.0
United States	66.9	67.1	66.9	67.4	67.3	68.2	68.3	67.9
Uruguay	..	..	88.9	88.7	87.9	88.4	..	89.7
OECD Total	72.6	72.7	73.3	73.5	73.4	73.0	73.0	72.4

.. Not available

Note: Detailed metadata at: *http://metalinks.oecd.org/ins/20190221/0f8b.*

1. Information on data for Israel: *http://oe.cd/israel-disclaimer.*

Source: Insurance activity indicators, OECD Insurance Statistics (database)

Table 24. Ratio of reinsurance accepted (Life and Non-life)

Per cent

	2010	2011	2012	2013	2014	2015	2016	2017
Argentina	..	..	0.5	0.3	7.2	7.0	6.7	6.6
Australia	9.1	10.0	11.1	10.9	10.1	10.9	12.5	13.0
Austria	..	..	..	12.0	9.6	8.9	9.3	6.4
Belgium	2.9	3.1	2.7	3.2	3.5	3.0	2.9	2.3
Bolivia	..	..	0.6	..	..	..	1.0	3.9
Brazil	..	..	..	..	0.0	0.0	0.0	0.0
Canada	7.7	8.2	8.5	9.7	17.7	17.6	..	..
Chile	0.3	0.3	0.5	0.5	0.6	0.8	1.1	0.9
Colombia	..	..	0.6	..	..	..	1.0	3.9
Costa Rica	0.1	0.1	0.2	0.3	0.3	0.3	0.3	0.3
Cuba	..	..	..	..	..	..	..	..
Czech Republic	1.4	1.7	1.9	1.8	1.6	2.0	2.4	2.5
Denmark	..	0.3	0.8	84.9	0.8	0.8	2.9	3.3
Ecuador	..	..	..	..	..	2.0	1.7	..
El Salvador	..	..	..	..	..	..	..	..
Estonia	0.0	0.1	..	..	..	..	..	..
Finland	1.5	1.9	1.9	1.5	1.4	1.3	1.5	1.6
France	8.9	8.7	10.7	10.1	10.5	8.9	15.7	12.7
Germany	..	..	23.2	22.4	22.4	24.6	24.5	24.6
Greece	1.2	1.7	2.0	2.3	1.2	1.1	1.0	0.9
Guatemala	..	..	2.9	2.7	2.7	3.1	2.9	2.9
Honduras	..	..	..	0.0	0.0	0.0	..	..
Hong Kong, China	4.4	4.8	4.9	4.7	4.8	4.5	4.8	4.7
Hungary	0.6	0.7	1.0	1.3	0.9	1.0	1.0	1.5
India	..	1.7	..	..	..	0.7	..	5.8
Indonesia	..	..	4.2	4.9	2.5	2.1	2.0	1.8
Iceland	0.8	1.9	2.3	2.3	2.5	2.4	1.7	1.4
Ireland	1.2	1.6	2.0	1.8	1.9	1.9	2.2	0.7
Israel[1]	0.0	0.0	..	..	..	..	0.0	..
Italy	2.1	2.5	2.5	2.4	1.8	1.8	2.1	2.1
Japan	4.2	4.4	9.9	7.4	5.5	4.1	6.5	6.0
Korea	6.1	5.4	4.9	5.2	5.0	5.1	5.2	..
Latvia	0.6	1.5	1.4	0.0	0.0	0.0	0.0	0.0
Lithuania	0.1	0.1	0.1	0.1	0.0	0.0	0.0	0.0
Luxembourg	0.7	1.9	1.3	0.9	1.2	0.8	0.3	0.2
Malaysia	6.5	6.5	7.1	7.4	7.5	7.7	7.7	7.2
Mexico	1.6	2.0	1.8	1.7	1.8	1.7	1.6	1.7
Netherlands	7.1	0.7	1.4	1.5	1.5	1.7	0.5	1.8
New Zealand	1.6	..	1.3	0.6	0.6	3.8	1.8	5.3
Nicaragua	..	..	..	0.0	..	..	..	..
Norway	..	..	..	..	..	..	..	..
Panama	..	..	6.7	6.2	..	..	..	..
Paraguay	..	..	2.0	1.5	..	1.1	1.0	0.7
Peru	..	1.5	1.4	1.0	0.7	0.6	0.6	0.7
Poland	1.1	0.9	1.0	1.2	1.0	2.7	3.5	3.2
Portugal	2.8	3.7	4.1	3.5	3.3	3.9	5.1	5.3
Puerto Rico	..	..	..	0.5	0.9	0.8	0.6	..
Russia	..	4.0	..	..	3.5	2.8	3.0	2.7
Singapore	25.0	25.1	20.6	19.6	19.2	19.7	21.7	17.6
Slovak Republic	0.6	0.9	1.0	0.9	1.4	2.0	..	0.2
Slovenia	12.1	12.0	12.3	11.3	11.3	12.5	12.1	12.1
South Africa	..	..	..	2.3	2.3	2.2	2.9	..
Spain	2.0	6.0	2.6	7.7	7.8	8.2	8.2	8.1
Sri Lanka	..	..	..	..	2.2	1.5	..	2.4
Sweden	7.2	6.0	7.9	6.3	4.1	3.1	3.0	3.1
Switzerland	14.7	12.3	13.5	14.5	13.8	12.7	13.3	14.2
Thailand	1.7	1.7	..	..	..	..	..	..
Tunisia	..	..	..	..	..	..	1.2	5.3
Turkey	4.0	3.2	2.9	2.7	5.0	3.1	5.9	6.0
United Kingdom	5.7	7.9	8.1	9.7	9.9	11.1	35.8	14.3
United States	20.4	20.5	20.7	21.5	21.8	22.8	22.3	23.0
Uruguay	..	..	0.0	0.0	0.0	0.0	..	0.0
OECD Total	12.9	13.0	15.0	15.5	15.4	16.7	18.5	17.7

.. Not available

Note: Detailed metadata at: *http://metalinks.oecd.org/ins/20190221/0f8b.*

1. Information on data for Israel: *http://oe.cd/israel-disclaimer.*

Source: Insurance activity indicators, OECD Insurance Statistics (database)

Table 25. Ratio of reinsurance accepted (Life)

Per cent

	2010	2011	2012	2013	2014	2015	2016	2017
Argentina	..	..	1.1	0.6	3.0	2.3	3.0	2.9
Australia	5.8	6.4	7.6	8.1	7.5	8.4	9.7	12.2
Austria	..	..	..	0.2	0.2	0.2	0.2	0.2
Belgium	0.4	0.5	0.2	0.4	0.4	0.3	0.4	0.3
Bolivia	..	..	0.4	..	..	..	0.0	3.3
Brazil	..	..	..	..	0.0	0.0	0.0	0.0
Canada	6.9	8.3	8.8	9.7	16.6	17.5	..	..
Chile	0.1	0.1	0.0	0.0	0.1	0.4	1.0	0.8
Colombia	..	..	0.4	..	..	..	0.0	3.3
Costa Rica	0.1	0.0	0.1	0.0	0.0	0.0	0.0	0.0
Cuba	..	..	..	..	..	..	..	..
Czech Republic	0.0	0.0	0.0	0.0	0.0	0.0	0.6	0.6
Denmark	..	0.0	0.6	89.0	0.5	0.5	0.6	0.4
Ecuador	..	..	..	..	..	0.6	0.0	..
El Salvador	..	..	..	..	..	..	..	..
Estonia	0.0	0.0	..	..	..	..	..	..
Finland	0.1	0.1	0.1	0.1	0.2	0.0	0.0	0.0
France	12.0	5.6	9.1	8.0	8.9	6.3	15.5	8.8
Germany	..	..	0.7	0.7	0.6	0.6	0.6	0.8
Greece	0.3	1.1	0.2	0.2	0.2	0.2	0.1	0.0
Guatemala	..	..	2.1	1.0	1.6	1.7	1.9	1.4
Honduras	..	..	..	0.0	0.0	0.0	..	..
Hong Kong, China	1.1	1.0	1.0	1.1	1.6	1.7	2.8	2.5
Hungary	0.0	0.0	0.0	0.0	0.0	0.0	0.0	0.0
India	..	0.0	..	..	..	0.0	..	0.2
Indonesia	..	..	0.0	0.0	..	..	..	..
Iceland	0.0	0.0	0.0	0.0	0.0	0.1	..	0.0
Ireland	0.9	0.9	1.2	1.1	1.1	1.2	0.7	0.2
Israel[1]	0.0	0.0	..	..	..	..	0.0	..
Italy	2.1	2.4	2.6	1.9	1.3	1.3	1.5	1.5
Japan	1.8	2.0	9.9	7.4	5.5	4.1	3.4	2.6
Korea	2.7	1.4	1.1	1.1	1.1	1.1	1.3	..
Latvia	0.0	0.0	0.0	0.0	0.0	0.0	0.0	0.0
Lithuania	0.0	0.0	0.0	0.0	0.0	0.0	0.0	0.0
Luxembourg	0.7	1.9	1.3	1.0	1.3	0.8	0.4	0.2
Malaysia	1.1	1.1	1.2	1.3	1.4	1.4	1.4	1.6
Mexico	0.6	0.6	0.5	0.6	0.7	0.4	0.5	0.6
Netherlands	11.2	0.1	0.1	0.0	0.0	0.0	0.0	0.1
New Zealand	..	..	..	..	..	..	..	..
Nicaragua	..	..	..	0.0	..	..	..	..
Norway	..	..	..	..	..	..	..	..
Panama	..	..	5.1	5.5	..	..	..	..
Paraguay	..	..	..	0.8	..	0.7	0.0	0.2
Peru	..	1.8	1.6	1.2	0.6	0.5	0.3	0.1
Poland	0.2	0.1	0.1	0.1	0.1	0.1	0.1	0.1
Portugal	0.2	0.0	0.0	0.0	0.0	0.0	0.0	0.0
Puerto Rico	..	..	..	0.0	0.0	0.0	0.5	..
Russia	..	0.0	..	..	0.0	0.0	0.0	0.0
Singapore	12.3	10.2	11.8	10.9	10.8	10.4	14.7	11.0
Slovak Republic	0.0	0.0	0.0	0.0	0.0	0.0	..	0.0
Slovenia	0.0	0.0	..	..	..	..	..	..
South Africa	..	..	..	0.0	0.0	0.0	0.0	..
Spain	0.1	1.1	0.2	1.3	1.6	1.5	1.5	1.4
Sri Lanka	..	..	..	..	..	0.0	..	0.6
Sweden	0.3	0.2	2.3	0.2	0.0	0.0	0.0	0.0
Switzerland	1.0	0.5	1.1	1.5	1.4	1.5	1.7	1.3
Thailand	0.0	0.1	..	..	..	..	..	..
Tunisia	..	..	..	..	..	..	1.5	1.5
Turkey	1.7	2.0	1.6	2.1	1.5	1.6	4.3	3.6
United Kingdom	3.4	6.8	7.1	9.3	9.0	10.0	40.7	10.4
United States	8.4	9.2	9.8	11.3	10.4	15.1	13.8	14.9
Uruguay	..	..	0.0	0.0	0.0	0.0	..	0.0
OECD Total	5.0	5.5	7.4	7.5	6.8	8.8	12.4	9.2

.. Not available

Note: Detailed metadata at: *http://metalinks.oecd.org/ins/20190221/0f8b.*

1. Information on data for Israel: *http://oe.cd/israel-disclaimer.*

Source: *Insurance activity indicators, OECD Insurance Statistics (database)*

Table 26. Ratio of reinsurance accepted (Non-life)

Per cent

	2010	2011	2012	2013	2014	2015	2016	2017
Argentina	..	..	0.4	0.3	8.0	7.8	7.5	7.2
Australia	13.6	14.8	15.2	14.2	14.3	14.7	16.0	13.9
Austria	..	..	..	18.2	14.7	13.6	13.7	9.2
Belgium	7.4	7.5	7.3	7.1	7.6	6.4	5.8	4.7
Bolivia	..	..	0.6	..	..	..	1.4	4.2
Brazil	..	..	..	..	0.1	0.0	0.0	0.0
Canada	8.1	8.2	8.3	9.7	18.1	17.7	..	..
Chile	0.6	0.7	1.2	1.4	1.5	1.6	1.3	1.1
Colombia	..	..	0.6	..	..	..	1.4	4.2
Costa Rica	0.1	0.1	0.2	0.4	0.3	0.4	0.3	0.3
Cuba	..	..	..	..	..	..	..	..
Czech Republic	2.6	3.2	3.5	3.3	2.9	3.4	3.7	3.7
Denmark	..	0.8	1.1	1.1	1.3	1.4	8.0	9.8
Ecuador	..	..	..	..	..	2.4	2.2	..
El Salvador	..	..	..	..	..	..	..	..
Estonia	0.0	0.1	..	..	..	..	..	..
Finland	3.5	3.7	3.7	3.3	3.0	3.0	3.0	3.3
France	13.1	14.0	13.3	13.4	13.3	13.5	16.1	17.4
Germany	..	..	35.6	34.6	34.7	37.0	36.4	35.9
Greece	1.8	2.1	3.3	3.7	2.2	1.9	1.8	1.8
Guatemala	..	..	3.1	3.2	3.0	3.4	3.2	3.3
Honduras	..	..	..	0.0	0.0	0.0	..	..
Hong Kong, China	23.2	26.2	26.2	26.0	26.1	24.2	23.3	25.1
Hungary	1.2	1.5	2.2	2.9	1.9	2.1	2.0	2.9
India	..	11.6	..	..	..	3.0	..	19.4
Indonesia	..	..	14.4	15.2	7.3	6.8	7.5	7.2
Iceland	0.9	2.0	2.5	2.5	2.7	2.6	1.9	1.5
Ireland	2.4	4.1	5.3	5.0	5.3	4.6	5.5	3.3
Israel[1]	0.0	0.0	..	..	..	..	0.0	..
Italy	2.2	2.6	2.4	3.4	3.4	3.8	3.9	3.7
Japan	13.7	14.3	..	..	..	..	16.0	16.3
Korea	11.0	10.7	10.2	11.1	10.1	10.3	10.2	..
Latvia	0.8	1.8	1.7	0.0	0.0	0.0	0.0	0.0
Lithuania	0.1	0.2	0.2	0.2	0.0	0.0	0.0	0.0
Luxembourg	0.3	2.0	1.3	0.3	0.2	0.2	0.2	0.2
Malaysia	15.0	14.8	16.4	16.5	16.7	17.3	17.8	16.8
Mexico	2.4	3.1	2.9	2.7	2.7	2.7	2.6	2.6
Netherlands	2.8	1.5	2.5	2.9	2.8	2.9	0.6	0.7
New Zealand	1.6	..	1.3	0.6	0.6	3.8	1.8	5.3
Nicaragua	..	..	..	0.0	..	..	..	..
Norway	..	..	..	..	..	..	..	..
Panama	..	..	7.7	6.6	..	..	..	..
Paraguay	..	..	2.2	1.5	..	1.2	1.0	0.8
Peru	..	1.4	1.3	1.0	0.8	0.7	0.8	1.3
Poland	2.2	1.9	2.3	2.5	2.1	5.3	6.1	5.3
Portugal	10.3	10.3	11.0	11.7	12.3	12.1	12.6	12.9
Puerto Rico	..	..	..	0.5	1.0	0.9	0.6	..
Russia	..	4.5	..	..	5.0	3.3	3.7	3.7
Singapore	52.5	55.3	37.6	38.1	37.3	40.7	39.2	37.0
Slovak Republic	1.2	1.9	2.1	2.1	3.1	4.0	..	0.8
Slovenia	15.6	15.4	15.8	14.6	14.6	16.3	15.7	15.5
South Africa	..	..	..	10.8	11.6	11.1	14.2	..
Spain	3.8	10.3	4.8	12.9	12.6	13.5	14.1	13.4
Sri Lanka	..	..	..	..	3.5	2.6	..	3.7
Sweden	13.8	11.8	14.6	12.9	13.5	11.4	11.8	13.0
Switzerland	27.0	23.3	24.9	26.6	25.4	23.4	23.6	24.8
Thailand	5.5	5.2	..	..	..	..	..	..
Tunisia	..	..	..	..	..	..	1.1	6.2
Turkey	4.5	3.5	3.1	2.8	5.4	3.3	6.1	6.5
United Kingdom	12.2	11.0	11.2	10.9	12.6	14.1	25.0	22.7
United States	28.2	28.1	28.2	27.8	28.2	27.4	27.0	27.4
Uruguay	..	..	0.0	0.0	0.0	0.0	..	0.0
OECD Total	22.0	21.6	23.6	23.5	24.2	24.3	23.8	24.6

.. Not available

Note: Detailed metadata at: *http://metalinks.oecd.org/ins/20190221/0f8b*.

1. Information on data for Israel: *http://oe.cd/israel-disclaimer*.

Source: Insurance activity indicators, OECD Insurance Statistics (database)

Table 27. Market share of foreign companies in the domestic market (Life)

Per cent

	2010	2011	2012	2013	2014	2015	2016	2017
Argentina	..	..	18.3	31.8	31.4	30.8	30.4	30.0
Australia	15.0	10.3	15.8	16.8	15.5	17.7	20.8	25.5
Austria	..	..	..	37.5	39.2	37.7	39.3	39.7
Belgium	..	..	..	..	..	..	..	..
Bolivia	..	..	..	..	..	..	29.9	20.8
Brazil	..	..	..	..	18.6	18.3	17.2	21.3
Canada	10.1	7.9	6.3	5.6	26.0	21.0	..	..
Chile	49.0	37.6	43.7	46.7	45.0	41.8	41.6	44.5
Colombia	..	..	..	..	..	..	29.9	20.8
Costa Rica	0.2	3.4	5.5	12.4	17.0	23.0	25.0	33.9
Cuba	..	..	..	..	..	..	..	..
Czech Republic	97.4	97.2	97.1	96.8	96.7	96.3	96.8	96.4
Denmark	..	20.4	19.3	2.5	19.5	18.6	18.8	19.9
Ecuador	..	..	..	..	..	..	11.7	..
El Salvador	..	9.3	9.7	17.4	9.6	9.4	9.6	..
Estonia	100.0	100.0	100.0	100.0	100.0	100.0	100.0	100.0
Finland	..	..	38.3	42.0	43.0	38.5	..	..
France	..	..	..	..	..	..	..	..
Germany	27.0	27.4	30.1	27.4	26.0	26.7	25.3	24.6
Greece	57.2	63.4	63.3	53.8	48.0	55.7	76.9	74.0
Guatemala	..	..	..	..	..	..	..	..
Honduras	..	..	..	13.8	59.6	62.2	..	..
Hong Kong, China	..	..	..	..	..	..	..	..
Hungary	93.4	92.8	93.5	95.6	96.2	95.8	96.9	96.6
India	..	0.0	..	..	..	0.0	..	0.1
Indonesia	..	..	..	..	..	..	..	..
Iceland	3.0	3.6	3.9	4.3	5.0	5.8	..	..
Ireland	8.2	4.7	3.9	4.9	4.5	4.7	..	..
Israel[1]	30.6	30.4	0.3	0.4	0.4	0.4	0.4	0.4
Italy	30.2	30.1	27.4	28.9	31.3	30.5	33.1	32.1
Japan	17.6	19.2	22.4	20.7	20.1	20.6	21.8	22.7
Korea	19.7	18.9	16.3	16.1	13.2	12.4	14.7	..
Latvia	97.3	90.1	90.0	91.8	91.0	89.8	90.8	91.3
Lithuania	97.0	96.9	96.8	97.0	97.4	97.4	97.5	97.1
Luxembourg	95.1	95.6	94.6	96.2	96.4	92.5	77.2	90.6
Malaysia	62.0	67.9	68.1	68.6	68.8	69.6	69.7	71.8
Mexico	72.5	69.9	71.1	6.3	74.0	72.3	70.6	68.0
Netherlands	25.2	21.1	21.1	19.2	4.6	18.5	19.2	23.3
New Zealand	..	..	..	..	..	..	..	..
Nicaragua	..	..	32.6	29.1	26.6	26.4	18.0	..
Norway	9.7	9.3	10.7	12.3	13.3	15.1	0.7	0.7
Panama	..	..	54.1	59.9	..	..	..	..
Paraguay	..	..	..	6.2	..	0.0	0.0	5.5
Peru	..	22.3	20.7	23.5	30.7	56.8	28.1	27.6
Poland	49.8	50.9	51.1	48.8	50.0	50.7	54.3	45.2
Portugal	5.8	9.3	7.9	6.8	54.0	64.2	77.5	93.8
Puerto Rico	..	..	..	10.4	7.8	0.0	38.0	..
Russia	..	..	..	..	8.5	18.1	15.5	10.2
Singapore	44.0	61.0	66.3	67.2	71.3	70.6	70.0	53.3
Slovak Republic	91.0	90.4	90.2	90.4	90.0	89.0	..	5.6
Slovenia	16.6	17.1	16.8	17.6	17.2	17.0	17.1	15.7
South Africa	..	20.8	33.0	31.9	35.2	33.3	34.6	..
Spain	10.3	8.8	19.1	12.4	12.8	12.3	..	..
Sri Lanka	..	..	..	..	2.4	1.7	..	..
Sweden	16.8	17.3	18.4	19.5	7.9	8.8	11.2	12.2
Switzerland	30.5	29.9	30.6	31.2	27.9	26.9	25.6	25.3
Thailand	30.9	28.8	..	..	..	..	..	..
Tunisia	..	..	..	..	..	..	..	..
Turkey	27.5	27.7	27.1	47.1	47.9	59.7	54.2	56.4
United Kingdom	18.8	21.0	26.4	23.3	16.0	16.9	..	..
United States	20.6	19.8	19.6	20.0	21.0	17.4	22.5	21.7
Uruguay	..	..	33.5	32.8	33.4	30.1	..	21.3

.. Not available

Note: Detailed metadata at: *http://metalinks.oecd.org/ins/20190221/0f8b*.

1. Information on data for Israel: *http://oe.cd/israel-disclaimer*.

Source: Insurance activity indicators, OECD Insurance Statistics (database)

Table 28. Market share of foreign undertakings in total domestic business (Life)

Branches or agencies

Per cent

	2010	2011	2012	2013	2014	2015	2016	2017
Argentina	..	..	1.5	1.8	3.9	3.2	3.4	3.5
Australia	..	..	..	..	..	..	..	..
Austria	..	..	..	0.0	0.0	0.0	0.0	0.0
Belgium	..	..	..	..	..	..	..	..
Bolivia	..	..	..	..	..	..	..	..
Brazil	..	..	..	..	..	0.0	0.0	0.0
Canada	2.8	2.4	2.6	2.2	15.5	15.8	..	..
Chile	0.0	..	..	..	..	..	..	..
Colombia	..	..	..	..	..	..	..	..
Costa Rica	0.0	0.0	0.0	0.2	0.6	1.1	1.0	1.3
Cuba	..	..	..	..	..	..	..	..
Czech Republic	8.4	8.3	8.1	7.5	7.2	10.8	10.9	11.4
Denmark	..	..	..	..	..	..	..	..
Ecuador	..	..	..	..	..	..	..	..
El Salvador	..	9.3	9.7	17.4	9.6	9.4	9.6	..
Estonia	0.0	0.0	2.9	2.5	2.7	2.8	2.2	3.1
Finland	..	..	..	..	..	..	..	..
France	..	..	..	..	..	..	..	..
Germany	0.4	3.1	4.0	4.0	3.9	4.0	3.9	4.0
Greece	13.6	6.2	0.4	0.0	0.0	0.0	0.0	0.0
Guatemala	..	..	..	..	..	..	..	..
Honduras	..	..	..	13.8	25.6	23.1	..	..
Hong Kong, China	..	..	..	..	..	..	..	..
Hungary	..	..	..	..	..	..	..	..
India	..	0.0	..	..	..	0.0	..	0.1
Indonesia	..	..	..	..	..	..	..	..
Iceland	0.0	0.0	..	..	..	..	..	..
Ireland	8.2	4.7	3.9	4.9	4.5	4.7	..	..
Israel[1]	0.0	..	..	..	..	..	..	..
Italy	0.0	0.0	0.0	0.0	0.0	0.0	0.0	0.0
Japan	7.7	9.2	5.5	4.9	4.2	4.1	4.3	4.5
Korea	2.9	2.7	2.2	2.2	2.4	0.2	2.0	..
Latvia	38.0	51.5	55.7	56.3	58.5	59.3	61.4	63.1
Lithuania	47.7	46.7	41.5	41.6	43.1	41.8	40.8	41.4
Luxembourg	0.2	0.4	0.3	0.5	0.1	0.1	0.1	0.1
Malaysia	0.4	0.4	0.4	0.5	0.5	0.5	0.5	0.6
Mexico	..	..	..	..	..	..	..	..
Netherlands	3.0	2.7	2.7	2.0	0.0	0.0	..	..
New Zealand	..	..	..	..	..	..	..	..
Nicaragua	..	..	..	..	..	..	..	..
Norway	1.2	1.0	0.8	1.3	1.4	0.7	0.7	0.7
Panama	..	..	10.3	10.0	..	..	..	..
Paraguay	..	..	..	..	..	0.0	0.0	..
Peru	..	..	..	..	..	..	..	..
Poland	..	..	..	..	..	..	..	..
Portugal	0.5	0.8	0.0	0.0	0.0	0.0	0.0	0.0
Puerto Rico	..	..	..	..	..	..	..	..
Russia	..	..	..	..	..	..	..	0.0
Singapore	30.0	29.8	15.1	15.0	32.6	30.7	32.3	8.7
Slovak Republic	4.2	4.5	4.3	5.4	4.4	4.8	..	5.6
Slovenia	..	..	..	..	..	..	..	..
South Africa	..	..	..	0.0	..	..	..	..
Spain	0.3	0.3	0.2	0.0	0.0	0.0	..	..
Sri Lanka	..	..	..	..	..	0.0	..	..
Sweden	..	..	..	..	0.7	..	..	..
Switzerland	4.0	1.6	2.1	1.5	0.0	0.0	0.0	0.0
Thailand	30.9	28.8	..	..	..	..	..	..
Tunisia	..	..	..	..	..	..	..	..
Turkey	0.0	..	..	..	..	..	0.0	0.0
United Kingdom	0.9	0.1	0.0	0.0	0.0	0.0	..	0.0
United States	0.0	0.0	..	..	..	..	0.0	0.0
Uruguay	..	..	..	0.0	0.0	0.0	..	0.0

.. Not available

Note: Detailed metadata at: *http://metalinks.oecd.org/ins/20190221/0f8b*.

1. Information on data for Israel: *http://oe.cd/israel-disclaimer*.

Source: Insurance activity indicators, OECD Insurance Statistics (database)

Table 29. Market share of foreign companies in the domestic market (Non-life)

Per cent

	2010	2011	2012	2013	2014	2015	2016	2017
Argentina	..	..	17.6	20.1	21.1	22.0	23.4	30.5
Australia	28.7	27.3	27.1	27.7	28.7	28.2	28.7	29.5
Austria	..	..	..	35.2	37.5	36.9	36.6	33.2
Belgium	..	..	..	..	..	..	..	..
Bolivia	..	..	..	..	..	..	27.9	29.1
Brazil	..	..	..	..	51.3	32.4	35.7	39.4
Canada	30.9	29.8	29.0	27.9	44.8	41.6	..	..
Chile	66.8	66.5	65.7	63.7	63.5	62.7	79.0	75.6
Colombia	..	..	..	..	..	..	27.9	29.1
Costa Rica	0.9	5.8	7.6	10.0	14.2	17.5	20.5	22.8
Cuba	..	..	..	..	..	..	..	..
Czech Republic	89.0	88.6	88.6	88.2	89.4	90.0	89.1	88.6
Denmark	..	16.0	16.6	16.4	27.5	27.9	28.3	25.3
Ecuador	..	..	..	..	..	..	0.4	..
El Salvador	..	2.3	2.4	0.0	0.0	0.0	0.0	..
Estonia	91.7	90.4	92.7	94.3	95.1	95.2	94.8	100.0
Finland	..	..	25.0	23.8	23.7	100.0	..	..
France	0.1	0.1	0.1	0.1	0.1	0.1	..	..
Germany	17.1	18.2	13.2	14.0	14.5	14.3	13.3	13.6
Greece	33.8	36.6	41.2	34.5	41.2	43.0	57.3	57.3
Guatemala	..	..	..	..	..	..	..	..
Honduras	..	..	..	10.5	40.3	42.8	..	..
Hong Kong, China	..	..	..	..	..	..	..	..
Hungary	97.3	96.8	95.7	94.9	94.7	92.8	91.7	91.4
India	..	0.0	..	..	..	..	..	2.9
Indonesia	..	..	..	..	..	..	..	..
Iceland	9.2	9.7	9.9	10.4	10.9	11.3	..	..
Ireland	8.9	8.2	17.6	14.3	24.3	22.2	..	..
Israel[1]	11.1	11.2	3.3	3.3	3.4	4.0	3.8	3.8
Italy	27.3	27.6	27.5	27.8	28.9	32.2	31.8	31.1
Japan	10.9	12.8	..	..	..	..	9.4	7.5
Korea	4.7	3.9	3.8	4.0	3.7	3.7	3.7	..
Latvia	58.6	44.3	48.1	49.4	48.7	57.1	79.0	77.2
Lithuania	95.9	98.0	98.5	98.8	99.0	99.0	99.3	99.5
Luxembourg	61.6	62.7	58.9	52.1	53.3	52.8	51.7	51.1
Malaysia	32.3	42.7	43.9	45.8	46.6	47.8	48.5	51.9
Mexico	53.5	51.1	52.4	9.7	48.7	52.2	48.5	50.3
Netherlands	17.0	29.4	29.4	22.7	11.6	16.3	2.6	2.3
New Zealand	..	..	..	..	..	..	..	..
Nicaragua	..	..	24.6	25.7	24.7	25.7	26.0	..
Norway	42.6	42.3	43.9	43.4	41.1	40.2	40.3	37.8
Panama	..	..	39.2	47.0	..	..	..	..
Paraguay	..	..	0.0	26.4	..	0.0	22.8	24.7
Peru	..	18.8	19.1	19.9	20.6	45.9	24.8	25.7
Poland	59.3	61.1	62.8	61.3	61.3	61.8	59.1	58.4
Portugal	28.3	26.7	26.5	26.6	84.2	84.3	91.0	91.6
Puerto Rico	..	..	..	52.6	51.8	41.0	55.6	..
Russia	..	..	..	..	2.2	13.7	13.7	14.0
Singapore	67.0	85.6	86.8	86.2	89.0	89.2	90.2	80.0
Slovak Republic	94.7	94.4	94.0	93.8	93.6	93.2	..	8.3
Slovenia	4.9	5.1	4.9	5.1	5.2	5.3	5.7	5.9
South Africa	..	27.3	63.5	45.2	39.5	34.6	37.4	..
Spain	18.6	17.0	32.2	29.1	28.8	23.6	..	..
Sri Lanka	..	..	..	..	4.7	4.8	..	16.0
Sweden	53.1	51.9	63.8	57.6	55.4	44.8	46.7	48.0
Switzerland	19.9	19.8	20.4	20.6	19.6	20.3	20.1	18.7
Thailand	7.7	7.1	..	..	..	..	..	..
Tunisia	..	..	..	..	..	..	..	..
Turkey	55.2	57.9	53.8	62.2	59.3	66.7	63.7	57.1
United Kingdom	53.1	55.2	55.2	58.0	57.8	57.5	0.3	0.4
United States	13.9	13.9	10.1	10.4	9.4	9.5	10.2	10.0
Uruguay	..	..	31.3	31.4	32.2	33.6	..	34.7

.. Not available

Note: Detailed metadata at: *http://metalinks.oecd.org/ins/20190221/0f8b*.

1. Information on data for Israel: *http://oe.cd/israel-disclaimer*.

Source: Insurance activity indicators, OECD Insurance Statistics (database)

Table 30. Market share of foreign undertakings in total domestic business (Non-life)

Branches or agencies

Per cent

	2010	2011	2012	2013	2014	2015	2016	2017
Argentina	..	..	0.1	0.1	3.2	2.5	2.4	2.6
Australia	11.6	9.7	9.7	9.7	10.1	9.1	9.9	9.6
Austria	..	..	..	0.1	0.1	0.0	0.0	0.1
Belgium	..	..	..	..	..	..	..	..
Bolivia	..	..	..	..	..	..	..	..
Brazil	..	..	..	..	..	0.0	0.0	0.0
Canada	15.1	14.3	13.4	13.1	23.2	21.0	..	..
Chile	0.0	..	..	..	..	..	..	..
Colombia	..	..	..	..	..	..	..	..
Costa Rica	0.0	0.0	0.1	0.3	0.4	0.8	1.3	1.5
Cuba	..	..	..	..	..	..	..	..
Czech Republic	3.2	3.1	2.7	3.7	4.7	4.9	5.3	5.4
Denmark	..	..	..	..	..	..	..	..
Ecuador	..	..	..	..	..	..	..	..
El Salvador	..	2.3	2.4	0.0	0.0	0.0	0.0	..
Estonia	0.0	0.0	14.5	13.6	14.8	13.5	15.0	15.1
Finland	..	..	..	..	..	..	..	..
France	0.1	0.1	0.1	0.1	0.1	0.1	..	..
Germany	1.5	3.0	3.1	2.7	3.2	3.5	3.1	3.8
Greece	4.0	4.6	7.9	0.0	0.0	0.0	0.0	0.0
Guatemala	..	..	..	..	..	..	..	..
Honduras	..	..	..	10.5	4.4	3.6	..	..
Hong Kong, China	..	..	..	..	..	..	..	..
Hungary	..	..	..	..	..	..	..	..
India	..	0.0	..	..	..	..	..	2.9
Indonesia	..	..	..	..	..	..	..	..
Iceland	0.0	0.0	..	..	..	..	..	..
Ireland	8.9	8.2	17.6	14.3	24.3	22.2	..	..
Israel[1]	0.0	..	..	..	..	..	..	..
Italy	1.0	1.1	1.1	1.1	1.1	1.4	1.6	1.5
Japan	5.6	7.8	..	..	..	..	2.3	2.5
Korea	3.2	2.6	2.0	3.1	2.3	2.3	2.3	..
Latvia	11.2	10.9	13.3	18.5	20.4	20.2	22.6	27.0
Lithuania	19.8	40.4	39.7	52.9	53.1	53.9	46.8	48.4
Luxembourg	7.9	7.2	7.5	6.5	3.6	3.6	3.5	3.3
Malaysia	3.8	4.4	5.8	6.7	7.3	8.4	9.6	8.9
Mexico	..	..	..	..	..	..	..	..
Netherlands	1.9	1.9	1.9	0.3	0.3	0.0	..	..
New Zealand	..	..	..	..	..	..	..	..
Nicaragua	..	..	..	..	..	..	..	..
Norway	41.4	41.5	43.2	43.4	41.1	40.2	40.3	37.8
Panama	..	..	7.9	7.7	..	..	..	..
Paraguay	..	..	..	..	..	0.0	0.0	..
Peru	..	..	..	..	..	..	..	..
Poland	..	..	..	..	..	..	..	..
Portugal	0.3	0.3	0.0	0.0	0.0	0.0	0.0	0.0
Puerto Rico	..	..	..	..	..	..	..	..
Russia	..	..	..	..	..	..	0.1	0.0
Singapore	44.1	44.0	42.7	46.8	39.6	38.2	37.4	36.5
Slovak Republic	6.2	6.2	7.1	8.0	8.7	8.5	..	8.3
Slovenia	..	..	..	..	..	..	..	..
South Africa	..	..	..	0.0	..	..	..	..
Spain	0.2	0.2	0.2	0.0	0.0	0.0	..	..
Sri Lanka	..	..	..	..	..	0.0	..	..
Sweden	..	..	..	..	8.2	..	..	..
Switzerland	4.8	4.8	4.9	5.0	5.5	6.0	7.1	7.5
Thailand	7.7	7.1	..	..	..	..	..	..
Tunisia	..	..	..	..	..	..	..	..
Turkey	0.2	0.2	0.3	0.3	0.3	0.4	0.4	0.5
United Kingdom	5.3	5.4	4.7	3.7	4.1	4.6	0.3	0.4
United States	0.1	0.1	0.1	0.0	0.0	0.1	0.1	0.1
Uruguay	..	..	..	0.0	0.0	0.0	..	0.0

.. Not available

Note: Detailed metadata at: *http://metalinks.oecd.org/ins/20190221/0f8b*.

1. Information on data for Israel: *http://oe.cd/israel-disclaimer*.

Source: Insurance activity indicators, OECD Insurance Statistics (database)

Country tables

AUSTRALIA

Table 1. Selected aggregates

Million AUD

	2010	2011	2012	2013	2014	2015	2016	2017
1.1 Insurance business written in the reporting country								
1.1.1 Insurance business, by ownership								
Gross premiums								
Domestic undertakings	73 331	78 509	79 230	86 754	103 414	100 992	95 348	90 032
Foreign controlled undertakings	12 274	11 038	13 757	15 722	17 983	19 150	19 836	21 498
Foreign companies (branches)	3 844	3 450	3 713	3 977	4 206	3 893	4 393	4 353
All undertakings	77 176	81 959	82 943	90 731	107 620	104 885	99 741	94 385
Premiums ceded								
Domestic undertakings	9 989	11 246	11 507	12 121	13 268	15 209	17 826	19 711
Foreign controlled undertakings	2 770	3 170	4 111	4 666	5 483	5 986	6 268	8 647
Foreign companies (branches)	1 402	1 442	1 659	1 947	1 842	1 739	1 759	1 873
All undertakings	11 391	12 688	13 166	14 068	15 110	16 948	19 585	21 584
Net written premiums								
Domestic undertakings	63 343	67 263	67 724	74 633	90 147	85 783	77 522	70 321
Foreign controlled undertakings	9 439	7 868	9 646	11 055	12 500	13 164	13 568	12 851
Foreign companies (branches)	2 441	2 008	2 054	2 030	2 365	2 154	2 634	2 480
All undertakings	65 785	69 271	69 778	76 663	92 511	87 937	80 156	72 801
1.1.2 Insurance business on foreign risks, gross premiums								
Life	495	475	491	574	686	701	711	706
Non-life	..	..	..	..	..	..	..	..
Composite total	..	..	..	..	..	..	..	..
Total	495	475	491	574	686	701	711	706
1.1.3 Life insurance payments, by class, gross premiums								
Annuities	..	..	..	..	..	..	..	..
Unit linked	..	..	..	..	..	..	..	..
Other life insurance	..	..	..	..	..	..	..	..
Total life insurance	..	..	41 091	45 794	60 881	56 868	49 890	43 141
***of which:** Pension contracts*	..	..	..	..	..	..	..	..
1.1.4 Non-life insurance payments, by class, gross premiums								
Motor vehicle insurance	..	11 474	12 114	12 924	13 467	13 749	14 512	15 447
Marine, aviation and other transport insurance	..	1 457	1 484	1 523	1 598	1 673	1 648	1 739
Freight insurance	..	..	..	..	..	..	..	..
Fire and other property damage insurance	..	9 537	10 918	12 038	11 836	12 031	12 297	12 713
Pecuniary loss insurance	..	1 161	1 207	1 258	1 454	1 493	1 443	1 352
General liability insurance	..	4 821	5 008	5 283	5 418	5 435	5 348	5 491
Accident and health	..	1 038	1 049	1 134	1 124	1 130	1 064	1 021
***of which:** Health*	..	..	..	..	..	..	..	..
Other non-life insurance	..	751	835	900	951	1 029	1 071	1 205
Treaty reinsurance	..	5 235	5 836	5 823	5 970	6 271	7 115	6 269
Total non-life insurance	33 223	35 475	38 450	40 884	41 818	42 811	44 498	45 237
1.2 Gross claims payments								
Life								
Domestic undertakings	41 639	44 988	45 777	47 647	64 828	56 547	59 350	47 307
Foreign controlled undertakings	5 355	4 301	4 181	5 212	5 876	6 681	7 133	9 207
Foreign companies (branches)	..	..	..	..	..	..	..	..
All undertakings	41 639	44 988	45 777	47 647	64 828	56 547	59 350	47 307
Non-life								
Domestic undertakings	21 552	31 597	22 048	24 141	26 293	29 311	28 026	29 946
Foreign controlled undertakings	4 120	6 668	4 538	4 542	5 446	6 183	5 534	6 453
Foreign companies (branches)	2 401	7 061	1 749	1 984	3 318	2 585	3 217	3 124
All undertakings	23 953	38 658	23 797	26 126	29 611	31 896	31 243	33 070
Composite, all undertakings	..	..	..	..	..	..	..	..
Total								
Domestic undertakings	63 191	76 585	67 825	71 788	91 121	85 858	87 376	77 253
Foreign controlled undertakings	9 475	10 969	8 719	9 754	11 322	12 864	12 667	15 660
Foreign companies (branches)	2 401	7 061	1 749	1 984	3 318	2 585	3 217	3 124
All undertakings	65 592	83 646	69 574	73 773	94 439	88 443	90 593	80 377
1.3 Commissions								
Life								
Domestic undertakings	2 738	2 852	3 007	3 015	3 118	3 087	3 129	2 514
Foreign controlled undertakings	440	455	252	447	451	460	464	494
Foreign companies (branches)	..	..	..	..	..	..	..	..
All undertakings	2 738	2 852	3 007	3 015	3 118	3 087	3 129	2 514
Non-life								
Domestic undertakings	..	..	..	506	566	816	1 038	1 070
Foreign controlled undertakings	..	..	..	239	270	276	308	341
Foreign companies (branches)	..	..	..	264	287	301	327	324
All undertakings	..	..	..	770	853	1 117	1 364	1 394
Composite, all undertakings	..	..	..	..	..	..	..	..
Total								
Domestic undertakings	2 738	2 852	3 007	3 521	3 684	3 903	4 167	3 584
Foreign controlled undertakings	440	455	252	686	721	736	772	835
Foreign companies (branches)	..	..	..	264	287	301	327	324
All undertakings	2 738	2 852	3 007	3 785	3 971	4 204	4 493	3 908

AUSTRALIA

Table 1. Selected aggregates (cont.)

Million AUD

	2010	2011	2012	2013	2014	2015	2016	2017
1.4 Gross operating expenses								
Life								
Domestic undertakings	6 640	6 777	7 274	7 830	8 128	8 041	8 666	8 457
Foreign controlled undertakings	1 608	1 709	1 430	2 392	2 393	2 487	3 038	3 239
Foreign companies (branches)	..	..	..	..	..	..	..	..
All undertakings	6 640	6 777	7 274	7 830	8 128	8 041	8 666	8 457
Non-life								
Domestic undertakings	6 027	6 658	7 197	7 361	7 502	7 497	7 368	7 475
Foreign controlled undertakings	1 172	1 370	1 490	1 618	1 704	1 850	1 829	1 975
Foreign companies (branches)	559	571	559	597	629	660	618	563
All undertakings	6 586	7 229	7 756	7 959	8 131	8 157	7 987	8 038
Composite, all undertakings	..	..	..	..	..	..	..	..
Total								
Domestic undertakings	12 667	13 435	14 471	15 191	15 630	15 538	16 034	15 932
Foreign controlled undertakings	2 780	3 079	2 920	4 010	4 097	4 337	4 867	5 214
Foreign companies (branches)	559	571	559	597	629	660	618	563
All undertakings	13 226	14 006	15 030	15 789	16 259	16 198	16 653	16 495
1.5 Insurance business written abroad by branches, gross premiums								
Life								
Branches and agencies	..	..	..	..	..	..	..	..
Subsidaries	..	..	..	..	..	..	..	..
Total	..	..	..	..	..	..	..	..
Non-life								
Branches and agencies	..	..	..	..	..	..	..	..
Subsidaries	..	..	..	..	..	..	..	..
Total	..	..	..	..	..	..	..	..
Composite total	..	..	..	..	..	..	..	..
Total								
Branches and agencies	..	..	..	..	..	..	..	..
Subsidaries	..	..	..	..	..	..	..	..
Total	..	..	..	..	..	..	..	..

.. Not available

Note: Detailed metadata at: *http://metalinks.oecd.org/ins/20190221/48bf.*

Source: *OECD Insurance Statistics (database)*

AUSTRALIA

Table 2. Number of companies and employees

	2010	2011	2012	2013	2014	2015	2016	2017
2.1 Number of companies								
Life								
Domestic undertakings	26	31	28	28	28	28	29	29
Foreign controlled undertakings	8	14	14	14	14	13	13	13
Foreign companies (branches)	..	..	..	..	..	..	..	..
All undertakings	26	31	28	28	28	28	29	29
Non-life								
Domestic undertakings	84	81	79	75	74	70	68	58
Foreign controlled undertakings	20	19	17	18	19	19	17	15
Foreign companies (branches)	34	31	30	29	29	29	31	28
All undertakings	118	112	109	104	103	99	99	86
Composite, all undertakings	..	..	..	..	..	0	..	..
Reinsurance								
Domestic undertakings	2	3	3	3	3	2	2	2
Foreign controlled undertakings	1	1	1	1	1	1	1	1
Foreign companies (branches)	10	9	9	9	9	9	8	8
All undertakings	12	12	12	12	12	11	10	10
Total								
Domestic undertakings	112	115	110	106	105	100	99	89
Foreign controlled undertakings	29	34	32	33	34	33	31	29
Foreign companies (branches)	44	40	39	38	38	38	39	36
All undertakings	156	155	149	144	143	138	138	125
2.2 Number of employees								
Insurance undertakings	..	..	..	..	..	..	..	..
Intermediaries	..	..	..	..	..	..	..	..
Total	..	..	..	..	..	..	..	..

.. Not available

Note: Detailed metadata at: *http://metalinks.oecd.org/ins/20190221/48bf.*

Source: OECD Insurance Statistics (database)

AUSTRIA

Table 1. Selected aggregates

Million EUR

	2010	2011	2012	2013	2014	2015	2016	2017
1.1 Insurance business written in the reporting country								
1.1.1 Insurance business, by ownership								
Gross premiums								
Domestic undertakings	..	..	..	18 879	18 889	19 003	18 647	18 126
Foreign controlled undertakings	..	..	..	6 781	7 196	7 060	6 979	6 390
Foreign companies (branches)	..	..	..	8	6	6	6	7
All undertakings	..	..	..	18 887	18 895	19 009	18 653	18 134
Premiums ceded								
Domestic undertakings	..	..	..	3 539	3 102	2 996	3 521	3 130
Foreign controlled undertakings	..	..	..	1 127	1 171	1 113	1 636	1 280
Foreign companies (branches)	..	..	..	0	0	0	0	0
All undertakings	..	..	..	3 539	3 102	2 996	3 522	3 131
Net written premiums								
Domestic undertakings	..	..	..	15 340	15 787	16 007	15 126	14 996
Foreign controlled undertakings	..	..	..	5 654	6 024	5 948	5 343	5 110
Foreign companies (branches)	..	..	..	8	6	6	6	7
All undertakings	..	..	..	15 348	15 793	16 013	15 131	15 003
1.1.2 Insurance business on foreign risks, gross premiums								
Life	991	174	72	157	22	20	14	3
Non-life	4 630	722	662	717	726	702	753	777
Composite	13 176	523	626	595	489	391	371	363
of which:								
Life	6 471	252	188	202	158	111	95	89
Non-life	6 704	270	438	393	331	280	276	274
Total	18 797	1 419	1 360	1 469	1 237	1 114	1 138	1 143
1.1.3 Life insurance payments, by class, gross premiums								
Annuities	..	..	..	1 441	1 822	1 946	1 531	1 434
Unit linked	2 860	2 255	1 846	1 248	1 011	933	864	812
Other life insurance	4 578	4 644	4 588	3 738	3 852	3 812	3 646	3 488
Total life insurance	7 438	6 899	6 434	6 427	6 685	6 692	6 041	5 735
***of which:** Pension contracts*	..	..	..	997	1 116	1 031	940	964
1.1.4 Non-life insurance payments, by class, gross premiums								
Motor vehicle insurance	1 260	1 316	1 386	1 487	1 447	3 920	4 043	3 980
Marine, aviation and other transport insurance	124	140	165	174	138	11	9	10
Freight insurance	..	..	..	..	..	155	148	137
Fire and other property damage insurance	973	978	1 008	1 081	1 058	3 153	3 178	3 013
Pecuniary loss insurance	220	237	167	174	183	178	176	166
General liability insurance	888	922	834	860	886	889	905	868
Accident and health	2 572	2 873	3 024	3 150	3 143	3 257	3 391	3 473
***of which:** Health*	1 653	1 704	1 762	1 841	1 905	2 007	2 096	2 167
Other non-life insurance	5 193	5 517	5 672	5 517	5 340	742	749	739
Treaty reinsurance	..	..	..	..	..	..	..	..
Total non-life insurance	11 230	11 983	12 255	12 444	12 195	12 303	12 599	12 386
1.2 Gross claims payments								
Life								
Domestic undertakings	256	314	360	358	1 110	1 254	947	977
Foreign controlled undertakings	0	0	145	140	714	837	920	959
Foreign companies (branches)	0	0	..	0	0	0	0	0
All undertakings	256	314	360	358	1 110	1 254	947	977
Non-life								
Domestic undertakings	3 019	2 290	2 675	1 107	1 632	2 072	2 203	1 939
Foreign controlled undertakings	1 531	875	1 490	905	873	1 288	2 620	1 893
Foreign companies (branches)	5	5	5	4	3	2	3	3
All undertakings	3 024	2 296	2 681	1 111	1 636	2 075	2 206	1 942
Composite								
Domestic undertakings	10 023	10 854	11 652	11 676	11 289	12 780	12 440	12 173
Foreign controlled undertakings	3 565	3 751	3 829	3 846	3 026	3 760	10 479	9 813
Foreign companies (branches)	0	0	..	0	0	0	0	0
All undertakings	10 023	10 854	11 652	11 676	11 289	12 780	12 440	12 173
of which:								
Life	5 599	6 338	6 047	6 011	5 955	7 193	6 817	6 194
Domestic undertakings	5 599	6 338	6 047	6 011	5 955	7 193	6 817	6 194
Foreign controlled undertakings	2 117	2 297	2 281	2 274	1 630	2 235	3 500	3 281
Foreign companies (branches)	0	0	..	0	0	0	0	0
All undertakings	5 599	6 338	6 047	6 011	5 955	7 193	6 817	6 194
Non-life	4 425	4 516	5 605	5 665	5 335	5 588	5 623	5 980
Domestic undertakings	4 425	4 516	5 605	5 665	5 335	5 588	5 623	5 980
Foreign controlled undertakings	1 448	1 454	1 549	1 572	1 396	1 525	6 979	6 532
Foreign companies (branches)	0	0	..	0	0	0	0	0
All undertakings	4 425	4 516	5 605	5 665	5 335	5 588	5 623	5 980
Total								
Domestic undertakings	13 298	13 458	14 687	13 141	14 032	16 107	15 590	15 089
Foreign controlled undertakings	5 096	4 626	5 464	4 891	4 613	5 885	14 018	12 665
Foreign companies (branches)	5	5	5	4	3	2	3	3
All undertakings	13 304	13 463	14 692	13 145	14 036	16 109	15 593	15 092

AUSTRIA

Table 1. Selected aggregates (cont.)

Million EUR

	2010	2011	2012	2013	2014	2015	2016	2017
1.3 Commissions								
Life								
Domestic undertakings	129	138	75	99	98	98	80	73
Foreign controlled undertakings	0	0	17	5	70	70	79	72
Foreign companies (branches)	0	0	..	0	0	0	0	0
All undertakings	129	138	75	99	98	98	80	73
Non-life								
Domestic undertakings	519	548	338	354	398	386	399	408
Foreign controlled undertakings	295	302	309	319	329	341	348	352
Foreign companies (branches)	1	2	2	2	1	1	1	2
All undertakings	521	549	340	356	399	387	400	410
Composite								
Domestic undertakings	1 916	1 962	2 309	2 285	2 279	2 354	2 392	2 365
Foreign controlled undertakings	712	717	750	752	666	739	734	725
Foreign companies (branches)	0	0	..	0	0	0	0	0
All undertakings	1 916	1 962	2 309	2 285	2 279	2 354	2 392	2 365
of which:								
Life	688	669	692	644	624	623	579	538
Domestic undertakings	688	669	692	644	624	623	579	538
Foreign controlled undertakings	256	255	253	238	163	188	163	149
Foreign companies (branches)	0	0	..	0	0	0	0	0
All undertakings	688	669	692	644	624	623	579	538
Non-life	1 228	1 292	1 616	1 641	1 655	1 731	1 812	1 827
Domestic undertakings	1 228	1 292	1 616	1 641	1 655	1 731	1 812	1 827
Foreign controlled undertakings	456	462	497	514	503	551	571	576
Foreign companies (branches)	0	0	..	0	0	0	0	0
All undertakings	1 228	1 292	1 616	1 641	1 655	1 731	1 812	1 827
Total								
Domestic undertakings	2 564	2 647	2 722	2 738	2 775	2 839	2 871	2 846
Foreign controlled undertakings	1 008	1 019	1 077	1 076	1 065	1 150	1 161	1 149
Foreign companies (branches)	1	2	2	2	1	1	1	2
All undertakings	2 565	2 649	2 724	2 740	2 776	2 840	2 872	2 848
1.4 Gross operating expenses								
Life								
Domestic undertakings	146	157	95	120	43	40	37	42
Foreign controlled undertakings	0	0	0	14	30	30	36	41
Foreign companies (branches)	0	0	..	0	0	0	0	0
All undertakings	146	157	95	120	43	40	37	42
Non-life								
Domestic undertakings	906	672	860	697	153	143	192	191
Foreign controlled undertakings	443	263	447	414	116	92	111	105
Foreign companies (branches)	3	3	3	3	1	1	1	1
All undertakings	909	675	863	700	154	144	193	192
Composite								
Domestic undertakings	2 115	2 054	1 918	2 306	623	678	702	696
Foreign controlled undertakings	723	667	695	699	167	185	177	181
Foreign companies (branches)	0	0	..	0	0	0	0	0
All undertakings	2 115	2 054	1 918	2 306	623	678	702	696
of which:								
Life	908	879	513	848	194	202	223	224
Domestic undertakings	908	879	513	848	194	202	223	224
Foreign controlled undertakings	341	344	339	323	61	68	63	58
Foreign companies (branches)	0	0	..	0	0	0	0	0
All undertakings	908	879	513	848	194	202	223	224
Non-life	1 208	1 175	1 405	1 458	428	476	479	472
Domestic undertakings	1 208	1 175	1 405	1 458	428	476	479	472
Foreign controlled undertakings	382	323	356	376	106	117	114	123
Foreign companies (branches)	0	0	..	0	0	0	0	0
All undertakings	1 208	1 175	1 405	1 458	428	476	479	472
Total								
Domestic undertakings	3 167	2 883	2 873	3 124	819	861	930	929
Foreign controlled undertakings	1 166	930	1 143	1 128	313	308	324	328
Foreign companies (branches)	3	3	3	3	1	1	1	1
All undertakings	3 170	2 885	2 876	3 127	820	862	931	930

Table 1. Selected aggregates (cont.)

Million EUR

	2010	2011	2012	2013	2014	2015	2016	2017
1.5 Insurance business written abroad by branches, gross premiums								
Life								
Branches and agencies	139	174	72	157	22	19	13	11
Subsidaries	..	..	..	..	..	..	..	..
Total	139	174	72	157	22	19	13	11
Non-life								
Branches and agencies	141	219	149	159	198	204	217	215
Subsidaries	..	..	..	..	..	..	..	..
Total	141	219	149	159	198	204	217	215
Composite								
Branches and agencies	539	480	557	480	368	284	251	275
Subsidaries	..	..	..	..	..	..	..	..
Total	539	480	557	480	368	284	251	275
of which:								
Life	407	233	168	140	103	78	83	78
Branches and agencies	407	233	168	140	103	78	83	78
Subsidaries	..	..	..	..	..	..	..	..
Total	407	233	168	140	103	78	83	78
Non-life	132	246	389	340	266	206	168	198
Branches and agencies	132	246	389	340	266	206	168	198
Subsidaries	..	..	..	..	..	..	..	..
Total	132	246	389	340	266	206	168	198
Total								
Branches and agencies	818	873	778	796	587	507	481	501
Subsidaries	..	..	..	..	..	..	..	..
Total	818	873	778	796	587	507	481	501

.. Not available

Note: Detailed metadata at: *http://metalinks.oecd.org/ins/20190221/c1c6.*

Source: *OECD Insurance Statistics (database)*

AUSTRIA

Table 2. Number of companies and employees

	2010	2011	2012	2013	2014	2015	2016	2017
2.1 Number of companies								
Life								
Domestic undertakings	3	3	3	3	7	7	6	6
Foreign controlled undertakings	0	0	1	1	3	3	4	4
Foreign companies (branches)	0	0	0	0	0	0	0	0
All undertakings	3	3	3	3	7	7	6	6
Non-life								
Domestic undertakings	17	17	14	14	12	12	12	12
Foreign controlled undertakings	9	8	7	7	8	8	8	8
Foreign companies (branches)	1	1	1	1	1	1	1	1
All undertakings	18	18	15	15	13	13	13	13
Composite								
Domestic undertakings	28	28	27	26	21	20	17	17
Foreign controlled undertakings	10	10	10	9	6	5	4	4
Foreign companies (branches)	0	0	0	0	0	0	0	0
All undertakings	28	28	27	26	21	20	17	17
Reinsurance								
Domestic undertakings	3	3	3	3	3	2	3	2
Foreign controlled undertakings	2	2	2	1	2	1	1	0
Foreign companies (branches)	0	0	0	0	0	0	0	0
All undertakings	3	3	3	3	3	2	3	2
Total								
Domestic undertakings	51	51	47	46	43	41	38	37
Foreign controlled undertakings	21	20	20	18	19	17	17	16
Foreign companies (branches)	1	1	1	1	1	1	1	1
All undertakings	52	52	48	47	44	42	39	38
2.2 Number of employees								
Insurance undertakings	27 755	27 671	27 430	27 738	27 791	27 911	28 336	28 367
Intermediaries	9 872	9 839	9 255	..	..	..	..	..
Total	27 755	27 671	27 430	27 738	27 791	27 911	28 336	28 367

.. Not available

Note: Detailed metadata at: *http://metalinks.oecd.org/ins/20190221/c1c6.*

Source: OECD Insurance Statistics (database)

BELGIUM

Table 1. Selected aggregates

Million EUR

	2010	2011	2012	2013	2014	2015	2016	2017
1.1 Insurance business written in the reporting country								
1.1.1 Insurance business, by ownership								
Gross premiums								
Domestic undertakings	29 575	29 363	32 640	28 251	28 863	27 712	27 493	27 299
Foreign controlled undertakings	..	..	..	..	..	..	..	..
Foreign companies (branches)	..	..	..	..	..	..	..	..
All undertakings	29 575	29 363	32 640	28 251	28 863	27 712	27 493	27 299
Premiums ceded								
Domestic undertakings	1 773	1 441	2 417	2 474	3 251	3 183	3 520	3 412
Foreign controlled undertakings	..	..	..	..	..	..	..	..
Foreign companies (branches)	..	..	..	..	..	..	..	..
All undertakings	1 773	1 441	2 417	2 474	3 251	3 183	3 520	3 412
Net written premiums								
Domestic undertakings	27 802	27 922	30 223	25 777	25 612	24 529	23 973	23 887
Foreign controlled undertakings	..	..	..	..	..	..	..	..
Foreign companies (branches)	..	..	..	..	..	..	..	..
All undertakings	27 802	27 922	30 223	25 777	25 612	24 529	23 973	23 887
1.1.2 Insurance business on foreign risks, gross premiums								
Life	..	..	31	25	15	24	20	17
Non-life	..	..	242	268	563	436	515	553
Composite	..	..	230	218	223	321	331	331
of which:								
Life	..	..	77	53	39	38	23	17
Non-life	..	..	153	165	184	282	308	313
Total	..	..	502	511	801	781	866	901
1.1.3 Life insurance payments, by class, gross premiums								
Annuities	..	..	..	..	..	..	..	..
Unit linked	2 049	2 142	4 844	2 743	2 524	3 008	2 221	3 182
Other life insurance	17 092	16 324	16 235	13 501	13 723	12 302	12 674	11 424
Total life insurance	19 141	18 467	21 078	16 244	16 247	15 310	14 895	14 606
of which: *Pension contracts*	..	..	..	..	..	..	..	..
1.1.4 Non-life insurance payments, by class, gross premiums								
Motor vehicle insurance	..	..	3 459	3 487	3 542	3 585	..	..
Marine, aviation and other transport insurance	..	..	78	71	69	81	..	..
Freight insurance	..	..	116	104	100	73	..	..
Fire and other property damage insurance	..	..	2 573	2 696	2 755	2 708	..	..
Pecuniary loss insurance	..	..	407	404	725	598	..	..
General liability insurance	..	..	780	770	785	762	..	..
Accident and health	..	..	3 361	3 592	3 695	3 653	..	..
of which: *Health*	..	..	1 517	1 618	1 708	1 849	..	..
Other non-life insurance	..	..	737	825	885	888	..	..
Treaty reinsurance	..	..	7	..	..	..	..	..
Total non-life insurance	..	..	11 516	11 949	12 556	12 349	12 532	12 652
1.2 Gross claims payments								
Life								
Domestic undertakings	514	547	592	528	626	469	642	521
Foreign controlled undertakings	..	..	..	..	..	..	..	..
Foreign companies (branches)	..	..	..	..	..	..	..	..
All undertakings	..	..	592	528	626	469	642	521
Non-life								
Domestic undertakings	1 496	1 512	1 898	1 960	2 272	2 363	2 539	2 316
Foreign controlled undertakings	..	..	..	..	..	..	..	..
Foreign companies (branches)	..	..	..	..	..	..	..	..
All undertakings	..	..	1 898	1 960	2 272	2 363	2 539	2 316
Composite								
Domestic undertakings	17 461	20 798	23 438	23 890	24 323	25 926	25 229	24 184
Foreign controlled undertakings	..	..	..	..	..	..	..	..
Foreign companies (branches)	..	..	..	..	..	..	..	..
All undertakings	..	..	23 438	23 890	24 323	25 926	25 229	24 184
of which:								
Life	..	..	17 427	17 746	17 418	19 244	18 328	17 466
Domestic undertakings	12 194	15 232	17 427	17 746	17 418	19 244	18 328	17 466
Foreign controlled undertakings	..	..	..	..	..	..	..	..
Foreign companies (branches)	..	..	..	..	..	..	..	..
All undertakings	..	..	17 427	17 746	17 418	19 244	18 328	17 466
Non-life	..	..	6 010	6 144	6 905	6 682	6 901	6 717
Domestic undertakings	5 267	5 566	6 010	6 144	6 905	6 682	6 901	6 717
Foreign controlled undertakings	..	..	..	..	..	..	..	..
Foreign companies (branches)	..	..	..	..	..	..	..	..
All undertakings	..	..	6 010	6 144	6 905	6 682	6 901	6 717
Total								
Domestic undertakings	19 470	22 857	25 928	26 378	27 222	28 758	28 410	27 020
Foreign controlled undertakings	..	..	..	..	..	..	..	..
Foreign companies (branches)	..	..	..	..	..	..	..	..
All undertakings	..	..	25 928	26 378	27 222	28 758	28 410	27 020

BELGIUM

Table 1. Selected aggregates (cont.)

Million EUR

	2010	2011	2012	2013	2014	2015	2016	2017
1.3 Commissions								
Life								
Domestic undertakings	74	54	59	55	45	47	55	56
Foreign controlled undertakings	..	..	..	..	..	..	..	..
Foreign companies (branches)	..	..	..	..	..	..	..	..
All undertakings	..	..	59	55	45	47	55	56
Non-life								
Domestic undertakings	340	318	394	391	450	550	616	607
Foreign controlled undertakings	..	..	..	..	..	..	..	..
Foreign companies (branches)	..	..	..	..	..	..	..	..
All undertakings	..	..	394	391	450	550	616	607
Composite								
Domestic undertakings	2 118	2 209	2 397	2 446	2 478	2 493	2 484	2 536
Foreign controlled undertakings	..	..	..	..	..	..	..	..
Foreign companies (branches)	..	..	..	..	..	..	..	..
All undertakings	..	..	2 397	2 446	2 478	2 493	2 484	2 536
of which:								
Life	..	..	905	875	852	833	765	756
Domestic undertakings	808	826	905	875	852	833	765	756
Foreign controlled undertakings	..	..	..	..	..	..	..	..
Foreign companies (branches)	..	..	..	..	..	..	..	..
All undertakings	..	..	905	875	852	833	765	756
Non-life	..	..	1 493	1 572	1 626	1 660	1 719	1 779
Domestic undertakings	1 310	1 382	1 493	1 572	1 626	1 660	1 719	1 779
Foreign controlled undertakings	..	..	..	..	..	..	..	..
Foreign companies (branches)	..	..	..	..	..	..	..	..
All undertakings	..	..	1 493	1 572	1 626	1 660	1 719	1 779
Total								
Domestic undertakings	2 531	2 581	2 851	2 892	2 973	3 090	3 155	3 198
Foreign controlled undertakings	..	..	..	..	..	..	..	..
Foreign companies (branches)	..	..	..	..	..	..	..	..
All undertakings	..	..	2 851	2 892	2 973	3 090	3 155	3 198
1.4 Gross operating expenses								
Life								
Domestic undertakings	135	115	118	58	41	45	47	51
Foreign controlled undertakings	..	..	..	..	..	..	..	..
Foreign companies (branches)	..	..	..	..	..	..	..	..
All undertakings	..	..	118	58	41	45	47	51
Non-life								
Domestic undertakings	648	621	806	386	643	618	641	678
Foreign controlled undertakings	..	..	..	..	..	..	..	..
Foreign companies (branches)	..	..	..	..	..	..	..	..
All undertakings	..	..	806	386	643	618	641	678
Composite								
Domestic undertakings	4 007	4 176	4 401	2 084	2 197	2 205	2 320	2 402
Foreign controlled undertakings	..	..	..	..	..	..	..	..
Foreign companies (branches)	..	..	..	..	..	..	..	..
All undertakings	..	..	4 401	2 084	2 197	2 205	2 320	2 402
of which:								
Life	..	..	1 702	830	833	824	859	869
Domestic undertakings	1 560	1 597	1 702	830	833	824	859	869
Foreign controlled undertakings	..	..	..	..	..	..	..	..
Foreign companies (branches)	..	..	..	..	..	..	..	..
All undertakings	..	..	1 702	830	833	824	859	869
Non-life	..	..	2 699	1 254	1 364	1 382	1 461	1 533
Domestic undertakings	2 446	2 579	2 699	1 254	1 364	1 382	1 461	1 533
Foreign controlled undertakings	..	..	..	..	..	..	..	..
Foreign companies (branches)	..	..	..	..	..	..	..	..
All undertakings	..	..	2 699	1 254	1 364	1 382	1 461	1 533
Total								
Domestic undertakings	4 790	4 912	5 325	2 528	2 881	2 868	3 008	3 130
Foreign controlled undertakings	..	..	..	..	..	..	..	..
Foreign companies (branches)	..	..	..	..	..	..	..	..
All undertakings	..	..	5 325	2 528	2 881	2 868	3 008	3 130

BELGIUM

Table 1. Selected aggregates (cont.)

Million EUR

	2010	2011	2012	2013	2014	2015	2016	2017
1.5 Insurance business written abroad by branches, gross premiums								
Life								
Branches and agencies	..	..	2	2	2	0	0	0
Subsidaries	..	..	..	..	..	..	..	..
Total	..	..	2	2	2	..	0	0
Non-life								
Branches and agencies	..	..	698	727	1 572	1 931	1 854	1 843
Subsidaries	..	..	..	..	..	..	..	..
Total	..	..	698	727	1 572	1 931	1 854	1 843
Composite								
Branches and agencies	..	..	442	448	1 121	1 156	1 197	1 337
Subsidaries	..	..	..	..	..	..	..	..
Total	..	..	442	448	1 121	1 156	1 197	1 337
of which:								
Life	..	..	32	28	16	16	14	61
Branches and agencies	..	..	32	28	16	16	14	61
Subsidaries	..	..	..	..	..	..	..	..
Total	..	..	32	28	16	16	14	61
Non-life	..	..	409	421	1 105	1 141	1 183	1 276
Branches and agencies	..	..	409	421	1 105	1 141	1 183	1 276
Subsidaries	..	..	..	..	..	..	..	..
Total	..	..	409	421	1 105	1 141	1 183	1 276
Total								
Branches and agencies	..	..	1 142	1 178	2 696	3 087	3 051	3 181
Subsidaries	..	..	..	..	..	..	..	..
Total	..	..	1 142	1 178	2 696	3 087	3 051	3 181

.. Not available

Note: Detailed metadata at: *http://metalinks.oecd.org/ins/20190221/e710.*

Source: OECD Insurance Statistics (database)

BELGIUM

Table 2. Number of companies and employees

	2010	2011	2012	2013	2014	2015	2016	2017
2.1 Number of companies								
Life								
Domestic undertakings	20	18	17	16	15	15	12	10
Foreign controlled undertakings	..	..	..	..	..	..	..	..
Foreign companies (branches)	8	8	7	7	8	8	10	10
All undertakings	28	26	24	23	23	23	22	20
Non-life								
Domestic undertakings	54	53	49	44	42	41	38	34
Foreign controlled undertakings	..	..	..	..	..	..	..	..
Foreign companies (branches)	40	44	36	36	36	32	32	33
All undertakings	94	97	85	80	78	73	70	67
Composite								
Domestic undertakings	23	24	23	23	23	23	22	23
Foreign controlled undertakings	..	..	..	..	..	..	..	..
Foreign companies (branches)	2	2	2	2	2	2	2	2
All undertakings	25	26	25	25	25	25	24	25
Reinsurance								
Domestic undertakings	2	2	1	1	1	1	1	1
Foreign controlled undertakings	..	..	..	..	..	..	..	..
Foreign companies (branches)	0	0	1	1	1	1	1	1
All undertakings	2	2	2	2	2	2	2	2
Total								
Domestic undertakings	99	97	90	84	81	80	73	68
Foreign controlled undertakings	..	..	..	..	..	..	..	..
Foreign companies (branches)	50	54	46	46	47	43	45	46
All undertakings	149	151	136	130	128	123	118	114
2.2 Number of employees								
Insurance undertakings	23 833	25 083	..	..	..	..	..	..
Intermediaries	18 075	..	..	..	..	..	..	..
Total	41 908	..	..	..	..	..	..	..

.. Not available

Note: Detailed metadata at: *http://metalinks.oecd.org/ins/20190221/e710.*

Source: OECD Insurance Statistics (database)

CANADA

Table 1. Selected aggregates

Million CAD

	2010	2011	2012	2013	2014	2015	2016	2017
1.1 Insurance business written in the reporting country								
1.1.1 Insurance business, by ownership								
Gross premiums								
Domestic undertakings	78 875	83 513	87 337	91 830	81 347	86 082	..	..
Foreign controlled undertakings	11 288	11 273	11 465	11 237	18 957	17 321	..	..
Foreign companies (branches)	9 464	9 502	9 621	9 651	21 604	20 840	..	..
All undertakings	88 339	93 014	96 958	101 481	102 951	106 922	..	..
Premiums ceded								
Domestic undertakings	16 638	21 174	23 483	25 176	22 771	25 855	..	..
Foreign controlled undertakings	2 465	2 550	2 413	2 504	5 070	4 912	..	..
Foreign companies (branches)	2 014	1 923	2 405	2 094	4 469	4 735	..	..
All undertakings	18 651	23 097	25 888	27 270	27 240	30 590	..	..
Net written premiums								
Domestic undertakings	62 237	62 338	63 854	66 655	58 576	60 227	..	..
Foreign controlled undertakings	8 823	8 723	9 052	8 733	13 888	12 410	..	..
Foreign companies (branches)	7 450	7 579	7 216	7 557	17 135	16 104	..	..
All undertakings	69 687	69 917	71 070	74 212	75 710	76 331	..	..
1.1.2 Insurance business on foreign risks, gross premiums								
Life	..	..	..	..	..	..	..	..
Non-life	..	..	..	..	..	..	..	..
Composite	..	..	..	..	..	..	..	..
of which:								
Life	..	..	..	..	..	..	..	..
Non-life	..	..	..	..	..	..	..	..
Total	..	..	..	..	..	..	..	..
1.1.3 Life insurance payments, by class, gross premiums								
Annuities	7 815	6 457	5 276	6 263	5 562	5 539	..	..
Unit linked	70	..	..	..	..	..	..	..
Other life insurance	19 212	..	..	..	..	..	..	..
Total life insurance	39 093	..	..	..	..	..	..	..
***of which:** Pension contracts*	1 598	..	..	..	..	..	..	..
1.1.4 Non-life insurance payments, by class, gross premiums								
Motor vehicle insurance	18 191	20 277	21 805	22 857	21 007	21 426	..	..
Marine, aviation and other transport insurance	650	656	672	630	773	716	..	..
Freight insurance	..	..	..	..	..	..	..	..
Fire and other property damage insurance	13 483	15 268	16 577	16 687	18 994	19 992	..	..
Pecuniary loss insurance	1 643	1 716	1 785	1 748	2 271	2 613	..	..
General liability insurance	4 797	5 054	5 197	5 267	5 830	6 289	..	..
Accident and health	18 043	25 743	19 672	20 262	25 708	26 370	..	..
***of which:** Health*	..	..	..	..	..	..	..	..
Other non-life insurance	6	8	14	32	138	275	..	..
Treaty reinsurance	..	..	..	..	..	..	..	..
Total non-life insurance	56 813	68 723	65 723	67 482	74 721	77 682	..	..
1.2 Gross claims payments								
Life								
Domestic undertakings	0	0	0	0	0	0	..	..
Foreign controlled undertakings	0	0	0	0	0	0	..	..
Foreign companies (branches)	25	27	28	36	41	13	..	..
All undertakings	25	27	28	36	41	13	..	..
Non-life								
Domestic undertakings	21 444	23 354	24 435	28 506	25 194	25 500	..	..
Foreign controlled undertakings	4 666	5 150	4 939	5 566	8 332	8 552	..	..
Foreign companies (branches)	5 971	5 840	4 875	5 242	5 901	4 694	..	..
All undertakings	27 415	29 193	29 310	33 748	31 095	30 193	..	..
Composite								
Domestic undertakings	13 016	10 525	10 851	11 227	9 477	10 030	..	..
Foreign controlled undertakings	773	666	731	736	881	303	..	..
Foreign companies (branches)	220	160	163	159	7 182	7 161	..	..
All undertakings	13 236	10 685	11 014	11 386	16 659	17 190	..	..
of which:								
Life	5 224	4 599	4 749	4 969	5 480	5 747	..	..
Domestic undertakings	5 096	4 523	4 650	4 869	3 858	4 186	..	..
Foreign controlled undertakings	301	190	189	190	344	188	..	..
Foreign companies (branches)	128	76	99	99	1 622	1 561	..	..
All undertakings	5 224	4 599	4 749	4 969	5 480	5 747	..	..
Non-life	8 012	6 085	6 264	6 417	11 179	11 444	..	..
Domestic undertakings	7 920	6 002	6 201	6 357	5 620	5 844	..	..
Foreign controlled undertakings	472	475	542	546	537	115	..	..
Foreign companies (branches)	92	83	63	60	5 560	5 600	..	..
All undertakings	8 012	6 085	6 264	6 417	11 179	11 444	..	..
Total								
Domestic undertakings	34 460	33 879	35 286	39 733	34 671	35 529	..	..
Foreign controlled undertakings	5 440	5 816	5 670	6 301	9 213	8 854	..	..
Foreign companies (branches)	6 216	6 026	5 066	5 437	13 124	11 867	..	..
All undertakings	40 676	39 905	40 351	45 170	47 795	47 396	..	..

CANADA

Table 1. Selected aggregates (cont.)

Million CAD

	2010	2011	2012	2013	2014	2015	2016	2017
1.3 Commissions								
Life								
Domestic undertakings	0	0	0	0	..	0	..	..
Foreign controlled undertakings	0	0	0	0	..	..	..	..
Foreign companies (branches)	11	10	12	10	..	0	..	..
All undertakings	11	10	12	10	..	0	..	..
Non-life								
Domestic undertakings	4 055	4 305	4 719	4 781	..	5 441	..	..
Foreign controlled undertakings	932	91	1 115	1 092	..	1 882	..	..
Foreign companies (branches)	1 070	1 102	1 077	1 095	..	1 104	..	..
All undertakings	5 125	5 407	5 796	5 876	..	6 545	..	..
Composite								
Domestic undertakings	5 232	5 539	5 505	5 558	..	4 787	..	..
Foreign controlled undertakings	377	377	258	239	..	97	..	..
Foreign companies (branches)	169	158	147	145	..	193	..	..
All undertakings	5 401	5 697	5 652	5 703	..	4 980	..	..
of which:								
Life	4 026	4 212	4 239	4 291	..	3 572	..	..
Domestic undertakings	3 920	4 115	4 150	4 213	..	3 457	..	..
Foreign controlled undertakings	273	285	172	173	..	65	..	..
Foreign companies (branches)	106	97	89	78	..	115	..	..
All undertakings	4 026	4 212	4 239	4 291	..	3 572	..	..
Non-life	1 375	1 485	1 413	1 412	..	1 408	..	..
Domestic undertakings	1 312	1 424	1 355	1 345	..	1 330	..	..
Foreign controlled undertakings	104	91	86	66	..	32	..	..
Foreign companies (branches)	63	61	58	67	..	78	..	..
All undertakings	1 375	1 485	1 413	1 412	..	1 408	..	..
Total								
Domestic undertakings	9 287	9 844	10 224	10 339	..	10 228	..	..
Foreign controlled undertakings	1 309	467	1 373	1 331	..	1 979	..	..
Foreign companies (branches)	1 250	1 270	1 235	1 249	..	1 298	..	..
All undertakings	10 537	11 114	11 460	11 588	..	11 526	..	..
1.4 Gross operating expenses								
Life								
Domestic undertakings	18	20	22	23	24	22	..	..
Foreign controlled undertakings	0	0	0	..	0	0	..	..
Foreign companies (branches)	27	29	32	27	28	15	..	..
All undertakings	45	49	53	50	52	37	..	..
Non-life								
Domestic undertakings	4 707	5 235	5 774	6 023	4 032	4 493	..	..
Foreign controlled undertakings	1 310	1 385	1 465	1 409	1 385	1 488	..	..
Foreign companies (branches)	929	931	1 001	1 017	855	689	..	..
All undertakings	5 636	6 166	6 775	7 040	4 887	5 182	..	..
Composite								
Domestic undertakings	13 129	10 675	12 274	13 728	12 612	14 400	..	..
Foreign controlled undertakings	557	558	557	571	736	187	..	..
Foreign companies (branches)	124	119	110	117	206	272	..	..
All undertakings	13 253	10 794	12 384	13 845	12 818	14 672	..	..
of which:								
Life	..	..	..	..	..	..	..	..
Domestic undertakings	..	..	..	..	..	..	..	..
Foreign controlled undertakings	..	..	..	..	..	..	..	..
Foreign companies (branches)	..	..	..	..	..	..	..	..
All undertakings	..	..	..	..	..	..	..	..
Non-life	..	..	..	..	..	..	..	..
Domestic undertakings	..	..	..	..	..	..	..	..
Foreign controlled undertakings	..	..	..	..	..	..	..	..
Foreign companies (branches)	..	..	..	..	..	..	..	..
All undertakings	..	..	..	..	..	..	..	..
Total								
Domestic undertakings	17 854	15 930	18 069	19 774	16 668	18 915	..	..
Foreign controlled undertakings	1 868	1 943	2 021	1 981	2 121	1 675	..	..
Foreign companies (branches)	1 079	1 079	1 143	1 161	1 089	976	..	..
All undertakings	18 933	17 009	19 212	20 934	17 757	19 891	..	..

CANADA

Table 1. Selected aggregates (cont.)

Million CAD

	2010	2011	2012	2013	2014	2015	2016	2017
1.5 Insurance business written abroad by branches, gross premiums								
Life								
Branches and agencies	..	..	..	..	..	..	..	..
Subsidaries	..	..	..	..	..	..	..	..
Total	..	..	..	..	0	0	..	..
Non-life								
Branches and agencies	..	..	..	..	..	..	..	..
Subsidaries	..	..	..	..	..	..	..	..
Total	250	545	548	1 018	1 320	1 500	..	..
Composite								
Branches and agencies	..	..	..	..	..	..	..	..
Subsidaries	..	..	..	..	..	..	..	..
Total	36 677	34 423	37 741	7 942	31 162	40 235	..	..
of which:								
Life	..	..	..	..	27 224	..	..	..
Branches and agencies	..	..	..	..	..	..	..	..
Subsidaries	..	..	..	..	..	..	..	..
Total	..	..	..	..	27 224	..	..	..
Non-life	..	..	..	..	3 939	..	..	..
Branches and agencies	..	..	..	..	..	..	..	..
Subsidaries	..	..	..	..	..	..	..	..
Total	..	..	..	..	3 939	..	..	..
Total								
Branches and agencies	..	..	..	..	..	..	..	..
Subsidaries	..	..	..	..	..	..	..	..
Total	36 927	34 968	38 289	8 959	32 482	41 736	..	..

.. Not available

Note: Detailed metadata at: *http://metalinks.oecd.org/ins/20190221/39e0.*

Source: OECD Insurance Statistics (database)

CANADA

Table 2. Number of companies and employees

	2010	2011	2012	2013	2014	2015	2016	2017
2.1 Number of companies								
Life								
Domestic undertakings	1	1	1	1	1	1	..	..
Foreign controlled undertakings	0	0	0	0	0	0	..	..
Foreign companies (branches)	7	5	5	5	5	5	..	..
All undertakings	8	6	6	6	6	6	..	..
Non-life								
Domestic undertakings	87	86	84	60	66	66	..	..
Foreign controlled undertakings	23	23	23	22	28	28	..	..
Foreign companies (branches)	66	61	60	60	60	58	..	..
All undertakings	153	147	144	120	126	124	..	..
Composite								
Domestic undertakings	44	43	43	34	34	33	..	..
Foreign controlled undertakings	11	10	10	10	9	7	..	..
Foreign companies (branches)	26	26	21	26	23	22	..	..
All undertakings	70	69	64	60	57	55	..	..
Reinsurance								
Domestic undertakings	6	6	6	6	5	5	..	..
Foreign controlled undertakings	5	6	6	6	5	5	..	..
Foreign companies (branches)	24	28	27	28	25	26	..	..
All undertakings	30	34	33	34	30	31	..	..
Total								
Domestic undertakings	138	136	134	101	106	105	..	..
Foreign controlled undertakings	39	39	39	38	42	40	..	..
Foreign companies (branches)	123	120	113	119	113	111	..	..
All undertakings	261	256	247	220	219	216	..	..
2.2 Number of employees								
Insurance undertakings	..	..	..	..	..	..	..	..
Intermediaries	..	..	..	..	..	..	..	..
Total	..	..	..	..	..	..	..	..

.. Not available

Note: Detailed metadata at: *http://metalinks.oecd.org/ins/20190221/39e0.*

Source: OECD Insurance Statistics (database)

CHILE

Table 1. Selected aggregates

Million CLP

	2010	2011	2012	2013	2014	2015	2016	2017
1.1 Insurance business written in the reporting country								
1.1.1 Insurance business, by ownership								
Gross premiums								
Domestic undertakings	4 239 694	4 691 200	5 496 223	5 832 221	6 260 019	7 465 743	8 394 971	8 344 320
Foreign controlled undertakings	2 335 007	2 270 671	2 821 041	3 056 166	3 211 682	3 614 011	4 422 880	4 504 671
Foreign companies (branches)	0	..	..	..	..	..	..	..
All undertakings	4 239 694	4 691 200	5 496 223	5 832 221	6 260 019	7 465 743	8 394 971	8 344 320
Premiums ceded								
Domestic undertakings	..	911 543	930 906	906 942	998 507	1 135 872	1 310 392	1 382 346
Foreign controlled undertakings	..	648 512	671 333	647 814	676 439	749 522	953 240	901 373
Foreign companies (branches)	..	..	..	..	..	..	..	..
All undertakings	..	911 543	930 906	906 942	998 507	1 135 872	1 310 392	1 382 346
Net written premiums								
Domestic undertakings	..	3 779 657	4 565 317	4 925 279	5 261 513	6 329 871	7 084 578	6 961 974
Foreign controlled undertakings	..	1 622 159	2 149 709	2 408 352	2 535 243	2 864 489	3 469 640	3 603 299
Foreign companies (branches)	..	..	..	..	..	..	..	..
All undertakings	..	3 779 657	4 565 317	4 925 279	5 261 513	6 329 871	7 084 578	6 961 974
1.1.2 Insurance business on foreign risks, gross premiums								
Life	..	0	..	..	..	..	..	..
Non-life	..	0	..	..	..	..	..	..
Composite total	..	..	..	..	..	..	..	..
Total	..	0	..	..	..	..	..	..
1.1.3 Life insurance payments, by class, gross premiums								
Annuities	1 067 841	1 105 236	1 623 894	1 729 819	1 692 693	2 343 736	2 759 473	2 456 649
Unit linked	196 316	201 183	213 028	318 975	475 508	613 110	712 539	728 441
Other life insurance	1 531 021	1 625 966	1 761 476	1 827 419	1 948 628	2 123 123	2 373 130	2 560 094
Total life insurance	2 795 177	2 932 385	3 598 399	3 876 213	4 116 829	5 079 969	5 845 142	5 745 185
***of which:** Pension contracts*	0	1 340 726	..	..	..	..	..	..
1.1.4 Non-life insurance payments, by class, gross premiums								
Motor vehicle insurance	348 409	420 964	480 767	467 370	509 632	554 020	607 928	658 852
Marine, aviation and other transport insurance	75 737	92 530	93 208	117 884	129 698	148 074	132 318	134 870
Freight insurance	0	0	0	0	0	0	0	0
Fire and other property damage insurance	539 516	663 739	726 707	711 066	788 536	901 636	926 988	899 548
Pecuniary loss insurance	49 420	58 737	62 661	55 877	62 708	73 291	81 763	83 750
General liability insurance	52 327	69 048	80 035	52 154	56 828	41 342	34 468	30 188
Accident and health	123 267	115 563	117 127	25 789	30 296	46 180	53 105	66 796
***of which:** Health*	571	943	1 362	1 349	6 186	2 268	8 145	7 442
Other non-life insurance	252 717	336 427	335 850	524 059	561 863	602 569	651 596	675 973
Treaty reinsurance	0	0	0	0	0	0	0	0
Total non-life insurance	1 441 393	1 757 008	1 896 354	1 954 198	2 139 562	2 367 113	2 488 165	2 549 976
1.2 Gross claims payments								
Life								
Domestic undertakings	2 989 991	2 914 714	3 393 850	3 714 398	4 027 828	2 853 170	3 342 724	3 838 076
Foreign controlled undertakings	1 103 085	989 305	1 353 122	1 551 286	1 580 430	1 020 903	1 219 666	1 524 203
Foreign companies (branches)	0	0	..	..	..	..	..	..
All undertakings	2 989 991	2 914 714	3 393 850	3 714 398	4 027 828	2 853 170	3 342 724	3 838 076
Non-life								
Domestic undertakings	4 196 890	658 815	874 913	896 672	260 092	1 421 296	1 491 740	1 515 015
Foreign controlled undertakings	3 421 645	420 283	524 939	541 982	157 970	889 183	1 193 951	1 168 469
Foreign companies (branches)	0	0	..	..	..	..	..	..
All undertakings	4 196 890	658 815	874 913	896 672	260 092	1 421 296	1 491 740	1 515 015
Composite, all undertakings	..	..	..	..	..	..	..	..
Total								
Domestic undertakings	7 186 881	3 573 529	4 268 763	4 611 070	4 287 920	4 274 466	4 834 464	5 353 090
Foreign controlled undertakings	4 524 730	1 409 588	1 878 061	2 093 268	1 738 400	1 910 087	2 413 617	2 692 672
Foreign companies (branches)	0	0	..	..	..	..	..	..
All undertakings	7 186 881	3 573 529	4 268 763	4 611 070	4 287 920	4 274 466	4 834 464	5 353 090
1.3 Commissions								
Life								
Domestic undertakings	183 002	182 335	228 573	248 645	263 060	301 418	318 445	330 472
Foreign controlled undertakings	97 836	86 321	118 560	131 550	139 650	164 172	159 299	171 055
Foreign companies (branches)	0	0	..	..	..	..	..	..
All undertakings	183 002	182 335	228 573	248 645	263 060	301 418	318 445	330 472
Non-life								
Domestic undertakings	171 903	205 222	224 665	230 945	260 092	287 918	312 001	322 793
Foreign controlled undertakings	114 424	134 674	142 291	140 238	157 970	171 469	242 835	238 778
Foreign companies (branches)	0	0	..	..	..	..	..	..
All undertakings	171 903	205 222	224 665	230 945	260 092	287 918	312 001	322 793
Composite, all undertakings	..	..	..	..	..	..	..	..
Total								
Domestic undertakings	354 905	387 557	453 238	479 590	523 153	589 336	630 445	653 265
Foreign controlled undertakings	212 260	220 996	260 851	271 787	297 621	335 641	402 134	409 832
Foreign companies (branches)	0	0	..	..	..	..	..	..
All undertakings	354 905	387 557	453 238	479 590	523 153	589 336	630 445	653 265

CHILE

Table 1. Selected aggregates (cont.)

Million CLP

	2010	2011	2012	2013	2014	2015	2016	2017
1.4 Gross operating expenses								
Life								
Domestic undertakings	497 317	502 620	519 184	549 344	583 313	612 178	664 997	732 176
Foreign controlled undertakings	271 689	242 660	250 271	268 515	284 692	308 320	316 103	364 993
Foreign companies (branches)	0	0	..	..	..	..	..	..
All undertakings	497 317	502 620	519 184	549 344	583 313	612 178	664 997	732 176
Non-life								
Domestic undertakings	290 845	331 560	339 044	359 066	382 886	412 676	457 861	501 804
Foreign controlled undertakings	214 753	241 486	239 100	251 791	266 721	288 658	367 114	406 682
Foreign companies (branches)	0	0	..	..	..	..	..	..
All undertakings	290 845	331 560	339 044	359 066	382 886	412 676	457 861	501 804
Composite, all undertakings	..	..	..	..	..	..	..	..
Total								
Domestic undertakings	788 162	834 180	858 228	908 410	966 199	1 024 854	1 122 857	1 233 980
Foreign controlled undertakings	486 443	484 145	489 370	520 306	551 413	596 978	683 216	771 674
Foreign companies (branches)	0	0	..	..	..	..	..	..
All undertakings	788 162	834 180	858 228	908 410	966 199	1 024 854	1 122 857	1 233 980
1.5 Insurance business written abroad by branches, gross premiums								
Life								
Branches and agencies	..	0	..	..	..	..	..	..
Subsidaries	..	0	..	..	..	..	..	..
Total	..	0	..	..	..	..	..	..
Non-life								
Branches and agencies	..	0	..	..	..	..	..	..
Subsidaries	..	0	..	..	..	..	..	..
Total	..	0	..	..	..	..	..	..
Composite total	..	..	..	..	..	..	..	..
Total								
Branches and agencies	..	0	..	..	..	..	..	..
Subsidaries	..	0	..	..	..	..	..	..
Total	..	0	..	..	..	..	..	..

.. Not available

Note: Detailed metadata at: *http://metalinks.oecd.org/ins/20190221/f4f6*.

Source: OECD Insurance Statistics (database)

CHILE

Table 2. Number of companies and employees

	2010	2011	2012	2013	2014	2015	2016	2017
2.1 Number of companies								
Life								
Domestic undertakings	31	30	32	33	34	36	36	36
Foreign controlled undertakings	12	12	11	12	12	13	13	15
Foreign companies (branches)	0	0	..	..	..	..	0	..
All undertakings	31	30	32	33	34	36	36	36
Non-life								
Domestic undertakings	26	27	28	29	29	30	30	32
Foreign controlled undertakings	15	16	16	18	17	18	11	19
Foreign companies (branches)	0	0	..	..	..	..	0	..
All undertakings	26	27	28	29	29	30	30	32
Composite, all undertakings	**0**	**0**	**0**	**0**	**0**	**0**	**0**	**..**
Reinsurance								
Domestic undertakings	1	1	1	1	1	1	1	1
Foreign controlled undertakings	1	1	1	1	1	..	1	1
Foreign companies (branches)	0	0	..	..	..	..	0	..
All undertakings	1	1	1	1	1	1	1	1
Total								
Domestic undertakings	58	58	61	63	64	67	67	69
Foreign controlled undertakings	28	29	28	31	30	31	25	35
Foreign companies (branches)	0	0	..	..	..	..	0	..
All undertakings	58	58	61	63	64	67	67	69
2.2 Number of employees								
Insurance undertakings	13 554	14 366	16 304	16 686	17 039	15 368	16 414	16 859
Intermediaries	6 828	7 211	6 828	7 046	6 959	7 499	7 599	7 663
Total	20 382	21 577	23 132	23 732	23 998	22 867	24 013	24 522

.. Not available

Note: Detailed metadata at: *http://metalinks.oecd.org/ins/20190221/f4f6.*

Source: OECD Insurance Statistics (database)

CZECH REPUBLIC

Table 1. Selected aggregates

Million CZK

	2010	2011	2012	2013	2014	2015	2016	2017
1.1 Insurance business written in the reporting country								
1.1.1 Insurance business, by ownership								
Gross premiums								
Domestic undertakings	147 259	146 494	145 572	147 955	148 755	140 688	135 581	138 186
Foreign controlled undertakings	136 170	134 999	134 114	135 671	137 200	129 432	124 165	125 585
Foreign companies (branches)	8 723	8 598	8 026	8 567	9 164	11 159	11 102	11 459
All undertakings	155 981	155 092	153 597	156 522	157 919	151 846	146 683	149 645
Premiums ceded								
Domestic undertakings	26 327	27 642	27 730	29 333	29 915	29 857	28 913	30 449
Foreign controlled undertakings	23 843	24 903	24 826	26 054	26 601	26 578	25 450	26 230
Foreign companies (branches)	1 174	1 120	984	1 016	1 250	1 561	1 993	1 484
All undertakings	27 502	28 762	28 714	30 349	31 165	31 418	30 905	31 933
Net written premiums								
Domestic undertakings	120 931	118 852	117 842	118 623	118 839	110 831	106 669	107 737
Foreign controlled undertakings	112 327	110 096	109 288	109 617	110 598	102 854	98 714	99 356
Foreign companies (branches)	7 548	7 478	7 041	7 550	7 914	9 598	9 109	9 976
All undertakings	128 480	126 330	124 884	126 173	126 754	120 429	115 778	117 713
1.1.2 Insurance business on foreign risks, gross premiums								
Life	..	2	3	0	0	0	0	0
Non-life	..	814	931	741	993	524	274	738
Composite	..	1 553	1 681	1 780	2 121	1 867	1 843	2 777
of which:								
Life	..	1	0	37	360	4	0	1 805
Non-life	..	1 553	1 681	1 742	1 761	1 863	1 843	972
Total	..	2 370	2 614	2 521	3 113	2 390	2 117	3 515
1.1.3 Life insurance payments, by class, gross premiums								
Annuities	2 082	1 881	1 810	1 775	1 505	1 413	..	..
Unit linked	33 956	36 584	37 799	34 764	37 632	35 125	26 131	25 608
Other life insurance	35 710	33 543	32 437	35 030	32 042	25 876	33 110	31 425
Total life insurance	71 748	72 008	72 046	71 569	71 179	62 414	59 240	57 033
***of which:** Pension contracts*	..	..	..	..	..	..	..	0
1.1.4 Non-life insurance payments, by class, gross premiums								
Motor vehicle insurance	38 467	35 827	34 350	35 804	37 855	39 633	38 212	40 533
Marine, aviation and other transport insurance	289	274	243	214	294	331	912	1 073
Freight insurance	378	385	336	393	461	466	0	..
Fire and other property damage insurance	20 151	20 586	20 832	21 442	21 687	22 655	23 042	24 244
Pecuniary loss insurance	5 047	5 413	5 190	5 920	4 933	3 770	3 959	4 030
General liability insurance	12 128	12 416	12 420	12 869	13 164	13 810	13 609	14 559
Accident and health	5 491	5 708	5 523	5 482	5 342	5 393	5 136	5 460
***of which:** Health*	0	0	0	0	0	0	0	2 474
Other non-life insurance	2 284	2 477	2 656	2 825	3 002	3 374	2 223	2 364
Treaty reinsurance	0	0	0	0	0	0	0	..
Total non-life insurance	84 234	83 084	81 550	84 950	86 738	89 431	87 092	92 263
1.2 Gross claims payments								
Life								
Domestic undertakings	247	934	968	765	1 307	702	c	c
Foreign controlled undertakings	247	934	968	765	1 307	702	c	c
Foreign companies (branches)	4 041	4 193	4 402	7 219	6 044	6 376	6 094	6 249
All undertakings	4 287	5 127	5 370	7 984	7 352	7 077	6 456	6 567
Non-life								
Domestic undertakings	3 939	2 981	3 594	5 208	6 045	2 285	2 103	2 172
Foreign controlled undertakings	1 983	1 463	1 648	2 171	1 734	1 288	1 072	1 070
Foreign companies (branches)	1 001	922	746	1 184	1 353	1 216	1 674	1 764
All undertakings	4 940	3 903	4 340	6 392	7 398	3 501	3 777	3 936
Composite								
Domestic undertakings	72 968	76 178	78 484	86 244	90 284	84 909	81 024	80 221
Foreign controlled undertakings	69 071	72 105	74 012	81 355	84 712	79 681	75 835	75 301
Foreign companies (branches)	0	0	0	0	0	0	0	0
All undertakings	72 968	76 178	78 484	86 244	90 284	84 909	81 024	80 221
of which:								
Life	31 760	36 944	41 040	43 395	50 972	44 105	37 676	36 087
Domestic undertakings	31 760	36 944	41 040	43 395	50 972	44 105	37 676	36 087
Foreign controlled undertakings	30 834	35 822	39 685	42 174	49 092	42 631	36 570	35 018
Foreign companies (branches)	0	0	0	0	0	0	0	0
All undertakings	31 760	36 944	41 040	43 395	50 972	44 105	37 676	36 087
Non-life	41 208	39 235	37 444	42 849	39 312	40 805	43 348	44 134
Domestic undertakings	41 208	39 235	37 444	42 849	39 312	40 805	43 348	44 134
Foreign controlled undertakings	38 237	36 283	34 327	39 180	35 620	37 050	39 265	40 283
Foreign companies (branches)	0	0	0	0	0	0	0	0
All undertakings	41 208	39 235	37 444	42 849	39 312	40 805	43 348	44 134
Total								
Domestic undertakings	77 154	80 094	83 046	92 217	97 636	87 896	83 490	82 712
Foreign controlled undertakings	71 301	74 502	76 628	84 291	87 754	81 671	77 269	76 690
Foreign companies (branches)	5 041	5 116	5 148	8 403	7 397	7 592	7 767	8 012
All undertakings	82 196	85 209	88 194	100 620	105 033	95 488	91 257	90 724

CZECH REPUBLIC

Table 1. Selected aggregates (cont.)

Million CZK

	2010	2011	2012	2013	2014	2015	2016	2017
1.3 Commissions								
Life								
Domestic undertakings	9	628	..	..	..	..	..	..
Foreign controlled undertakings	9	628	..	..	..	..	..	..
Foreign companies (branches)	0	486	..	..	..	..	..	..
All undertakings	9	1 114	..	..	..	..	..	..
Non-life								
Domestic undertakings	313	466	..	..	..	..	..	..
Foreign controlled undertakings	257	273	..	..	..	..	..	..
Foreign companies (branches)	214	418	..	..	..	..	..	..
All undertakings	528	884	..	..	..	..	..	..
Composite								
Domestic undertakings	5 035	12 386	..	..	..	..	..	..
Foreign controlled undertakings	4 607	11 419	..	..	..	..	..	..
Foreign companies (branches)	0	0	..	..	..	..	..	..
All undertakings	5 035	12 386	..	..	..	..	..	..
of which:								
Life	414	7 407	..	..	..	..	..	..
Domestic undertakings	414	7 407	..	..	..	..	..	..
Foreign controlled undertakings	414	7 243	..	..	..	..	..	..
Foreign companies (branches)	0	0	..	..	..	..	..	..
All undertakings	414	7 407	..	..	..	..	..	..
Non-life	4 620	4 980	..	..	..	..	..	..
Domestic undertakings	4 620	4 980	..	..	..	..	..	..
Foreign controlled undertakings	4 193	4 176	..	..	..	..	..	..
Foreign companies (branches)	0	0	..	..	..	..	..	..
All undertakings	4 620	4 980	..	..	..	..	..	..
Total								
Domestic undertakings	5 357	13 481	..	..	..	..	..	..
Foreign controlled undertakings	4 873	12 320	..	..	..	..	..	..
Foreign companies (branches)	214	904	..	..	..	..	..	..
All undertakings	5 572	14 384	..	..	..	..	..	..
1.4 Gross operating expenses								
Life								
Domestic undertakings	1 060	1 085	1 132	748	759	739	c	c
Foreign controlled undertakings	1 060	1 085	1 132	748	759	739	c	c
Foreign companies (branches)	1 440	1 617	1 659	1 587	1 459	2 036	2 015	1 894
All undertakings	2 499	2 702	2 791	2 335	2 219	2 775	2 520	2 251
Non-life								
Domestic undertakings	2 303	2 559	1 970	1 795	1 805	1 571	1 203	2 170
Foreign controlled undertakings	1 446	1 509	1 152	987	937	883	622	979
Foreign companies (branches)	874	933	277	715	841	1 203	1 224	1 412
All undertakings	3 177	3 491	2 247	2 510	2 646	2 773	2 427	3 582
Composite								
Domestic undertakings	31 688	33 219	21 405	21 863	22 207	20 341	21 319	36 095
Foreign controlled undertakings	25 999	31 001	20 417	20 499	21 233	19 120	19 893	32 685
Foreign companies (branches)	0	0	0	0	0	0	0	0
All undertakings	31 688	33 219	21 405	21 863	22 207	20 341	21 319	36 095
of which:								
Life	12 087	13 363	12 009	11 670	11 475	9 613	9 217	11 707
Domestic undertakings	12 087	13 363	12 009	11 670	11 475	9 613	9 217	11 707
Foreign controlled undertakings	11 605	12 861	11 604	11 231	11 050	9 059	8 637	10 795
Foreign companies (branches)	0	0	0	0	0	0	0	0
All undertakings	12 087	13 363	12 009	11 670	11 475	9 613	9 217	11 707
Non-life	19 601	19 856	9 396	10 193	10 733	10 728	12 102	24 388
Domestic undertakings	19 601	19 856	9 396	10 193	10 733	10 728	12 102	24 388
Foreign controlled undertakings	17 994	18 140	8 814	9 268	10 184	10 061	11 256	21 890
Foreign companies (branches)	0	0	0	0	0	0	0	0
All undertakings	19 601	19 856	9 396	10 193	10 733	10 728	12 102	24 388
Total								
Domestic undertakings	35 050	36 863	24 507	24 407	24 772	22 650	23 027	38 621
Foreign controlled undertakings	28 505	33 595	22 701	22 234	22 929	20 742	21 020	34 020
Foreign companies (branches)	2 314	2 550	1 936	2 302	2 301	3 239	3 239	3 307
All undertakings	37 364	39 413	26 443	26 708	27 072	25 889	26 266	41 928

CZECH REPUBLIC

Table 1. Selected aggregates (cont.)

Million CZK

	2010	2011	2012	2013	2014	2015	2016	2017
1.5 Insurance business written abroad by branches, gross premiums								
Life								
Branches and agencies	0 |	0	0	0	0	0	0	0
Subsidaries	..	..	..	..	..	..	..	..
Total	0 |	0	0	0	0	0	..	0
Non-life								
Branches and agencies	437 |	318	307	323	313	351	377	596
Subsidaries	..	..	..	..	..	..	..	..
Total	437 |	318	307	323	313	351	377	596
Composite								
Branches and agencies	1 264 |	1 294	1 359	3 714	4 528	5 164	1 697	1 805
Subsidaries	..	..	..	..	..	..	..	..
Total	1 264 |	1 294	1 359	3 714	4 528	5 164	1 697	1 805
of which:								
Life	1 254 |	1 244	1 317	1 737	1 434	1 460	1 697	1 805
Branches and agencies	1 254 |	1 244	1 317	1 737	1 434	1 460	1 697	1 805
Subsidaries	..	..	..	..	..	..	..	..
Total	1 254 |	1 244	1 317	1 737	1 434	1 460	1 697	1 805
Non-life	10 |	49	42	1 977	3 095	3 704	..	0
Branches and agencies	10 |	49	42	1 977	3 095	3 704	0	0
Subsidaries	..	..	..	..	..	..	..	..
Total	10 |	49	42	1 977	3 095	3 704	..	0
Total								
Branches and agencies	1 701	1 612	1 666	4 037	4 841	5 516	2 074	2 401
Subsidaries	..	..	..	..	..	..	..	..
Total	1 701	1 612	1 666	4 037	4 841	5 516	2 074	2 401

.. Not available; c Confidential data; | Break in series

Note: Detailed metadata at: *http://metalinks.oecd.org/ins/20190221/3bbb.*

Source: OECD Insurance Statistics (database)

CZECH REPUBLIC

Table 2. Number of companies and employees

	2010	2011	2012	2013	2014	2015	2016	2017
2.1 Number of companies								
Life								
Domestic undertakings	3	3	3	2	2	2	1	1
Foreign controlled undertakings	3	3	3	2	2	2	1	1
Foreign companies (branches)	4	4	3	3	4	5	5	5
All undertakings	7	7	6	5	6	7	6	6
Non-life								
Domestic undertakings	17	17	16	16	15	15	13	11
Foreign controlled undertakings	9	9	8	8	7	5	4	3
Foreign companies (branches)	13	14	15	15	16	18	19	17
All undertakings	30	31	31	31	31	33	32	28
Composite								
Domestic undertakings	15	15	15	15	15	14	14	14
Foreign controlled undertakings	12	12	12	12	12	11	11	11
Foreign companies (branches)	0	0	0	0	0	0	0	0
All undertakings	15	15	15	15	15	14	14	14
Reinsurance								
Domestic undertakings	1	1	1	1	1	1	1	1
Foreign controlled undertakings	1	1	1	1	1	1	1	1
Foreign companies (branches)	0	..	..	..	..	..	..	0
All undertakings	1	1	1	1	1	1	1	1
Total								
Domestic undertakings	36	36	35	34	33	32	29	27
Foreign controlled undertakings	25	25	24	23	22	19	17	16
Foreign companies (branches)	17	18	18	18	20	23	24	22
All undertakings	53	54	53	52	53	55	53	49
2.2 Number of employees								
Insurance undertakings	..	..	..	..	..	..	..	..
Intermediaries	..	..	..	..	..	..	..	..
Total	..	..	..	..	..	..	..	..

.. Not available

Note: Detailed metadata at: *http://metalinks.oecd.org/ins/20190221/3bbb.*

Source: OECD Insurance Statistics (database)

DENMARK

Table 1. Selected aggregates

Million DKK

	2010	2011	2012	2013	2014	2015	2016	2017
1.1 Insurance business written in the reporting country								
1.1.1 Insurance business, by ownership								
Gross premiums								
Domestic undertakings	171 554	181 700	189 673	1 268 025	208 213	215 276	225 500	247 934
Foreign controlled undertakings	27 763	34 560	34 996	39 736	46 022	46 192	49 042	53 373
Foreign companies (branches)	..	..	..	..	..	..	..	..
All undertakings	..	181 700	189 673	1 268 025	208 213	215 276	225 500	247 934
Premiums ceded								
Domestic undertakings	6 015	7 676	7 009	7 417	5 875	6 309	6 943	8 079
Foreign controlled undertakings	1 456	3 427	3 293	3 199	2 080	2 462	2 355	2 024
Foreign companies (branches)	..	..	..	..	..	..	..	..
All undertakings	..	7 676	7 009	7 417	5 875	6 309	6 943	8 079
Net written premiums								
Domestic undertakings	165 540	174 024	182 664	1 260 608	202 338	208 966	218 557	239 855
Foreign controlled undertakings	26 307	31 132	31 703	36 537	43 942	43 730	46 687	51 349
Foreign companies (branches)	..	..	..	..	..	..	..	..
All undertakings	..	174 024	182 664	1 260 608	202 338	208 966	218 557	239 855
1.1.2 Insurance business on foreign risks, gross premiums								
Life	..	3 099	3 530	1 125	631	631	..	..
Non-life	..	13 950	14 359	14 611	23 099	22 611	..	..
Composite total	..	..	..	..	..	..	..	..
Total	..	17 050	17 889	15 737	23 730	23 242	..	..
1.1.3 Life insurance payments, by class, gross premiums								
Annuities	..	..	..	..	..	..	..	..
Unit linked	..	..	..	..	..	..	..	..
Other life insurance	..	..	..	..	..	..	..	..
Total life insurance	..	..	129 477	133 294	140 314	147 662	153 907	170 623
***of which:** Pension contracts*	..	..	..	..	..	..	..	..
1.1.4 Non-life insurance payments, by class, gross premiums								
Motor vehicle insurance	..	16 520	16 511	16 304	19 310	19 146	21 247	23 487
Marine, aviation and other transport insurance	..	1 328	1 397	1 263	1 174	1 105	1 857	1 844
Freight insurance	..	..	..	..	..	0	..	..
Fire and other property damage insurance	..	15 003	20 461	20 737	22 855	22 642	25 107	26 732
Pecuniary loss insurance	..	336	359	372	402	417	1 113	2 045
General liability insurance	..	1 857	2 023	2 061	2 377	2 314	3 203	3 411
Accident and health	..	13 403	13 553	12 611	15 063	15 282	15 965	16 727
***of which:** Health*	..	900	1 013	1 051	1 265	1 337	4 498	4 657
Other non-life insurance	..	3 983	4 465	4 659	5 156	5 052	1 635	1 759
Treaty reinsurance	..	451	638	653	867	937	538	616
Total non-life insurance	..	52 882	59 407	58 661	67 204	66 895	70 665	76 621
1.2 Gross claims payments								
Life								
Domestic undertakings	77 577	86 498	92 230	111 119	124 323	98 376	115 270	112 996
Foreign controlled undertakings	16 488	20 780	22 286	24 154	24 385	20 765	23 573	22 740
Foreign companies (branches)	..	..	..	..	..	..	..	..
All undertakings	77 577	86 498	92 230	111 119	124 323	98 376	115 270	112 996
Non-life								
Domestic undertakings	42 282	45 935	40 906	43 547	46 601	47 833	44 773	45 620
Foreign controlled undertakings	6 002	7 484	6 308	6 731	13 007	13 316	11 816	11 605
Foreign companies (branches)	..	..	..	..	..	..	..	..
All undertakings	42 282	45 935	40 906	43 547	46 601	47 833	44 773	45 620
Composite, all undertakings	..	..	..	..	..	..	..	..
Total								
Domestic undertakings	119 859	132 433	133 136	154 666	170 924	146 209	160 043	158 616
Foreign controlled undertakings	22 490	28 264	28 594	30 885	37 392	34 081	35 389	34 345
Foreign companies (branches)	..	..	..	..	..	..	..	..
All undertakings	119 859	132 433	133 136	154 666	170 924	146 209	160 043	158 616
1.3 Commissions								
Life								
Domestic undertakings	226	235	194	182	195	199	175	207
Foreign controlled undertakings	97	77	59	43	60	36	34	26
Foreign companies (branches)	..	..	..	..	..	..	..	..
All undertakings	..	235	194	182	195	199	175	207
Non-life								
Domestic undertakings	1 309	1 257	1 434	1 380	1 613	1 879	1 361	1 320
Foreign controlled undertakings	292	257	367	361	579	891	494	463
Foreign companies (branches)	..	..	..	..	..	..	..	..
All undertakings	..	1 257	1 434	1 380	1 613	1 879	1 361	1 320
Composite, all undertakings	..	..	..	..	..	..	..	..
Total								
Domestic undertakings	1 535	1 492	1 629	1 562	1 808	2 079	1 536	1 527
Foreign controlled undertakings	389	334	426	405	639	927	528	489
Foreign companies (branches)	..	..	..	..	..	..	..	..
All undertakings	..	1 492	1 629	1 562	1 808	2 079	1 536	1 527

DENMARK

Table 1. Selected aggregates (cont.)

Million DKK

	2010	2011	2012	2013	2014	2015	2016	2017
1.4 Gross operating expenses								
Life								
Domestic undertakings	4 685	5 136	5 088	4 954	4 887	4 570	4 788	4 971
Foreign controlled undertakings	1 340	1 325	1 316	1 326	1 377	1 284	1 268	1 386
Foreign companies (branches)	..	..	..	..	..	..	..	..
All undertakings	4 685	5 136	5 088	4 954	4 887	4 570	4 788	4 971
Non-life								
Domestic undertakings	9 713	10 241	10 292	10 391	11 564	11 856	12 050	12 003
Foreign controlled undertakings	1 577	1 940	2 124	2 200	3 867	4 065	3 780	3 542
Foreign companies (branches)	..	..	..	..	..	..	..	..
All undertakings	9 713	10 241	10 292	10 391	11 564	11 856	12 050	12 003
Composite, all undertakings	..	..	..	..	..	..	..	..
Total								
Domestic undertakings	14 398	15 377	15 380	15 345	16 451	16 426	16 838	16 974
Foreign controlled undertakings	2 917	3 265	3 440	3 526	5 244	5 349	5 048	4 928
Foreign companies (branches)	..	..	..	..	..	..	..	..
All undertakings	14 398	15 377	15 380	15 345	16 451	16 426	16 838	16 974
1.5 Insurance business written abroad by branches, gross premiums								
Life								
Branches and agencies	423	353	..	..	..	..	..	..
Subsidaries	..	..	..	..	..	..	..	..
Total	..	353	..	..	..	..	..	..
Non-life								
Branches and agencies	8 805	9 995	10 646	10 031	9 286	8 607	19 043	19 072
Subsidaries	..	..	..	..	..	..	..	..
Total	..	9 995	10 646	10 031	9 286	8 607	19 043	19 072
Composite total	..	..	..	..	..	..	..	..
Total								
Branches and agencies	9 227	10 348	10 646	10 031	9 286	8 607	19 043	19 072
Subsidaries	..	..	..	..	..	..	..	..
Total	..	10 348	10 646	10 031	9 286	8 607	19 043	19 072

.. Not available

Note: Detailed metadata at: *http://metalinks.oecd.org/ins/20190221/6aeb.*

Source: OECD Insurance Statistics (database)

DENMARK

Table 2. Number of companies and employees

	2010	2011	2012	2013	2014	2015	2016	2017
2.1 Number of companies								
Life								
Domestic undertakings	55	55	47	39	37	33	33	33
Foreign controlled undertakings	8	8	7	5	4	4	4	4
Foreign companies (branches)	4	6	6	1	1	1	1	2
All undertakings	59	61	53	40	38	34	34	35
Non-life								
Domestic undertakings	87	85	76	77	63	63	63	59
Foreign controlled undertakings	8	8	6	6	6	6	6	6
Foreign companies (branches)	45	41	38	48	49	49	53	56
All undertakings	132	126	114	125	112	112	116	115
Composite, all undertakings	**0**	**0**	**0**	**0**	**0**	**0**	**0**	**..**
Reinsurance								
Domestic undertakings	9	9	9	7	7	7	5	6
Foreign controlled undertakings	0	0	..	..	..	..	0	..
Foreign companies (branches)	..	..	..	..	..	..	..	..
All undertakings	..	9	9	7	7	7	5	6
Total								
Domestic undertakings	..	149	132	123	107	103	101	98
Foreign controlled undertakings	..	16	13	11	10	10	10	10
Foreign companies (branches)	..	47	44	49	50	50	54	58
All undertakings	..	196	176	172	157	153	155	156
2.2 Number of employees								
Insurance undertakings	16 051	16 130	15 835	15 377	17 057	16 472	16 112	13 640
Intermediaries	..	..	..	..	..	..	..	..
Total	..	16 130	15 835	15 377	17 057	16 472	16 112	13 640

.. Not available

Note: Detailed metadata at: *http://metalinks.oecd.org/ins/20190221/6aeb.*

Source: OECD Insurance Statistics (database)

ESTONIA

Table 1. Selected aggregates

Million EUR

	2010	2011	2012	2013	2014	2015	2016	2017
1.1 Insurance business written in the reporting country								
1.1.1 Insurance business, by ownership								
Gross premiums								
Domestic undertakings	427	403	430	523	561	619	654	721
Foreign controlled undertakings	406	380	407	499	539	596	627	721
Foreign companies (branches)	0	0	51	60	70	70	82	97
All undertakings	427	403	480	583	631	689	736	818
Premiums ceded								
Domestic undertakings	20	20	..	27	28	29	31	31
Foreign controlled undertakings	13	11	..	18	2	20	22	22
Foreign companies (branches)	0	0	..	..	..	..	..	..
All undertakings	20	20	..	..	..	..	..	..
Net written premiums								
Domestic undertakings	406	383	..	496	534	590	624	690
Foreign controlled undertakings	393	368	..	481	217	576	605	670
Foreign companies (branches)	0	0	..	..	..	..	..	..
All undertakings	406	383	..	..	..	..	..	..
1.1.2 Insurance business on foreign risks, gross premiums								
Life	96	90	..	..	..	..	..	..
Non-life	62	68	..	..	..	..	..	..
Composite	..	..	..	..	..	..	..	..
of which:								
Life	..	..	..	..	..	..	..	..
Non-life	..	..	..	..	..	..	..	..
Total	158	158	..	..	..	..	..	..
1.1.3 Life insurance payments, by class, gross premiums								
Annuities	8	9	10	17	19	24	27	27
Unit linked	104	84	27	87	109	118	116	116
Other life insurance	61	67	30	66	63	72	80	80
Total life insurance	173	160	68	171	191	215	221	223
of which: *Pension contracts*	1	26	30	33	37	36	40	39
1.1.4 Non-life insurance payments, by class, gross premiums								
Motor vehicle insurance	148	142	143	229	244	259	292	345
Marine, aviation and other transport insurance	1	1	3	2	2	2	6	6
Freight insurance	2	2	..	3	4	4	..	..
Fire and other property damage insurance	63	63	59	99	107	115	127	140
Pecuniary loss insurance	4	5	5	8	9	9	12	17
General liability insurance	8	9	6	15	16	19	21	22
Accident and health	28	30	15	40	42	42	54	43
of which: *Health*	..	..	..	9	..	..	..	..
Other non-life insurance	1	1	1	9	16	23	4	7
Treaty reinsurance	0	0	..	8	..	..	..	..
Total non-life insurance	254	253	231	412	440	474	515	580
1.2 Gross claims payments								
Life								
Domestic undertakings	82	115	112	101	..	97	87	c
Foreign controlled undertakings	82	115	112	101	..	97	87	c
Foreign companies (branches)	0	0	..	..	..	..	0	2
All undertakings	82	115	112	101	..	97	87	93
Non-life								
Domestic undertakings	153	154	147	197	..	230	243	270
Foreign controlled undertakings	139	141	134	184	..	217	228	253
Foreign companies (branches)	0	0	..	33	..	40	43	49
All undertakings	153	154	147	230	246	271	287	319
Composite								
Domestic undertakings	..	..	..	..	..	..	38	36
Foreign controlled undertakings	..	..	..	..	..	..	38	36
Foreign companies (branches)	..	..	..	..	..	..	3	4
All undertakings	..	..	..	..	..	..	42	40
of which:								
Life	..	..	..	..	..	..	34	40
Domestic undertakings	..	..	..	..	..	..	31	36
Foreign controlled undertakings	..	..	..	..	..	..	31	36
Foreign companies (branches)	..	..	..	..	..	..	3	4
All undertakings	..	..	..	..	..	..	34	40
Non-life	..	..	..	..	..	..	8	0
Domestic undertakings	..	..	..	..	..	..	8	0
Foreign controlled undertakings	..	..	..	..	..	..	8	0
Foreign companies (branches)	..	..	..	..	..	..	0	0
All undertakings	..	..	..	..	..	..	8	0
Total								
Domestic undertakings	235	270	259	298	..	328	369	397
Foreign controlled undertakings	221	256	246	285	..	314	354	380
Foreign companies (branches)	0	0	..	33	..	40	47	55
All undertakings	235	270	259	331	246	368	416	452

ESTONIA

Table 1. Selected aggregates (cont.)

Million EUR

	2010	2011	2012	2013	2014	2015	2016	2017
1.3 Commissions								
Life								
Domestic undertakings	3	8	9	19	21	23	..	..
Foreign controlled undertakings	3	8	9	19	21	23	..	..
Foreign companies (branches)	0	0	..	..	..	..	..	..
All undertakings	3	8	9	19	..	23	..	..
Non-life								
Domestic undertakings	17	17	4	72	73	78	..	..
Foreign controlled undertakings	16	15	2	67	69	73	..	..
Foreign companies (branches)	0	0	..	..	..	..	..	..
All undertakings	17	17	4	72	..	78	..	..
Composite								
Domestic undertakings	..	..	..	..	..	..	..	..
Foreign controlled undertakings	..	..	..	..	..	..	..	..
Foreign companies (branches)	..	..	..	..	..	..	..	..
All undertakings	..	..	..	..	..	..	..	..
of which:								
Life	..	..	..	..	..	..	..	..
Domestic undertakings	..	..	..	..	..	..	..	..
Foreign controlled undertakings	..	..	..	..	..	..	..	..
Foreign companies (branches)	..	..	..	..	..	..	..	..
All undertakings	..	..	..	..	..	..	..	..
Non-life	..	..	..	..	..	..	..	..
Domestic undertakings	..	..	..	..	..	..	..	..
Foreign controlled undertakings	..	..	..	..	..	..	..	..
Foreign companies (branches)	..	..	..	..	..	..	..	..
All undertakings	..	..	..	..	..	..	..	..
Total								
Domestic undertakings	20	25	13	90	94	101	..	..
Foreign controlled undertakings	18	23	11	86	89	95	..	..
Foreign companies (branches)	0	0	..	..	..	..	..	..
All undertakings	20	25	13	90	..	101	..	..
1.4 Gross operating expenses								
Life								
Domestic undertakings	21	24	23	9	9	11	..	..
Foreign controlled undertakings	21	24	23	9	9	11	..	..
Foreign companies (branches)	0	0	..	..	..	..	..	..
All undertakings	21	24	23	9	..	11	..	..
Non-life								
Domestic undertakings	71	74	73	27	30	27	115	137
Foreign controlled undertakings	64	67	67	25	29	26	..	..
Foreign companies (branches)	0	0	..	..	..	..	..	..
All undertakings	71	74	73	27	..	27	..	..
Composite								
Domestic undertakings	..	..	..	..	..	..	..	..
Foreign controlled undertakings	..	..	..	..	..	..	..	..
Foreign companies (branches)	..	..	..	..	..	..	..	..
All undertakings	..	..	..	..	..	..	..	..
of which:								
Life	..	..	..	..	..	..	..	..
Domestic undertakings	..	..	..	..	..	..	..	..
Foreign controlled undertakings	..	..	..	..	..	..	..	..
Foreign companies (branches)	..	..	..	..	..	..	..	..
All undertakings	..	..	..	..	..	..	..	..
Non-life	..	..	..	..	..	..	..	..
Domestic undertakings	..	..	..	..	..	..	..	..
Foreign controlled undertakings	..	..	..	..	..	..	..	..
Foreign companies (branches)	..	..	..	..	..	..	..	..
All undertakings	..	..	..	..	..	..	..	..
Total								
Domestic undertakings	92	98	96	37	40	38	115	137
Foreign controlled undertakings	85	91	90	35	38	36	..	..
Foreign companies (branches)	0	0	..	..	..	..	..	..
All undertakings	92	98	96	37	..	38	..	..

ESTONIA

Table 1. Selected aggregates (cont.)

Million EUR

	2010	2011	2012	2013	2014	2015	2016	2017
1.5 Insurance business written abroad by branches, gross premiums								
Life								
Branches and agencies	96	90	85	94	114	130	96	..
Subsidaries	0	0	..	..	..	..	..	..
Total	96	90	85	94	114	130	96	..
Non-life								
Branches and agencies	62	68	96	170	174	190	201	243
Subsidaries	0	0	..	..	..	..	..	..
Total	62	68	96	170	174	190	201	243
Composite								
Branches and agencies	..	..	..	..	..	..	52	..
Subsidaries	..	..	..	..	..	..	..	..
Total	..	..	..	..	..	..	52	..
of which:								
Life	..	..	..	..	..	..	42	..
Branches and agencies	..	..	..	..	..	..	42	..
Subsidaries	..	..	..	..	..	..	..	..
Total	..	..	..	..	..	..	42	..
Non-life	..	..	..	..	..	..	10	..
Branches and agencies	..	..	..	..	..	..	10	..
Subsidaries	..	..	..	..	..	..	..	..
Total	..	..	..	..	..	..	10	..
Total								
Branches and agencies	158	158	181	264	288	320	349	243
Subsidaries	0	0	..	..	..	..	..	..
Total	158	158	181	264	288	320	349	243

.. Not available; c Confidential data

Note: Detailed metadata at: *http://metalinks.oecd.org/ins/20190221/b8b6*.

Source: OECD Insurance Statistics (database)

ESTONIA

Table 2. Number of companies and employees

	2010	2011	2012	2013	2014	2015	2016	2017
2.1 Number of companies								
Life								
Domestic undertakings	5	4	4	4	4	4	2	1
Foreign controlled undertakings	5	4	4	4	4	4	2	1
Foreign companies (branches)	0	0	1	1	1	1	0	1
All undertakings	5	4	5	5	5	5	2	2
Non-life								
Domestic undertakings	8	8	8	8	8	8	8	7
Foreign controlled undertakings	5	5	5	5	5	5	5	4
Foreign companies (branches)	0	0	4	4	4	3	4	4
All undertakings	8	8	12	12	12	11	12	11
Composite								
Domestic undertakings	0	0	0	0	0	0	2	2
Foreign controlled undertakings	0	0	0	0	0	0	2	2
Foreign companies (branches)	0	0	0	0	0	0	1	1
All undertakings	0	0	0	0	0	0	3	3
Reinsurance								
Domestic undertakings	0	0	..	0	0	0	0	0
Foreign controlled undertakings	0	0	..	0	0	0	0	..
Foreign companies (branches)	0	0	..	..	..	0	0	..
All undertakings	0	0	..	..	..	0	0	..
Total								
Domestic undertakings	13	12	12	12	12	12	12	10
Foreign controlled undertakings	10	9	9	9	9	9	9	7
Foreign companies (branches)	0	0	5	5	5	4	5	6
All undertakings	13	12	17	17	17	16	17	16
2.2 Number of employees								
Insurance undertakings	2 702	1 867	1 903	2 596	2 561	2 581	..	..
Intermediaries	..	814	849	1 271	1 217	1 232	..	..
Total	..	2 681	2 752	3 867	3 778	3 813	..	..

.. Not available

Note: Detailed metadata at: *http://metalinks.oecd.org/ins/20190221/b8b6.*

Source: OECD Insurance Statistics (database)

FINLAND

Table 1. Selected aggregates

Million EUR

	2010	2011	2012	2013	2014	2015	2016	2017
1.1 Insurance business written in the reporting country								
1.1.1 Insurance business, by ownership								
Gross premiums								
Domestic undertakings	8 770	7 279	7 279	9 834	10 632	10 741	9 045	8 926
Foreign controlled undertakings	..	..	2 317	3 357	3 698	6 892	..	..
Foreign companies (branches)	..	..	..	..	..	..	..	..
All undertakings	8 770	7 279	7 279	9 834	10 632	10 741	9 045	8 926
Premiums ceded								
Domestic undertakings	242	240	240	257	259	246	241	230
Foreign controlled undertakings	..	..	20	19	15	217	..	..
Foreign companies (branches)	..	..	..	..	..	..	..	..
All undertakings	242	240	240	257	259	246	241	230
Net written premiums								
Domestic undertakings	8 528	7 039	7 039	9 577	10 373	10 495	8 804	8 696
Foreign controlled undertakings	..	..	2 297	3 338	3 683	6 675	..	..
Foreign companies (branches)	..	..	..	..	..	..	..	..
All undertakings	8 528	7 039	7 039	9 577	10 373	10 495	8 804	8 696
1.1.2 Insurance business on foreign risks, gross premiums								
Life	..	..	..	..	..	..	..	..
Non-life	..	..	..	..	..	..	..	..
Composite total	..	..	..	..	..	..	..	..
Total	..	..	..	..	..	..	..	..
1.1.3 Life insurance payments, by class, gross premiums								
Annuities	2 798	1 988	1 988	2 458	2 544	2 287	694	621
Unit linked	1 297	1 255	1 255	2 509	2 929	3 224	2 446	2 265
Other life insurance	1 120	505	505	614	619	745	1 433	1 641
Total life insurance	5 215	3 749	3 749	5 581	6 092	6 256	4 573	4 527
of which: *Pension contracts*	1 491	828	828	819	756	597	675	2 265
1.1.4 Non-life insurance payments, by class, gross premiums								
Motor vehicle insurance	1 282	1 389	1 474	1 520	1 591	1 639	1 639	1 586
Marine, aviation and other transport insurance	60	64	68	70	70	68	73	69
Freight insurance	49	50	53	55	56	52	57	55
Fire and other property damage insurance	750	828	864	929	985	1 030	1 028	972
Pecuniary loss insurance	41	38	33	33	30	28	22	20
General liability insurance	169	191	191	239	392	385	234	218
Accident and health	846	938	1 024	1 048	1 060	1 058	1 119	1 183
of which: *Health*	191	218	245	264	299	290	368	395
Other non-life insurance	117	129	131	144	152	88	163	151
Treaty reinsurance	122	132	149	149	135	135	136	144
Total non-life insurance	3 435	3 759	3 986	4 187	4 471	4 483	4 471	4 398
1.2 Gross claims payments								
Life								
Domestic undertakings	3 919	3 592	3 917	3 927	3 871	3 957	4 324	4 233
Foreign controlled undertakings	..	1 013	1 479	1 399	1 160	1 124	c	c
Foreign companies (branches)	..	..	..	..	..	..	..	..
All undertakings	3 919	3 592	3 917	3 927	3 871	3 957	4 324	4 233
Non-life								
Domestic undertakings	2 568	2 706	2 873	2 858	2 939	2 872	3 103	3 179
Foreign controlled undertakings	..	676	696	741	724	2 872	c	c
Foreign companies (branches)	..	..	..	..	..	..	..	..
All undertakings	2 568	2 706	2 873	2 858	2 939	2 872	3 103	3 179
Composite, all undertakings	..	..	..	..	..	..	..	..
Total								
Domestic undertakings	6 487	6 298	6 790	6 785	6 810	6 829	7 427	7 412
Foreign controlled undertakings	..	1 689	2 175	2 140	1 884	3 996	..	..
Foreign companies (branches)	..	..	..	..	..	..	..	..
All undertakings	6 487	6 298	6 790	6 785	6 810	6 829	7 427	7 412
1.3 Commissions								
Life								
Domestic undertakings	64	81	68	90	-83	101	126	121
Foreign controlled undertakings	..	7	6	9	-10	15	c	c
Foreign companies (branches)	..	..	..	..	..	..	..	..
All undertakings	64	81	68	90	-83	101	126	121
Non-life								
Domestic undertakings	99	90	102	58	-142	113	166	160
Foreign controlled undertakings	..	13	16	21	-18	23	c	c
Foreign companies (branches)	..	..	..	..	..	..	..	..
All undertakings	99	90	102	58	-142	113	166	160
Composite, all undertakings	..	..	..	..	..	..	..	..
Total								
Domestic undertakings	163	171	170	148	-225	214	292	281
Foreign controlled undertakings	..	21	22	30	-28	38	..	..
Foreign companies (branches)	..	..	..	..	..	..	..	..
All undertakings	163	171	170	148	-225	214	292	281

FINLAND

Table 1. Selected aggregates (cont.)

Million EUR

	2010	2011	2012	2013	2014	2015	2016	2017
1.4 Gross operating expenses								
Life								
Domestic undertakings	255	275	283	302	317	316	341	355
Foreign controlled undertakings	..	39	36	34	36	34	c	c
Foreign companies (branches)	..	..	..	..	..	..	..	..
All undertakings	255	275	283	302	317	316	341	355
Non-life								
Domestic undertakings	699	738	778	827	844	847	876	884
Foreign controlled undertakings	..	138	143	161	158	847	c	c
Foreign companies (branches)	..	..	..	..	..	..	..	..
All undertakings	699	738	778	827	844	847	876	884
Composite, all undertakings	..	..	..	..	..	..	..	..
Total								
Domestic undertakings	954	1 013	1 061	1 129	1 161	1 163	1 217	1 239
Foreign controlled undertakings	..	177	179	195	194	881	..	..
Foreign companies (branches)	..	..	..	..	..	..	..	..
All undertakings	954	1 013	1 061	1 129	1 161	1 163	1 217	1 239
1.5 Insurance business written abroad by branches, gross premiums								
Life								
Branches and agencies	598	614	203	162	107	17	..	..
Subsidaries	..	..	..	..	..	..	..	..
Total	598	614	203	162	107	17	..	..
Non-life								
Branches and agencies	..	..	..	..	..	..	..	..
Subsidaries	..	..	..	..	..	..	..	..
Total	..	..	..	..	..	..	..	..
Composite total	..	..	..	..	..	..	..	..
Total								
Branches and agencies	598	614	203	162	107	17	..	..
Subsidaries	..	..	..	..	..	..	..	..
Total	598	614	203	162	107	17	..	..

.. Not available; c Confidential data

Note: Detailed metadata at: *http://metalinks.oecd.org/ins/20190221/6ab0.*

Source: OECD Insurance Statistics (database)

FINLAND

Table 2. Number of companies and employees

	2010	2011	2012	2013	2014	2015	2016	2017
2.1 Number of companies								
Life								
Domestic undertakings	11	11	13	13	13	13	11	10
Foreign controlled undertakings	..	1	1	1	1	1	1	1
Foreign companies (branches)	..	..	..	..	..	..	..	..
All undertakings	11	11	13	13	13	13	11	10
Non-life								
Domestic undertakings	79	78	42	42	38	38	37	37
Foreign controlled undertakings	..	1	1	1	1	1	2	2
Foreign companies (branches)	..	..	..	..	..	..	..	..
All undertakings	79	78	42	42	38	38	37	37
Composite, all undertakings	..	..	..	..	..	..	..	..
Reinsurance								
Domestic undertakings	2	2	..	..	..	..	..	..
Foreign controlled undertakings	..	..	..	..	..	..	..	..
Foreign companies (branches)	..	..	..	..	..	..	..	..
All undertakings	2	2	..	..	..	..	..	..
Total								
Domestic undertakings	92	91	55	55	51	51	48	47
Foreign controlled undertakings	..	2	2	2	2	2	3	3
Foreign companies (branches)	..	..	..	..	..	..	..	..
All undertakings	92	91	55	55	51	51	48	47
2.2 Number of employees								
Insurance undertakings	9 221	9 321	9 321	9 231	8 980	8 750	8 815	7 751
Intermediaries	331	338	342	203	216	221	244	265
Total	9 552	9 659	9 663	9 434	9 196	8 971	9 059	8 016

.. Not available

Note: Detailed metadata at: *http://metalinks.oecd.org/ins/20190221/6ab0.*

Source: OECD Insurance Statistics (database)

FRANCE

Table 1. Selected aggregates

Million EUR

	2010	2011	2012	2013	2014	2015	2016	2017
1.1 Insurance business written in the reporting country								
1.1.1 Insurance business, by ownership								
Gross premiums								
Domestic undertakings	224 190	207 586	201 207	207 521	221 223	226 000	..	..
Foreign controlled undertakings	..	..	..	..	..	..	..	..
Foreign companies (branches)	84	95	104	103	103	111	..	..
All undertakings	224 274	207 680	201 310	207 624	221 327	226 111	283 901	278 237
Premiums ceded								
Domestic undertakings	19 192	20 994	21 638	22 115	19 932	25 840	..	..
Foreign controlled undertakings	..	..	..	..	..	..	..	..
Foreign companies (branches)	18	19	18	19	22	21	..	..
All undertakings	19 210	21 013	21 657	22 135	19 954	25 861	43 153	33 277
Net written premiums								
Domestic undertakings	204 998	186 592	179 568	185 406	201 291	200 160	..	..
Foreign controlled undertakings	..	..	..	..	..	..	..	..
Foreign companies (branches)	66	76	85	84	82	90	..	..
All undertakings	205 064	186 668	179 654	185 490	201 373	200 250	240 747	244 960
1.1.2 Insurance business on foreign risks, gross premiums								
Life	429	107	83	259	73	60	..	..
Non-life	391	1 592	1 589	1 735	1 876	2 188	..	..
Composite	..	227	206	636	468	485	..	..
of which:								
Life	..	226	206	167	456	482	..	..
Non-life	..	1	1	469	12	3	..	..
Total	821	1 926	1 879	2 631	2 416	2 734	..	..
1.1.3 Life insurance payments, by class, gross premiums								
Annuities	..	..	..	..	..	..	..	..
Unit linked	220 612	..	..	..	..	..	28 208	38 135
Other life insurance	..	..	..	..	..	..	111 059	102 007
Total life insurance	..	..	..	..	..	..	139 267	140 142
***of which:** Pension contracts*	..	..	..	..	..	..	..	..
1.1.4 Non-life insurance payments, by class, gross premiums								
Motor vehicle insurance	..	..	..	..	..	..	..	..
Marine, aviation and other transport insurance	..	..	..	..	..	..	..	..
Freight insurance	..	..	..	..	..	..	..	..
Fire and other property damage insurance	..	..	..	..	..	..	..	..
Pecuniary loss insurance	..	..	..	..	..	..	..	..
General liability insurance	..	..	..	..	..	..	..	..
Accident and health	..	..	..	..	..	..	..	..
***of which:** Health*	..	..	..	..	..	..	..	..
Other non-life insurance	..	..	..	..	..	..	..	..
Treaty reinsurance	..	..	..	..	..	..	..	..
Total non-life insurance	71 329	71 324	76 295	..	..	..	119 104	124 560
1.2 Gross claims payments								
Life								
Domestic undertakings	22 766	30 961	31 131	25 663	26 144	26 794	..	..
Foreign controlled undertakings	..	..	..	..	..	..	..	..
Foreign companies (branches)	..	..	..	..	..	..	..	..
All undertakings	22 766	30 961	31 131	25 663	26 144	26 794	133 135	145 577
Non-life								
Domestic undertakings	49 368	48 584	50 472	45 317	61 895	63 029	..	..
Foreign controlled undertakings	..	..	..	..	..	..	..	..
Foreign companies (branches)	44	51	59	59	52	51	..	..
All undertakings	49 412	48 635	50 531	45 376	61 947	63 080	95 217	101 007
Composite								
Domestic undertakings	73 529	93 502	98 016	97 287	86 518	91 862	..	..
Foreign controlled undertakings	..	..	..	..	..	..	..	..
Foreign companies (branches)	..	..	..	..	..	..	..	..
All undertakings	73 529	93 502	98 016	97 287	86 518	91 862	..	..
of which:								
Life	..	..	..	88 620	..	..	..	..
Domestic undertakings	..	..	..	88 620	..	..	..	..
Foreign controlled undertakings	..	..	..	..	..	..	..	..
Foreign companies (branches)	..	..	..	..	..	..	..	..
All undertakings	..	..	..	88 620	..	..	..	..
Non-life	..	..	..	8 667	..	..	..	..
Domestic undertakings	..	..	..	8 667	..	..	..	..
Foreign controlled undertakings	..	..	..	..	..	..	..	..
Foreign companies (branches)	..	..	..	..	..	..	..	..
All undertakings	..	..	..	8 667	..	..	..	..
Total								
Domestic undertakings	145 663	173 047	179 619	168 267	174 557	181 685	..	..
Foreign controlled undertakings	..	..	..	..	..	..	..	..
Foreign companies (branches)	44	51	59	59	52	51	..	..
All undertakings	145 707	173 098	179 678	168 326	174 608	181 736	228 352	246 584

FRANCE

Table 1. Selected aggregates (cont.)

Million EUR

	2010	2011	2012	2013	2014	2015	2016	2017
1.3 Commissions								
Life								
Domestic undertakings	1 323 |	1 682	1 705	..	..	..	..	..
Foreign controlled undertakings	..	..	..	..	..	..	..	..
Foreign companies (branches)	..	..	..	..	..	..	..	..
All undertakings	1 323 |	1 682	1 705	..	..	..	..	..
Non-life								
Domestic undertakings	10 198 |	10 449	10 610	..	..	..	..	..
Foreign controlled undertakings	..	..	..	..	..	..	..	..
Foreign companies (branches)	18	19	22	..	..	..	..	..
All undertakings	10 215 |	10 468	10 633	..	..	..	..	..
Composite								
Domestic undertakings	5 201 |	5 915	5 717	..	..	..	..	..
Foreign controlled undertakings	..	..	..	..	..	..	..	..
Foreign companies (branches)	..	..	..	..	..	..	..	..
All undertakings	5 201 |	5 915	5 717	..	..	..	..	..
of which:								
Life	|..	4 985	4 677	..	..	..	..	..
Domestic undertakings	|..	4 985	4 677	..	..	..	..	..
Foreign controlled undertakings	..	..	..	..	..	..	..	..
Foreign companies (branches)	..	..	..	..	..	..	..	..
All undertakings	|..	4 985	4 677	..	..	..	..	..
Non-life	|..	930	1 041	..	..	..	..	..
Domestic undertakings	|..	930	1 041	..	..	..	..	..
Foreign controlled undertakings	..	..	..	..	..	..	..	..
Foreign companies (branches)	..	..	..	..	..	..	..	..
All undertakings	|..	930	1 041	..	..	..	..	..
Total								
Domestic undertakings	16 722	18 046	18 033	..	..	..	..	..
Foreign controlled undertakings	..	..	..	..	..	..	..	..
Foreign companies (branches)	18	19	22	..	..	..	..	..
All undertakings	16 739	18 065	18 055	..	..	..	..	..
1.4 Gross operating expenses								
Life								
Domestic undertakings	719	842	2 982	2 828	2 893	2 914	..	..
Foreign controlled undertakings	..	..	..	..	..	..	..	..
Foreign companies (branches)	..	..	..	..	..	..	..	..
All undertakings	719	842	2 982	2 828	2 893	2 914	15 848	16 123
Non-life								
Domestic undertakings	5 842	5 487	15 726	15 969	16 156	15 936	..	..
Foreign controlled undertakings	..	..	..	..	..	..	..	..
Foreign companies (branches)	8	10	9	..	8	..	..	..
All undertakings	5 849	5 497	15 726	15 969	16 164	15 936	27 415	27 948
Composite								
Domestic undertakings	4 505	4 937	12 392	12 957	13 439	14 727	..	..
Foreign controlled undertakings	..	..	..	..	..	..	..	..
Foreign companies (branches)	..	..	..	..	..	..	..	..
All undertakings	4 505	4 937	12 392	12 957	13 439	14 727	..	..
of which:								
Life	..	..	..	10 533	10 808	11 414	..	..
Domestic undertakings	..	..	..	10 533	..	..	..	..
Foreign controlled undertakings	..	..	..	..	..	..	..	..
Foreign companies (branches)	..	..	..	..	..	..	..	..
All undertakings	..	..	..	10 533	10 808	11 414	..	..
Non-life	..	..	..	2 424	2 631	3 313	..	..
Domestic undertakings	..	..	..	2 424	..	..	..	..
Foreign controlled undertakings	..	..	..	..	..	..	..	..
Foreign companies (branches)	..	..	..	..	..	..	..	..
All undertakings	..	..	..	2 424	2 631	3 313	..	..
Total								
Domestic undertakings	11 066	11 266	31 100	31 754	32 488	33 578	..	..
Foreign controlled undertakings	..	..	..	..	..	..	..	..
Foreign companies (branches)	8	10	9	..	8	..	..	..
All undertakings	11 074	11 276	31 100	31 754	32 497	33 578	43 263	44 071

FRANCE

Table 1. Selected aggregates (cont.)

Million EUR

	2010	2011	2012	2013	2014	2015	2016	2017
1.5 Insurance business written abroad by branches, gross premiums								
Life								
Branches and agencies	1 761	1 929	1 895	2 691	2 860	3 373	4 393	5 050
Subsidaries	..	..	..	..	..	..	..	..
Total	1 761	1 929	1 895	2 691	2 860	3 373	4 393	5 050
Non-life								
Branches and agencies	5 111	5 592	4 107	4 176	4 960	5 460	8 837	9 719
Subsidaries	..	..	..	..	..	..	..	..
Total	5 111	5 592	4 107	4 176	4 960	5 460	8 837	9 719
Composite								
Branches and agencies	..	..	..	..	..	..	..	..
Subsidaries	..	..	..	..	..	..	..	..
Total	..	..	..	..	..	..	..	..
of which:								
Life	..	..	..	..	..	..	..	..
Branches and agencies	..	..	..	..	..	..	..	..
Subsidaries	..	..	..	..	..	..	..	..
Total	..	..	..	..	..	..	..	..
Non-life	..	..	..	..	..	..	..	..
Branches and agencies	..	..	..	..	..	..	..	..
Subsidaries	..	..	..	..	..	..	..	..
Total	..	..	..	..	..	..	..	..
Total								
Branches and agencies	6 872	7 521	6 001	6 867	7 820	8 834	13 230	14 769
Subsidaries	..	..	..	..	..	..	..	..
Total	6 872	7 521	6 001	6 867	7 820	8 834	13 230	14 769

.. Not available; | Break in series
Note: Detailed metadata at: *http://metalinks.oecd.org/ins/20190221/b6cf.*
Source: OECD Insurance Statistics (database)

FRANCE

Table 2. Number of companies and employees

	2010	2011	2012	2013	2014	2015	2016	2017
2.1 Number of companies								
Life								
Domestic undertakings	61	61	62	59	55	51	..	..
Foreign controlled undertakings	..	..	..	..	..	..	..	..
Foreign companies (branches)	..	..	..	..	..	..	..	..
All undertakings	61	61	62	59	55	51	..	..
Non-life								
Domestic undertakings	257	250	221	212	206	191	..	..
Foreign controlled undertakings	8	7	5	..	..	..	..	..
Foreign companies (branches)	..	..	..	4	4	4	..	..
All undertakings	257	250	221	216	210	195	394	381
Composite								
Domestic undertakings	39	40	40	38	38	39	..	..
Foreign controlled undertakings	..	..	..	..	..	..	..	..
Foreign companies (branches)	..	..	..	..	..	..	..	..
All undertakings	39	40	40	38	38	39	239	236
Reinsurance								
Domestic undertakings	24	20	16	16	15	16	..	..
Foreign controlled undertakings	..	..	..	..	..	..	..	..
Foreign companies (branches)	..	..	..	..	..	..	..	..
All undertakings	24	20	16	16	15	16	14	14
Total								
Domestic undertakings	381	371	339	325	314	297	..	..
Foreign controlled undertakings	..	7	5	..	..	..	..	..
Foreign companies (branches)	..	..	..	4	4	4	..	..
All undertakings	381	371	339	329	318	301	647	631
2.2 Number of employees								
Insurance undertakings	..	..	..	..	..	..	..	..
Intermediaries	..	..	..	..	..	..	..	..
Total	..	..	..	..	..	..	..	..

.. Not available

Note: Detailed metadata at: *http://metalinks.oecd.org/ins/20190221/b6cf.*

Source: OECD Insurance Statistics (database)

GERMANY

Table 1. Selected aggregates

Million EUR

	2010	2011	2012	2013	2014	2015	2016	2017
1.1 Insurance business written in the reporting country								
1.1.1 Insurance business, by ownership								
Gross premiums								
Domestic undertakings	180 083	178 145	233 661	243 304	246 201	254 407	257 208	264 933
Foreign controlled undertakings	37 912	35 602	37 194	39 396	38 694	39 170	36 978	36 644
Foreign companies (branches)	1 744	5 560	8 062	7 963	8 796	9 751	8 994	10 550
All undertakings	181 828	183 705	235 634	251 267	254 997	264 153	266 203	275 483
Premiums ceded								
Domestic undertakings	14 656	15 996	23 045	25 709	27 853	32 499	31 990	34 336
Foreign controlled undertakings	3 414	3 905	3 947	4 645	4 615	4 593	4 041	4 046
Foreign companies (branches)	..	..	100	108	103	114	112	132
All undertakings	..	..	23 145	25 817	27 956	32 613	32 102	34 469
Net written premiums								
Domestic undertakings	165 427	162 149	210 616	217 596	218 348	221 907	225 218	230 596
Foreign controlled undertakings	34 499	31 696	33 247	34 751	34 078	34 577	32 937	32 598
Foreign companies (branches)	..	..	1 873	7 854	8 693	9 637	8 882	10 418
All undertakings	..	..	212 489	225 450	227 041	231 545	234 100	241 014
1.1.2 Insurance business on foreign risks, gross premiums								
Life	..	..	..	..	..	..	..	..
Non-life	..	..	..	..	..	..	..	..
Composite total	..	..	..	..	..	..	..	..
Total	..	..	..	..	..	..	..	..
1.1.3 Life insurance payments, by class, gross premiums								
Annuities	27 898	27 237	29 443	32 863	34 019	31 782	31 215	30 000
Unit linked	13 466	12 808	12 721	12 919	13 863	13 863	15 351	15 994
Other life insurance	44 734	40 660	40 822	41 934	40 891	41 214	38 845	41 612
Total life insurance	86 098	80 705	82 986	87 716	88 774	86 859	85 411	87 606
***of which:** Pension contracts*	..	..	..	..	..	..	..	..
1.1.4 Non-life insurance payments, by class, gross premiums								
Motor vehicle insurance	24 680	26 350	27 577	28 592	31 425	32 589	36 521	40 579
Marine, aviation and other transport insurance	4 535	4 156	4 537	4 476	4 379	5 116	4 749	4 933
Freight insurance	..	..	..	..	..	..	..	..
Fire and other property damage insurance	33 154	36 611	34 420	36 832	35 422	38 830	42 499	46 541
Pecuniary loss insurance	2 910	2 979	2 754	2 815	2 088	2 197	2 376	3 872
General liability insurance	11 648	12 321	12 623	13 265	14 213	15 425	16 126	17 517
Accident and health	45 055	47 235	48 823	49 395	48 811	49 176	49 721	52 572
***of which:** Health*	37 290	39 555	41 036	41 747	40 924	41 627	37 178	39 328
Other non-life insurance	4 195	4 316	4 794	4 841	4 865	31 030	25 991	21 153
Treaty reinsurance	..	..	..	..	..	..	..	..
Total non-life insurance	126 177	133 968	135 526	140 215	141 203	174 363	177 983	187 167
1.2 Gross claims payments								
Life								
Domestic undertakings	71 181	85 244	66 288	69 267	74 625	73 307	78 596	69 073
Foreign controlled undertakings	..	..	15 284	17 017	17 510	17 929	17 942	16 501
Foreign companies (branches)	..	..	..	..	..	..	..	..
All undertakings	71 181	85 244	66 288	69 267	74 625	73 307	78 596	69 073
Non-life								
Domestic undertakings	84 864	93 574	101 839	113 293	72 709	77 667	78 086	84 787
Foreign controlled undertakings	..	..	12 192	12 402	8 955	3 653	9 227	9 500
Foreign companies (branches)	..	..	..	..	..	..	..	..
All undertakings	84 864	93 574	101 839	113 293	72 709	77 667	78 086	84 787
Composite, all undertakings	..	..	..	..	..	..	..	..
Total								
Domestic undertakings	156 045	178 818	168 127	182 560	147 334	150 974	156 682	153 859
Foreign controlled undertakings	..	..	27 475	29 419	26 465	21 581	27 169	26 001
Foreign companies (branches)	..	..	..	..	..	..	..	..
All undertakings	156 045	178 818	168 127	182 560	147 334	150 974	156 682	153 859
1.3 Commissions								
Life								
Domestic undertakings	5 875	6 312	6 005	5 367	5 583	5 069	4 987	4 794
Foreign controlled undertakings	..	..	1 771	1 604	1 533	1 488	1 238	1 138
Foreign companies (branches)	..	..	..	..	..	..	..	..
All undertakings	5 875	6 312	6 005	5 367	5 583	5 069	4 987	4 794
Non-life								
Domestic undertakings	9 627	9 908	10 069	10 048	10 221	10 740	11 105	12 173
Foreign controlled undertakings	..	..	1 985	1 720	1 626	257	1 594	1 623
Foreign companies (branches)	..	..	..	..	..	..	..	..
All undertakings	9 627	9 908	10 069	10 048	10 221	10 740	11 105	12 173
Composite, all undertakings	..	..	..	..	..	..	..	..
Total								
Domestic undertakings	15 502	16 220	16 074	15 416	15 805	15 810	16 092	16 967
Foreign controlled undertakings	..	..	3 756	3 323	3 159	1 745	2 832	2 760
Foreign companies (branches)	..	..	..	..	..	..	..	..
All undertakings	15 502	16 220	16 074	15 416	15 805	15 810	16 092	16 967

GERMANY

Table 1. Selected aggregates (cont.)

Million EUR

	2010	2011	2012	2013	2014	2015	2016	2017
1.4 Gross operating expenses								
Life								
Domestic undertakings	14 203	14 545	4 051	3 954	3 963	4 008	3 902	3 907
Foreign controlled undertakings	..	..	925	921	894	1 036	938	952
Foreign companies (branches)	..	..	..	..	..	..	..	..
All undertakings	14 203	14 545	4 051	3 954	3 963	4 008	3 902	3 907
Non-life								
Domestic undertakings	27 565	28 382	11 593	11 599	10 296	10 627	10 807	11 161
Foreign controlled undertakings	..	..	1 528	1 400	1 187	324	1 183	1 210
Foreign companies (branches)	..	..	..	..	..	..	..	..
All undertakings	27 565	28 382	11 593	11 599	10 296	10 627	10 807	11 161
Composite, all undertakings	..	..	..	..	..	..	..	..
Total								
Domestic undertakings	41 768	42 927	15 644	15 553	14 259	14 635	14 709	15 068
Foreign controlled undertakings	..	..	2 453	2 321	2 081	1 361	2 121	2 163
Foreign companies (branches)	..	..	..	..	..	..	..	..
All undertakings	41 768	42 927	15 644	15 553	14 259	14 635	14 709	15 068
1.5 Insurance business written abroad by branches, gross premiums								
Life								
Branches and agencies	..	..	..	..	..	..	..	..
Subsidaries	..	..	..	..	..	..	..	..
Total	..	..	..	..	..	..	..	..
Non-life								
Branches and agencies	..	..	..	..	..	..	..	..
Subsidaries	..	..	..	..	..	..	..	..
Total	..	..	..	..	..	..	..	..
Composite total	..	..	..	..	..	..	..	..
Total								
Branches and agencies	..	..	..	..	..	..	..	..
Subsidaries	..	..	..	..	..	..	..	..
Total	..	..	..	..	..	..	..	..

.. Not available

Note: Detailed metadata at: *http://metalinks.oecd.org/ins/20190221/cc08*.

Source: OECD *Insurance Statistics (database)*

GERMANY

Table 2. Number of companies and employees

	2010	2011	2012	2013	2014	2015	2016	2017
2.1 Number of companies								
Life								
Domestic undertakings	96	95	90	91	91	85	85	86
Foreign controlled undertakings	19	20	19	17	17	14	14	15
Foreign companies (branches)	21	20	19	2	2	2	2	1
All undertakings	117	115	109	93	93	87	87	87
Non-life								
Domestic undertakings	261	265	256	259	255	257	252	251
Foreign controlled undertakings	25	25	25	23	21	22	18	17
Foreign companies (branches)	72	69	62	3	3	3	2	2
All undertakings	333	334	318	262	258	260	254	253
Composite, all undertakings	**0**	**0**	**0**	**0**	**0**	**0**	**0**	**..**
Reinsurance								
Domestic undertakings	35	33	30	29	27	27	27	27
Foreign controlled undertakings	5	5	6	4	3	3	3	3
Foreign companies (branches)	7	7	7	1	1	1	1	1
All undertakings	42	40	37	30	28	28	28	28
Total								
Domestic undertakings	392	393	376	379	373	369	364	364
Foreign controlled undertakings	49	50	50	44	41	39	35	35
Foreign companies (branches)	100	96	88	6	6	6	5	4
All undertakings	492	489	464	385	379	375	369	368
2.2 Number of employees								
Insurance undertakings	123 595	125 783	126 625	128 755	126 755	128 784	..	..
Intermediaries	27 927	27 952	27 407	27 331	26 982	25 917	..	..
Total	151 522	153 735	154 032	156 086	153 737	154 701	156 675	154 262

.. Not available

Note: Detailed metadata at: *http://metalinks.oecd.org/ins/20190221/cc08.*

Source: OECD Insurance Statistics (database)

GREECE

Table 1. Selected aggregates

Million EUR

	2010	2011	2012	2013	2014	2015	2016	2017
1.1 Insurance business written in the reporting country								
1.1.1 Insurance business, by ownership								
Gross premiums								
Domestic undertakings	4 818	4 691	4 289	4 071	3 806	3 573	3 531	3 729
Foreign controlled undertakings	1 877	2 130	2 071	1 730	1 696	1 766	2 350	2 450
Foreign companies (branches)	427	261	211	0	0	0	0	0
All undertakings	5 246	4 952	4 499	4 071	3 806	3 573	3 531	3 729
Premiums ceded								
Domestic undertakings	523	737	534	824	471	459	396	402
Foreign controlled undertakings	226	439	235	214	206	201	244	260
Foreign companies (branches)	96	90	0	0	0	0	0	0
All undertakings	619	827	534	824	471	459	396	402
Net written premiums								
Domestic undertakings	4 295	3 954	3 754	3 247	3 334	3 114	3 135	3 328
Foreign controlled undertakings	1 651	1 691	1 836	1 516	1 490	1 565	2 106	2 190
Foreign companies (branches)	332	171	211	0	0	0	0	0
All undertakings	4 627	4 125	3 965	3 247	3 335	3 114	3 135	3 328
1.1.2 Insurance business on foreign risks, gross premiums								
Life	..	..	..	..	..	..	..	..
Non-life	..	..	..	..	..	..	..	..
Composite	..	..	..	..	..	..	..	..
of which:								
Life	..	..	..	..	..	..	..	..
Non-life	..	..	..	..	..	..	..	..
Total	..	..	..	..	..	..	..	..
1.1.3 Life insurance payments, by class, gross premiums								
Annuities	..	..	165	142	129	125	0	0
Unit linked	..	..	368	240	396	326	250	347
Other life insurance	..	..	1 406	1 299	1 353	1 348	1 416	1 533
Total life insurance	..	..	1 939	1 681	1 879	1 799	1 666	1 881
***of which:** Pension contracts*	..	..	205	143	151	156	..	..
1.1.4 Non-life insurance payments, by class, gross premiums								
Motor vehicle insurance	1 965	1 840	1 569	1 417	1 154	1 006	911	938
Marine, aviation and other transport insurance	28	25	21	19	19	20	32	34
Freight insurance	33	27	24	24	21	21	..	0
Fire and other property damage insurance	576	529	538	529	448	440	410	398
Pecuniary loss insurance	65	69	78	69	30	30	40	28
General liability insurance	81	73	78	76	67	68	65	63
Accident and health	76	76	68	64	57	57	300	242
***of which:** Health*	18	19	20	0	0	..	..	0
Other non-life insurance	153	146	179	188	128	129	137	146
Treaty reinsurance	0	0	0	0	0	..	..	0
Total non-life insurance	2 995	2 786	2 556	2 386	1 924	1 770	1 896	1 848
1.2 Gross claims payments								
Life								
Domestic undertakings	692	822	1 300	1 072	900	744	..	..
Foreign controlled undertakings	506	591	1 017	707	1	502	..	..
Foreign companies (branches)	269	263	0	0	0	0	..	..
All undertakings	961	1 085	1 300	1 072	900	744	..	..
Non-life								
Domestic undertakings	550	501	431	373	355	314	..	..
Foreign controlled undertakings	144	146	142	121	224	109	..	..
Foreign companies (branches)	35	47	0	1	1	0	..	..
All undertakings	586	549	431	375	356	314	..	..
Composite								
Domestic undertakings	1 317	1 408	1 291	1 096	1 018	931	..	..
Foreign controlled undertakings	422	430	441	364	412	347	..	..
Foreign companies (branches)	0	0	0	0	0	0	..	..
All undertakings	1 317	1 408	1 291	1 096	1 018	931	..	..
of which:								
Life	703	866	791	669	613	573	..	..
Domestic undertakings	703	866	791	669	613	573	..	..
Foreign controlled undertakings	255	285	282	226	7	220	..	..
Foreign companies (branches)	0	0	0	0	0	0	..	..
All undertakings	703	866	791	669	613	573	..	..
Non-life	614	541	501	426	405	358	..	..
Domestic undertakings	614	541	501	426	405	358	..	..
Foreign controlled undertakings	166	145	159	138	405	126	..	..
Foreign companies (branches)	0	0	0	0	0	0	..	..
All undertakings	614	541	501	426	405	358	..	..
Total								
Domestic undertakings	2 559	2 731	3 022	2 541	2 273	1 989	..	..
Foreign controlled undertakings	1 072	1 167	1 600	1 192	637	957	..	..
Foreign companies (branches)	304	310	0	1	1	0	..	..
All undertakings	2 864	3 042	3 022	2 542	2 274	1 989	..	..

Table 1. Selected aggregates (cont.)

Million EUR

	2010	2011	2012	2013	2014	2015	2016	2017
1.3 Commissions								
Life								
Domestic undertakings	..	..	..	..	95	91	..	..
Foreign controlled undertakings	..	..	..	..	70	70	..	..
Foreign companies (branches)	..	..	..	..	0	0	..	..
All undertakings	..	..	..	..	95	91	..	..
Non-life								
Domestic undertakings	..	..	..	..	161	158	..	..
Foreign controlled undertakings	..	..	..	..	63	66	..	..
Foreign companies (branches)	..	..	..	..	0	0	..	..
All undertakings	..	..	..	..	162	158	..	..
Composite								
Domestic undertakings	..	..	..	..	276	709	..	..
Foreign controlled undertakings	..	..	..	..	115	115	..	..
Foreign companies (branches)	..	..	..	..	0	0	..	..
All undertakings	..	..	..	..	276	709	..	..
of which:								
Life	..	..	..	..	102	544	..	..
Domestic undertakings	..	..	..	..	102	544	..	..
Foreign controlled undertakings	..	..	..	..	39	40	..	..
Foreign companies (branches)	..	..	..	..	0	0	..	..
All undertakings	..	..	..	..	102	544	..	..
Non-life	..	..	..	..	174	164	..	..
Domestic undertakings	..	..	..	..	174	164	..	..
Foreign controlled undertakings	..	..	..	..	76	75	..	..
Foreign companies (branches)	..	..	..	..	0	0	..	..
All undertakings	..	..	..	..	174	164	..	..
Total								
Domestic undertakings	..	..	..	..	532	957	..	..
Foreign controlled undertakings	..	..	..	..	248	251	..	..
Foreign companies (branches)	..	..	..	..	0	0	..	..
All undertakings	..	..	..	..	532	957	..	..
1.4 Gross operating expenses								
Life								
Domestic undertakings	177	182	82	79	176	163	35	38
Foreign controlled undertakings	137	139	75	66	141	132	32	35
Foreign companies (branches)	59	57	0	0	0	..	0	0
All undertakings	236	239	82	79	176	163	35	38
Non-life								
Domestic undertakings	395	373	104	124	264	247	248	301
Foreign controlled undertakings	135	137	59	61	115	116	145	168
Foreign companies (branches)	53	60	1	0	0	0	0	0
All undertakings	448	432	106	124	264	247	248	301
Composite								
Domestic undertakings	608	543	67	169	404	371	700	701
Foreign controlled undertakings	189	191	16	57	154	150	448	438
Foreign companies (branches)	0	0	0	0	0	..	0	0
All undertakings	608	543	67	169	404	371	700	701
of which:								
Life	195	176	36	53	144	145	315	322
Domestic undertakings	195	176	36	53	144	145	315	322
Foreign controlled undertakings	70	69	11	21	53	52	231	223
Foreign companies (branches)	0	0	0	0	0	..	0	0
All undertakings	195	176	36	53	144	145	315	322
Non-life	413	368	31	116	260	226	385	379
Domestic undertakings	413	368	31	116	260	226	385	379
Foreign controlled undertakings	119	122	4	36	101	98	217	215
Foreign companies (branches)	0	0	0	0	0	..	0	0
All undertakings	413	368	31	116	260	226	385	379
Total								
Domestic undertakings	1 179	1 098	253	372	844	781	983	1 041
Foreign controlled undertakings	461	467	150	184	410	398	625	641
Foreign companies (branches)	112	117	1	0	0	0	0	0
All undertakings	1 291	1 215	254	372	844	781	983	1 041

GREECE

Table 1. Selected aggregates (cont.)

Million EUR

	2010	2011	2012	2013	2014	2015	2016	2017
1.5 Insurance business written abroad by branches, gross premiums								
Life								
Branches and agencies	16	0	..	..	..	..	..	0
Subsidaries	..	..	..	..	..	..	..	0
Total	16	0	..	..	..	..	..	0
Non-life								
Branches and agencies	14	0	..	..	..	..	..	1
Subsidaries	..	..	..	..	..	..	..	0
Total	14	0	..	..	..	..	..	1
Composite								
Branches and agencies	..	..	..	..	..	..	..	0
Subsidaries	..	..	..	..	..	..	..	0
Total	..	..	..	..	..	..	..	0
of which:								
Life	..	..	..	..	..	..	..	0
Branches and agencies	..	..	..	..	..	..	..	0
Subsidaries	..	..	..	..	..	..	..	0
Total	..	..	..	..	..	..	..	0
Non-life	..	..	..	..	..	..	..	0
Branches and agencies	..	..	..	..	..	..	..	0
Subsidaries	..	..	..	..	..	..	..	0
Total	..	..	..	..	..	..	..	0
Total								
Branches and agencies	30	0	..	..	..	..	..	1
Subsidaries	..	..	..	..	..	..	..	0
Total	30	0	..	..	..	..	..	1

.. Not available

Note: Detailed metadata at: *http://metalinks.oecd.org/ins/20190221/a7da.*

Source: OECD Insurance Statistics *(database)*

GREECE

Table 2. Number of companies and employees

	2010	2011	2012	2013	2014	2015	2016	2017
2.1 Number of companies								
Life								
Domestic undertakings	11	10	11	11	11	11	4	3
Foreign controlled undertakings	6	6	7	7	7	7	2	2
Foreign companies (branches)	1	1	0	0	0	0	0	0
All undertakings	12	11	11	11	11	11	4	3
Non-life								
Domestic undertakings	32	31	31	28	24	24	24	22
Foreign controlled undertakings	7	7	7	7	6	5	7	6
Foreign companies (branches)	2	2	2	2	2	2	0	0
All undertakings	34	33	33	30	26	26	24	22
Composite								
Domestic undertakings	12	11	11	11	11	11	17	17
Foreign controlled undertakings	4	4	4	4	4	4	10	10
Foreign companies (branches)	0	0	0	0	0	0	0	0
All undertakings	12	11	11	11	11	11	17	17
Reinsurance								
Domestic undertakings	0	0	0	0	0	0	0	0
Foreign controlled undertakings	0	0	0	0	0	0	0	0
Foreign companies (branches)	0	0	0	0	0	0	0	0
All undertakings	0	0	0	0	0	0	0	0
Total								
Domestic undertakings	55	52	53	50	46	46	45	42
Foreign controlled undertakings	17	17	18	18	17	16	19	18
Foreign companies (branches)	3	3	2	2	2	2	0	0
All undertakings	58	55	55	52	48	48	45	42
2.2 Number of employees								
Insurance undertakings	..	..	..	..	..	..	..	..
Intermediaries	..	..	..	..	..	..	..	..
Total	..	..	..	..	..	..	..	..

.. Not available

Note: Detailed metadata at: *http://metalinks.oecd.org/ins/20190221/a7da*.

Source: OECD Insurance Statistics (database)

HUNGARY

Table 1. Selected aggregates

Million HUF

	2010	2011	2012	2013	2014	2015	2016	2017
1.1 Insurance business written in the reporting country								
1.1.1 Insurance business, by ownership								
Gross premiums								
Domestic undertakings	842 781	815 038	760 249	801 210	833 664	835 428	885 781	956 006
Foreign controlled undertakings	802 202	770 794	718 932	763 286	796 332	788 248	835 272	897 699
Foreign companies (branches)	..	..	..	..	..	..	..	..
All undertakings	842 781	815 038	760 249	801 210	833 664	835 428	885 781	956 006
Premiums ceded								
Domestic undertakings	134 572	131 231	127 261	111 755	116 117	115 801	118 081	120 524
Foreign controlled undertakings	123 702	120 088	118 373	104 254	108 557	104 464	107 021	106 729
Foreign companies (branches)	..	..	..	..	..	..	..	..
All undertakings	134 572	131 231	127 261	111 755	116 117	115 801	118 081	120 524
Net written premiums								
Domestic undertakings	708 209	683 807	632 989	689 455	717 547	719 627	767 700	835 482
Foreign controlled undertakings	678 500	650 706	600 559	659 032	687 774	683 784	728 251	790 970
Foreign companies (branches)	..	..	..	..	..	..	..	..
All undertakings	708 209	683 807	632 989	689 455	717 547	719 627	767 700	835 482
1.1.2 Insurance business on foreign risks, gross premiums								
Life	2 501	30 145	3 284	3 358	3 533	4 234	4 317	4 630
Non-life	1 568	2 165	1 257	1 840	1 923	1 052	2 308	2 657
Composite	5 030	5 326	7 943	4 500	2 829	4 368	8 142	9 004
of which:								
Life	64	80	279	781	228	216	177	172
Non-life	4 965	5 246	7 665	3 719	2 602	4 152	7 965	8 832
Total	9 099	37 636	12 484	9 698	8 285	9 654	14 767	16 291
1.1.3 Life insurance payments, by class, gross premiums								
Annuities	4 459	4 247	3 529	2 975	3 147	3 479	..	..
Unit linked	295 752	298 106	261 098	286 919	282 059	266 857	..	..
Other life insurance	147 947	142 599	138 251	146 439	171 738	156 617	..	..
Total life insurance	448 159	444 952	402 878	436 333	456 944	426 953	438 718	460 791
***of which:** Pension contracts*	51	37	..	19	..	10	..	..
1.1.4 Non-life insurance payments, by class, gross premiums								
Motor vehicle insurance	200 559	164 432	147 428	144 515	152 283	175 045	203 396	232 622
Marine, aviation and other transport insurance	1 098	933	663	661	793	879	142	172
Freight insurance	2 798	3 082	2 405	2 552	2 856	3 165	5 733	6 143
Fire and other property damage insurance	140 943	147 551	152 904	159 562	158 219	161 160	168 736	179 697
Pecuniary loss insurance	3 829	4 922	2 930	3 739	3 672	4 822	5 430	5 027
General liability insurance	17 560	17 956	18 856	20 074	21 904	23 585	21 274	24 525
Accident and health	20 323	22 596	23 361	25 922	28 358	29 859	22 389	24 898
***of which:** Health*	7 599	5 929	7 128	8 559	9 558	8 668	4 250	5 557
Other non-life insurance	7 479	8 811	8 758	7 781	8 557	9 909	19 916	22 112
Treaty reinsurance	..	..	..	..	..	..	..	..
Total non-life insurance	394 588	370 284	357 305	364 806	376 641	408 424	447 017	495 197
1.2 Gross claims payments								
Life								
Domestic undertakings	142 272	170 016	153 649	139 994	130 633	150 198	155 047	172 359
Foreign controlled undertakings	131 643	158 484	150 320	129 594	121 318	139 595	147 047	160 787
Foreign companies (branches)	..	..	..	..	..	..	..	..
All undertakings	142 272	170 016	153 649	139 994	130 633	150 198	155 047	172 359
Non-life								
Domestic undertakings	19 173	18 824	22 516	25 692	27 416	30 571	34 112	32 258
Foreign controlled undertakings	12 193	11 865	11 387	12 611	13 973	14 605	16 056	12 917
Foreign companies (branches)	..	..	..	..	..	..	..	..
All undertakings	19 173	18 824	22 516	25 692	27 416	30 571	34 112	32 258
Composite								
Domestic undertakings	441 811	411 093	413 298	422 789	379 879	356 926	361 448	389 622
Foreign controlled undertakings	441 811	411 093	413 298	422 789	379 879	356 926	361 448	389 622
Foreign companies (branches)	..	..	..	..	..	..	..	..
All undertakings	441 811	411 093	413 298	422 789	379 879	356 926	361 448	389 622
of which:								
Life	228 884	236 953	240 059	242 802	212 244	180 098	176 820	185 216
Domestic undertakings	228 884	236 953	240 059	242 802	212 244	180 098	176 820	185 216
Foreign controlled undertakings	228 884	236 953	240 059	242 802	212 244	180 098	176 820	185 216
Foreign companies (branches)	..	..	..	..	..	..	..	..
All undertakings	228 884	236 953	240 059	242 802	212 244	180 098	176 820	185 216
Non-life	212 928	174 139	173 240	179 988	167 635	176 829	184 628	204 406
Domestic undertakings	212 928	174 139	173 240	179 988	167 635	176 829	184 628	204 406
Foreign controlled undertakings	212 928	174 139	173 240	179 988	167 635	176 829	184 628	204 406
Foreign companies (branches)	..	..	..	..	..	..	..	..
All undertakings	212 928	174 139	173 240	179 988	167 635	176 829	184 628	204 406
Total								
Domestic undertakings	603 256	599 932	589 464	588 475	537 928	537 695	550 607	594 239
Foreign controlled undertakings	585 648	581 441	575 006	564 995	515 171	511 127	524 551	563 326
Foreign companies (branches)	..	..	..	..	..	..	..	..
All undertakings	603 256	599 932	589 464	588 475	537 928	537 695	550 607	594 239

HUNGARY

Table 1. Selected aggregates (cont.)

Million HUF

	2010	2011	2012	2013	2014	2015	2016	2017
1.3 Commissions								
Life								
Domestic undertakings	23 836	23 907	20 760	14 900	14 024	13 526	16 531	17 513
Foreign controlled undertakings	13 107	13 391	14 215	11 559	11 559	11 089	14 360	15 017
Foreign companies (branches)	..	..	..	..	..	..	..	..
All undertakings	23 836	23 907	20 760	14 900	14 024	13 526	16 531	17 513
Non-life								
Domestic undertakings	5 722	6 479	6 319	7 349	7 243	9 161	10 325	13 383
Foreign controlled undertakings	5 088	5 335	4 457	4 813	4 948	5 986	5 650	6 550
Foreign companies (branches)	..	..	..	..	..	..	..	..
All undertakings	5 722	6 479	6 319	7 349	7 243	9 161	10 325	13 383
Composite								
Domestic undertakings	74 369	74 891	69 058	75 007	72 592	79 086	108 207	114 286
Foreign controlled undertakings	74 369	74 891	69 058	75 007	72 592	79 086	108 207	114 286
Foreign companies (branches)	..	..	..	..	..	..	..	..
All undertakings	74 369	74 891	69 058	75 007	72 592	79 086	108 207	114 286
of which:								
Life	28 121	30 426	26 909	29 847	30 235	29 116	39 083	38 017
Domestic undertakings	28 121	30 426	26 909	29 847	30 235	29 116	39 083	38 017
Foreign controlled undertakings	28 121	30 426	26 909	29 847	30 235	29 116	39 083	38 017
Foreign companies (branches)	..	..	..	..	..	..	..	..
All undertakings	28 121	30 426	26 909	29 847	30 235	29 116	39 083	38 017
Non-life	46 248	44 465	42 148	45 160	42 357	49 970	69 124	76 269
Domestic undertakings	46 248	44 465	42 148	45 160	42 357	49 970	69 124	76 269
Foreign controlled undertakings	46 248	44 465	42 148	45 160	42 357	49 970	69 124	76 269
Foreign companies (branches)	..	..	..	..	..	..	..	..
All undertakings	46 248	44 465	42 148	45 160	42 357	49 970	69 124	76 269
Total								
Domestic undertakings	103 927	105 277	96 136	97 256	93 859	101 773	135 063	145 182
Foreign controlled undertakings	92 564	93 617	87 729	91 380	89 099	96 162	128 218	135 853
Foreign companies (branches)	..	..	..	..	..	..	..	..
All undertakings	103 927	105 277	96 136	97 256	93 859	101 773	135 063	145 182
1.4 Gross operating expenses								
Life								
Domestic undertakings	56 566	52 633	37 846	32 595	35 399	32 897	34 946	34 955
Foreign controlled undertakings	37 256	36 587	32 963	27 473	30 053	29 279	31 818	30 865
Foreign companies (branches)	..	..	..	..	..	..	..	..
All undertakings	56 566	52 633	37 846	32 595	35 399	32 897	34 946	34 955
Non-life								
Domestic undertakings	15 324	17 229	16 277	17 413	17 638	20 337	21 977	21 528
Foreign controlled undertakings	11 678	12 859	10 465	11 126	11 890	14 690	13 298	10 965
Foreign companies (branches)	..	..	..	..	..	..	..	..
All undertakings	15 324	17 229	16 277	17 413	17 638	20 337	21 977	21 528
Composite								
Domestic undertakings	175 554	170 062	155 577	172 680	181 142	167 842	176 431	185 944
Foreign controlled undertakings	175 554	170 062	155 577	172 680	181 142	167 842	176 431	185 944
Foreign companies (branches)	..	..	..	..	..	..	..	..
All undertakings	175 554	170 062	155 577	172 680	181 142	167 842	176 431	185 944
of which:								
Life	65 371	68 791	55 125	56 633	70 675	55 349	56 859	50 779
Domestic undertakings	65 371	68 791	55 125	56 633	70 675	55 349	56 859	50 779
Foreign controlled undertakings	65 371	68 791	55 125	56 633	70 675	55 349	56 859	50 779
Foreign companies (branches)	..	..	..	..	..	..	..	..
All undertakings	65 371	68 791	55 125	56 633	70 675	55 349	56 859	50 779
Non-life	110 183	101 271	100 451	116 047	110 467	112 493	119 571	135 165
Domestic undertakings	110 183	101 271	100 451	116 047	110 467	112 493	119 571	135 165
Foreign controlled undertakings	110 183	101 271	100 451	116 047	110 467	112 493	119 571	135 165
Foreign companies (branches)	..	..	..	..	..	..	..	..
All undertakings	110 183	101 271	100 451	116 047	110 467	112 493	119 571	135 165
Total								
Domestic undertakings	247 444	239 924	209 699	222 687	234 179	221 076	233 354	242 427
Foreign controlled undertakings	224 487	219 509	199 004	211 279	223 085	211 811	221 547	227 774
Foreign companies (branches)	..	..	..	..	..	..	..	..
All undertakings	247 444	239 924	209 699	222 687	234 179	221 076	233 354	242 427

HUNGARY

Table 1. Selected aggregates (cont.)

Million HUF

	2010	2011	2012	2013	2014	2015	2016	2017
1.5 Insurance business written abroad by branches, gross premiums								
Life								
Branches and agencies	..	..	..	..	..	..	..	..
Subsidaries	..	..	..	..	..	..	..	..
Total	..	..	..	..	..	..	..	..
Non-life								
Branches and agencies	..	..	..	..	..	..	..	..
Subsidaries	..	..	..	..	..	..	..	..
Total	..	..	..	..	..	..	..	..
Composite								
Branches and agencies	..	..	..	..	..	..	..	..
Subsidaries	..	..	..	..	..	..	..	..
Total	..	..	..	..	..	..	..	..
of which:								
Life	..	..	..	..	..	..	..	..
Branches and agencies	..	..	..	..	..	..	..	..
Subsidaries	..	..	..	..	..	..	..	..
Total	..	..	..	..	..	..	..	..
Non-life	..	..	..	..	..	..	..	..
Branches and agencies	..	..	..	..	..	..	..	..
Subsidaries	..	..	..	..	..	..	..	..
Total	..	..	..	..	..	..	..	..
Total								
Branches and agencies	..	..	..	..	..	..	..	..
Subsidaries	..	..	..	..	..	..	..	..
Total	..	..	..	..	..	..	..	..

.. Not available

Note: Detailed metadata at: *http://metalinks.oecd.org/ins/20190221/222a.*

Source: OECD Insurance Statistics (database)

HUNGARY

Table 2. Number of companies and employees

	2010	2011	2012	2013	2014	2015	2016	2017
2.1 Number of companies								
Life								
Domestic undertakings	12	12	12	10	10	10	8	7
Foreign controlled undertakings	9	9	9	7	7	7	7	6
Foreign companies (branches)	0	..	..	..	..	0	0	0
All undertakings	12	12	12	10	10	10	8	7
Non-life								
Domestic undertakings	15	15	13	12	12	11	10	9
Foreign controlled undertakings	9	9	7	6	6	6	6	5
Foreign companies (branches)	14	12	14	14	14	13	14	13
All undertakings	29	27	27	26	26	24	24	22
Composite								
Domestic undertakings	10	10	10	10	10	9	9	9
Foreign controlled undertakings	10	10	10	10	10	9	9	9
Foreign companies (branches)	0	1	1	1	1	2	2	2
All undertakings	10	11	11	11	11	11	11	11
Reinsurance								
Domestic undertakings	..	..	..	..	..	..	..	..
Foreign controlled undertakings	..	..	..	..	..	..	..	..
Foreign companies (branches)	..	..	..	..	..	..	..	..
All undertakings	..	..	..	..	..	..	..	..
Total								
Domestic undertakings	37	37	35	32	32	30	27	25
Foreign controlled undertakings	28	28	26	23	23	22	22	20
Foreign companies (branches)	14	13	15	15	15	15	16	15
All undertakings	51	50	50	47	47	45	43	40
2.2 Number of employees								
Insurance undertakings	10 547	9 580	9 701	9 363	9 229	8 728	8 542	8 133
Intermediaries	17 067	16 950	13 572	13 083	12 768	11 392	9 822	12 287
Total	27 615	26 530	23 273	22 445	21 997	20 121	18 364	20 420

.. Not available

Note: Detailed metadata at: *http://metalinks.oecd.org/ins/20190221/222a.*

Source: OECD Insurance Statistics (database)

ICELAND

Table 1. Selected aggregates

Million ISK

	2010	2011	2012	2013	2014	2015	2016	2017
1.1 Insurance business written in the reporting country								
1.1.1 Insurance business, by ownership								
Gross premiums								
Domestic undertakings	46 636	48 117	50 490	51 142	51 849	55 346	58 777	65 274
Foreign controlled undertakings	4 082	4 464	4 788	5 088	5 401	6 010	..	..
Foreign companies (branches)	0	0	..	..	..	..	..	..
All undertakings	46 636	48 117	50 490	51 142	51 849	55 346	58 777	65 274
Premiums ceded								
Domestic undertakings	3 621	3 425	3 371	3 136	2 918	2 882	2 725	2 613
Foreign controlled undertakings	476	328	318	310	310	272	..	..
Foreign companies (branches)	0	0	..	..	..	..	..	..
All undertakings	3 621	3 425	3 371	3 136	2 918	2 882	2 725	2 613
Net written premiums								
Domestic undertakings	43 015	44 692	47 118	48 005	48 931	52 465	56 052	62 662
Foreign controlled undertakings	3 606	4 136	4 470	4 779	5 091	5 737	..	..
Foreign companies (branches)	0	0	..	..	..	..	..	..
All undertakings	43 015	44 692	47 118	48 005	48 931	52 465	56 052	62 662
1.1.2 Insurance business on foreign risks, gross premiums								
Life	3 510	0	0	0	0	0	0	0
Non-life	43 506	2 528	2 632	2 156	2 563	3 018	1 010	1 737
Composite total	..	..	..	..	..	..	..	..
Total	47 016	2 528	2 632	2 156	2 563	3 018	1 010	1 737
1.1.3 Life insurance payments, by class, gross premiums								
Annuities	65	57	61	61	111	473	..	..
Unit linked	104	110	87	86	87	91	20	32
Other life insurance	3 216	3 227	3 532	3 913	4 042	4 087	5 141	5 789
Total life insurance	3 385	3 395	3 680	4 061	4 240	4 651	5 161	5 821
***of which:** Pension contracts*	0	0	0	0	0	0	0	0
1.1.4 Non-life insurance payments, by class, gross premiums								
Motor vehicle insurance	20 479	20 205	21 226	21 522	22 084	23 952	28 398	33 127
Marine, aviation and other transport insurance	2 483	2 629	2 746	3 372	3 419	3 690	3 631	3 139
Freight insurance	602	632	667	638	646	751	0	0
Fire and other property damage insurance	12 193	12 838	14 028	13 816	13 903	13 911	12 484	13 048
Pecuniary loss insurance	77	100	77	45	23	27	33	26
General liability insurance	2 372	2 782	2 932	2 556	2 565	2 672	3 078	3 561
Accident and health	5 012	5 318	5 108	5 102	4 947	5 646	5 960	6 509
***of which:** Health*	..	..	..	..	..	..	..	..
Other non-life insurance	12	27	27	30	22	42	32	42
Treaty reinsurance	0	0	0	0	0	0	0	0
Total non-life insurance	43 230	44 530	46 809	47 081	47 608	50 690	53 616	59 453
1.2 Gross claims payments								
Life								
Domestic undertakings	882	1 139	1 434	1 381	1 529	1 325	1 690	1 755
Foreign controlled undertakings	15	21	56	47	30	58	..	..
Foreign companies (branches)	0	..	..	..	..	..	..	..
All undertakings	882	1 139	1 434	1 381	1 529	1 325	1 690	1 755
Non-life								
Domestic undertakings	27 092	28 721	30 190	31 417	32 554	36 082	41 655	43 781
Foreign controlled undertakings	2 859	3 132	2 931	3 412	3 520	4 169	..	..
Foreign companies (branches)	0	..	..	..	..	..	..	..
All undertakings	27 092	28 721	30 190	31 417	32 554	36 082	41 655	43 781
Composite, all undertakings	..	..	..	..	..	..	..	..
Total								
Domestic undertakings	27 974	29 861	31 624	32 798	34 083	37 407	43 345	45 536
Foreign controlled undertakings	2 874	3 152	2 987	3 459	3 550	4 227	..	..
Foreign companies (branches)	0	..	..	..	..	..	..	..
All undertakings	27 974	29 861	31 624	32 798	34 083	37 407	43 345	45 536
1.3 Commissions								
Life								
Domestic undertakings	41	74	71	66	118	90	..	..
Foreign controlled undertakings	6	4	12	20	42	3	..	..
Foreign companies (branches)	0	..	..	..	..	..	..	..
All undertakings	41	74	71	66	118	90	..	..
Non-life								
Domestic undertakings	121	101	122	102	39	36	..	..
Foreign controlled undertakings	0	0	0	0	0	0	..	..
Foreign companies (branches)	0	..	..	..	..	..	..	..
All undertakings	121	101	122	102	39	36	..	..
Composite, all undertakings	..	..	..	..	..	..	..	..
Total								
Domestic undertakings	162	175	193	168	157	126	..	..
Foreign controlled undertakings	6	4	12	20	42	3	..	..
Foreign companies (branches)	0	..	..	..	..	..	..	..
All undertakings	162	175	193	168	157	126	..	..

ICELAND

Table 1. Selected aggregates (cont.)

Million ISK

	2010	2011	2012	2013	2014	2015	2016	2017
1.4 Gross operating expenses								
Life								
Domestic undertakings	851	945	1 119	1 384	1 098	1 498	1 231	1 528
Foreign controlled undertakings	52	57	77	90	18	161	..	..
Foreign companies (branches)	0	..	..	..	..	..	..	..
All undertakings	851	945	1 119	1 384	1 098	1 498	1 231	1 528
Non-life								
Domestic undertakings	8 563	9 081	9 987	9 860	9 680	4 314	6 931	7 422
Foreign controlled undertakings	859	965	996	1 084	1 086	1 225	..	..
Foreign companies (branches)	0	..	..	..	..	..	..	..
All undertakings	8 563	9 081	9 987	9 860	9 680	4 314	6 931	7 422
Composite, all undertakings	..	..	..	..	..	..	..	..
Total								
Domestic undertakings	9 414	10 027	11 106	11 244	10 778	5 812	8 162	8 950
Foreign controlled undertakings	911	1 022	1 072	1 173	1 104	1 387	..	..
Foreign companies (branches)	0	..	..	..	..	..	..	..
All undertakings	9 414	10 027	11 106	11 244	10 778	5 812	8 162	8 950
1.5 Insurance business written abroad by branches, gross premiums								
Life								
Branches and agencies	0	0	0	..	..	..	..	..
Subsidaries	0	0	0	..	..	..	..	..
Total	0	0	0	..	..	..	..	..
Non-life								
Branches and agencies	277	551	914	..	..	..	..	..
Subsidaries	0	0	0	..	..	..	..	..
Total	277	551	914	..	..	..	..	..
Composite total	..	..	..	..	..	..	..	..
Total								
Branches and agencies	277	551	914	..	..	..	..	..
Subsidaries	0	0	0	..	..	..	..	..
Total	277	551	914	..	..	..	..	..

.. Not available

Note: Detailed metadata at: *http://metalinks.oecd.org/ins/20190221/6934.*

Source: *OECD Insurance Statistics (database)*

ICELAND

Table 2. Number of companies and employees

	2010	2011	2012	2013	2014	2015	2016	2017
2.1 Number of companies								
Life								
Domestic undertakings	5	5	5	5	5	5	4	4
Foreign controlled undertakings	1	1	1	1	1	1	..	..
Foreign companies (branches)	0	0	1	1	1	1	..	..
All undertakings	5	5	6	6	6	6	4	4
Non-life								
Domestic undertakings	6	6	6	5	5	5	4	4
Foreign controlled undertakings	1	1	1	1	1	1	..	..
Foreign companies (branches)	0	0	1	1	1	1	..	..
All undertakings	6	6	7	6	6	6	4	4
Composite, all undertakings	**0**	**0**	**0**	**0**	**0**	**0**	**0**	**0**
Reinsurance								
Domestic undertakings	2	2	2	2	2	2	0	0
Foreign controlled undertakings	0	0	0	..	..	..	..	..
Foreign companies (branches)	0	0	0	..	..	..	..	..
All undertakings	2	2	2	2	2	2	0	0
Total								
Domestic undertakings	13	13	13	12	12	12	8	8
Foreign controlled undertakings	2	2	2	2	2	2	0	0
Foreign companies (branches)	0	0	2	2	2	2	0	0
All undertakings	13	13	15	14	14	14	8	8
2.2 Number of employees								
Insurance undertakings	617	652	641	614	..	582	..	..
Intermediaries	..	0	..	..	592	..	..	..
Total	617	652	..	614	592	582	..	..

.. Not available

Note: Detailed metadata at: *http://metalinks.oecd.org/ins/20190221/6934.*

Source: OECD Insurance Statistics (database)

IRELAND

Table 1. Selected aggregates

Million EUR

	2010	2011	2012	2013	2014	2015	2016	2017
1.1 Insurance business written in the reporting country								
1.1.1 Insurance business, by ownership								
Gross premiums								
Domestic undertakings	31 340	30 304	33 133	31 818	36 377	40 340	48 949	40 281
Foreign controlled undertakings	0	..	..	..	..	..	..	..
Foreign companies (branches)	2 840	1 731	2 348	2 301	3 184	3 645	..	..
All undertakings	34 180	32 035	35 481	34 119	39 561	43 985	48 949	40 281
Premiums ceded								
Domestic undertakings	2 950	3 478	3 755	3 908	3 891	4 933	9 985	..
Foreign controlled undertakings	0	..	..	..	..	..	..	..
Foreign companies (branches)	800	772	356	268	371	359	..	..
All undertakings	3 750	4 250	4 111	4 176	4 262	5 292	9 985	..
Net written premiums								
Domestic undertakings	28 390	26 826	29 379	27 910	32 486	35 407	38 964	..
Foreign controlled undertakings	0	..	..	..	..	..	..	..
Foreign companies (branches)	2 040	960	1 992	2 033	2 813	3 286	..	..
All undertakings	30 430	27 786	31 371	29 943	35 299	38 693	38 964	..
1.1.2 Insurance business on foreign risks, gross premiums								
Life	15 779	15 627	15 038	16 125	21 410	23 192	..	19 765
Non-life	3 016	3 195	3 676	3 826	3 960	4 263	..	1 927
Composite	..	..	..	..	..	..	..	..
of which:								
Life	..	..	..	..	..	..	..	..
Non-life	..	..	..	..	..	..	..	..
Total	18 796	18 821	18 714	19 951	25 370	27 455	..	21 692
1.1.3 Life insurance payments, by class, gross premiums								
Annuities	..	..	..	..	..	..	0	0
Unit linked	..	..	..	..	..	..	28 838	29 365
Other life insurance	..	..	..	..	..	..	4 477	3 804
Total life insurance	..	..	28 140	27 207	32 171	34 587	33 315	33 169
***of which:** Pension contracts*	..	..	..	..	..	..	..	..
1.1.4 Non-life insurance payments, by class, gross premiums								
Motor vehicle insurance	1 649	1 423	1 486	1 435	1 599	1 795	3 905	1 770
Marine, aviation and other transport insurance	204	237	243	183	143	163	421	143
Freight insurance	..	0	..	..	..	..	0	0
Fire and other property damage insurance	1 785	1 728	1 906	1 763	1 758	1 768	4 023	1 159
Pecuniary loss insurance	47	67	..	105	124	92	332	479
General liability insurance	1 108	1 072	1 147	1 127	1 301	1 400	2 887	965
Accident and health	1 267	1 432	1 288	1 171	1 235	2 750	1 935	2 322
***of which:** Health*	..	..	..	..	..	..	..	..
Other non-life insurance	518	485	563	504	494	585	1 159	4
Treaty reinsurance	168	284	374	330	373	414	746	217
Total non-life insurance	6 745	6 729	7 007	6 618	7 027	8 967	15 408	7 059
1.2 Gross claims payments								
Life								
Domestic undertakings	21 393	..	27 921	28 263	27 434	28 474	32 280	26 726
Foreign controlled undertakings	0	..	..	..	..	..	..	..
Foreign companies (branches)	626	..	..	1 235	1 114	1 356	..	..
All undertakings	22 019	..	27 921	29 498	28 548	29 830	32 280	26 726
Non-life								
Domestic undertakings	4 438	4 938	4 842	4 369	3 853	5 343	15 941	8 482
Foreign controlled undertakings	0	..	..	..	..	..	..	..
Foreign companies (branches)	474	1 023	983	677	1 177	1 179	..	..
All undertakings	4 912	5 961	5 825	5 046	5 030	6 522	15 941	8 482
Composite								
Domestic undertakings	..	..	..	..	..	..	..	..
Foreign controlled undertakings	..	..	..	..	..	..	..	..
Foreign companies (branches)	..	..	..	..	..	..	..	..
All undertakings	..	..	..	..	..	..	..	..
of which:								
Life	..	..	..	..	..	..	..	..
Domestic undertakings	..	..	..	..	..	..	..	..
Foreign controlled undertakings	..	..	..	..	..	..	..	..
Foreign companies (branches)	..	..	..	..	..	..	..	..
All undertakings	..	..	..	..	..	..	..	..
Non-life	..	..	..	..	..	..	..	..
Domestic undertakings	..	..	..	..	..	..	..	..
Foreign controlled undertakings	..	..	..	..	..	..	..	..
Foreign companies (branches)	..	..	..	..	..	..	..	..
All undertakings	..	..	..	..	..	..	..	..
Total								
Domestic undertakings	25 831	4 938	32 763	32 632	31 287	33 817	48 221	35 208
Foreign controlled undertakings	0	..	..	..	..	..	..	..
Foreign companies (branches)	1 099	1 023	983	1 912	2 291	2 535	..	..
All undertakings	26 931	5 961	33 746	34 544	33 578	36 352	48 221	35 208

IRELAND

Table 1. Selected aggregates (cont.)

Million EUR

	2010	2011	2012	2013	2014	2015	2016	2017
1.3 Commissions								
Life								
Domestic undertakings	1 310	..	1 593	1 844	2 051	2 281	2 198	1 517
Foreign controlled undertakings	0	..	..	..	..	..	..	..
Foreign companies (branches)	25	..	..	43	64	59	..	..
All undertakings	1 335	..	1 593	1 887	2 115	2 340	2 198	1 517
Non-life								
Domestic undertakings	767	764	657	737	764	896	2 292	957
Foreign controlled undertakings	0	..	..	..	..	..	..	..
Foreign companies (branches)	130	104	171	130	248	299	..	..
All undertakings	897	868	828	867	1 012	1 195	2 292	957
Composite								
Domestic undertakings	..	..	..	..	..	..	..	..
Foreign controlled undertakings	..	..	..	..	..	..	..	..
Foreign companies (branches)	..	..	..	..	..	..	..	..
All undertakings	..	..	..	..	..	..	..	..
of which:								
Life	..	..	..	..	..	..	..	..
Domestic undertakings	..	..	..	..	..	..	..	0
Foreign controlled undertakings	..	..	..	..	..	..	..	..
Foreign companies (branches)	..	..	..	..	..	..	..	..
All undertakings	..	..	..	..	..	..	..	..
Non-life	..	..	..	..	..	..	..	..
Domestic undertakings	..	..	..	..	..	..	..	..
Foreign controlled undertakings	..	..	..	..	..	..	..	..
Foreign companies (branches)	..	..	..	..	..	..	..	..
All undertakings	..	..	..	..	..	..	..	..
Total								
Domestic undertakings	2 077	764	2 250	2 581	2 815	3 177	4 490	2 474
Foreign controlled undertakings	0	..	..	..	..	..	..	..
Foreign companies (branches)	155	104	171	173	312	358	..	..
All undertakings	2 232	868	2 420	2 754	3 127	3 535	4 490	2 474
1.4 Gross operating expenses								
Life								
Domestic undertakings	1 127	..	1 268	1 346	1 429	1 437	1 319	444
Foreign controlled undertakings	0	..	..	..	..	..	..	..
Foreign companies (branches)	68	..	..	154	657	158	..	..
All undertakings	1 195	..	1 268	1 500	2 086	1 595	1 319	444
Non-life								
Domestic undertakings	726	688	622	650	589	484	1 873	932
Foreign controlled undertakings	0	..	..	..	..	..	..	..
Foreign companies (branches)	79	186	295	159	223	224	..	..
All undertakings	805	874	917	809	812	708	1 873	932
Composite								
Domestic undertakings	..	..	..	..	..	..	..	..
Foreign controlled undertakings	..	..	..	..	..	..	..	..
Foreign companies (branches)	..	..	..	..	..	..	..	..
All undertakings	..	..	..	..	..	..	..	..
of which:								
Life	..	..	..	..	..	..	..	..
Domestic undertakings	..	..	..	..	..	..	..	..
Foreign controlled undertakings	..	..	..	..	..	..	..	..
Foreign companies (branches)	..	..	..	..	..	..	..	..
All undertakings	..	..	..	..	..	..	..	..
Non-life	..	..	..	..	..	..	..	..
Domestic undertakings	..	..	..	..	..	..	..	..
Foreign controlled undertakings	..	..	..	..	..	..	..	..
Foreign companies (branches)	..	..	..	..	..	..	..	..
All undertakings	..	..	..	..	..	..	..	..
Total								
Domestic undertakings	1 853	688	1 891	1 996	2 018	1 921	3 192	1 376
Foreign controlled undertakings	0	..	..	..	..	..	..	..
Foreign companies (branches)	147	186	295	313	880	382	..	..
All undertakings	2 000	874	2 185	2 309	2 898	2 303	3 192	1 376

IRELAND

Table 1. Selected aggregates (cont.)

Million EUR

	2010	2011	2012	2013	2014	2015	2016	2017
1.5 Insurance business written abroad by branches, gross premiums								
Life								
Branches and agencies	3 701	2 434	3 422	5 563	5 970	6 234	..	6 438
Subsidaries	0	..	..	..	..	..	..	..
Total	3 701	2 434	3 422	5 563	5 970	6 234	..	6 438
Non-life								
Branches and agencies	8 628	9 626	9 599	9 228	9 640	9 835	..	8 739
Subsidaries	0	..	..	..	..	..	..	..
Total	8 628	9 626	9 599	9 228	9 640	9 835	..	8 739
Composite								
Branches and agencies	..	..	..	..	..	..	..	..
Subsidaries	..	..	..	..	..	..	..	..
Total	..	..	..	..	..	..	..	..
of which:								
Life	..	..	..	..	..	..	..	..
Branches and agencies	..	..	..	..	..	..	..	..
Subsidaries	..	..	..	..	..	..	..	..
Total	..	..	..	..	..	..	..	..
Non-life	..	..	..	..	..	..	..	..
Branches and agencies	..	..	..	..	..	..	..	..
Subsidaries	..	..	..	..	..	..	..	..
Total	..	..	..	..	..	..	..	..
Total								
Branches and agencies	12 329	12 060	13 021	14 791	15 610	16 069	..	15 177
Subsidaries	0	..	..	..	..	..	..	..
Total	12 329	12 060	13 021	14 791	15 610	16 069	..	15 177

.. Not available

Note: Detailed metadata at: *http://metalinks.oecd.org/ins/20190221/6298*.

Source: OECD *Insurance Statistics (database)*

IRELAND

Table 2. Number of companies and employees

	2010	2011	2012	2013	2014	2015	2016	2017
2.1 Number of companies								
Life								
Domestic undertakings	61	62	55	53	51	48	44	45
Foreign controlled undertakings	0	0	0	..	..	..	0	0
Foreign companies (branches)	10	9	8	8	8	11	11	12
All undertakings	71	71	63	61	59	59	55	57
Non-life								
Domestic undertakings	123	121	111	104	102	101	90	99
Foreign controlled undertakings	0	0	0	..	..	..	0	0
Foreign companies (branches)	30	28	28	27	30	32	31	30
All undertakings	153	149	139	131	132	133	121	129
Composite								
Domestic undertakings	0	0	0	0	0	0	0	1
Foreign controlled undertakings	0	0	0	0	0	0	0	0
Foreign companies (branches)	0	0	0	0	0	0	0	0
All undertakings	0	0	0	0	0	0	0	1
Reinsurance								
Domestic undertakings	115	102	87	77	75	67	61	64
Foreign controlled undertakings	0	0	0	..	..	..	0	0
Foreign companies (branches)	3	0	0	0	0	0	0	0
All undertakings	118	102	87	77	75	67	61	64
Total								
Domestic undertakings	299	285	253	234	228	216	196	209
Foreign controlled undertakings	0	..	..	..	..	..	0	0
Foreign companies (branches)	43	37	36	35	38	43	42	42
All undertakings	342	322	289	269	266	259	238	251
2.2 Number of employees								
Insurance undertakings	10 626	9 696	8 682	8 887	8 095	9 404	..	..
Intermediaries	..	..	..	..	..	..	..	..
Total	..	9 696	8 682	8 887	..	..	..	..

.. Not available

Note: Detailed metadata at: *http://metalinks.oecd.org/ins/20190221/6298.*

Source: OECD Insurance Statistics (database)

ISRAEL

Table 1. Selected aggregates

Million ILS

	2010	2011	2012	2013	2014	2015	2016	2017
1.1 Insurance business written in the reporting country								
1.1.1 Insurance business, by ownership								
Gross premiums								
Domestic undertakings	42 003	45 317	48 086	50 339	51 400	54 869	58 153	62 730
Foreign controlled undertakings	8 903	9 663	840	889	953	1 135	1 165	1 234
Foreign companies (branches)	0	..	..	..	..	..	..	..
All undertakings	42 003	45 317	48 086	50 339	51 400	54 869	58 153	62 730
Premiums ceded								
Domestic undertakings	5 868	6 529	6 877	6 418	5 934	6 356	8 756	8 468
Foreign controlled undertakings	816	894	185	164	162	232	225	228
Foreign companies (branches)	..	..	..	..	..	..	..	..
All undertakings	5 868	6 529	6 877	6 418	5 934	6 356	8 756	8 468
Net written premiums								
Domestic undertakings	36 135	38 788	41 209	43 921	45 466	48 512	49 398	54 263
Foreign controlled undertakings	8 087	8 769	656	726	791	903	940	1 006
Foreign companies (branches)	..	..	..	..	..	..	..	..
All undertakings	36 135	38 788	41 209	43 921	45 466	48 512	49 398	54 263
1.1.2 Insurance business on foreign risks, gross premiums								
Life	..	..	..	..	..	..	..	..
Non-life	..	..	..	..	..	..	..	..
Composite	..	3	..	..	..	..	..	..
of which:								
Life	..	..	..	..	..	..	..	..
Non-life	..	3	..	..	..	..	..	..
Total	..	3	..	..	..	..	..	..
1.1.3 Life insurance payments, by class, gross premiums								
Annuities	1 772	1 593	1 542	1 361	1 194	1 084	1 273	1 125
Unit linked	14 974	16 662	17 673	18 557	18 236	20 266	20 897	23 867
Other life insurance	4 911	5 654	6 242	6 709	7 141	8 066	8 492	8 730
Total life insurance	21 656	23 909	25 458	26 627	26 571	29 416	30 662	33 722
***of which:** Pension contracts*	14 762	..	..	..	..	..	..	..
1.1.4 Non-life insurance payments, by class, gross premiums								
Motor vehicle insurance	9 867	10 358	10 673	11 040	11 439	11 775	13 053	13 396
Marine, aviation and other transport insurance	43	41	41	38	38	39	38	36
Freight insurance	160	173	180	169	170	174	176	187
Fire and other property damage insurance	3 326	3 475	4 082	4 283	4 292	4 238	4 375	4 481
Pecuniary loss insurance	226	0	277	284	278	307	335	348
General liability insurance	2 353	2 354	2 487	2 575	2 697	2 814	2 917	3 094
Accident and health	3 607	3 950	4 396	4 869	5 425	5 678	6 086	6 961
***of which:** Health*	3 066	..	3 580	3 859	4 189	4 203	4 448	5 144
Other non-life insurance	766	1 056	492	452	492	426	502	506
Treaty reinsurance	0	..	..	..	0	0	0	..
Total non-life insurance	20 347	21 408	22 628	23 712	24 830	25 452	27 483	29 009
1.2 Gross claims payments								
Life								
Domestic undertakings	..	..	..	0	3	6	8	c
Foreign controlled undertakings	0	..	..	..	..	..	0	c
Foreign companies (branches)	..	..	..	..	..	..	..	..
All undertakings	0	..	..	0	3	6	8	c
Non-life								
Domestic undertakings	1 138	1 303	1 395	2 013	2 470	2 589	2 180	2 124
Foreign controlled undertakings	0	..	..	..	..	39	72	22
Foreign companies (branches)	..	..	..	..	..	..	..	..
All undertakings	1 138	1 303	1 395	2 013	2 470	2 589	2 180	2 124
Composite								
Domestic undertakings	22 199	24 636	25 830	24 594	27 644	30 828	31 879	35 461
Foreign controlled undertakings	4 398	5 004	393	280	462	640	538	0
Foreign companies (branches)	..	..	..	..	..	..	..	..
All undertakings	22 199	24 636	25 830	24 594	27 644	30 828	31 879	35 461
of which:								
Life	10 349	11 651	12 472	12 644	13 825	15 363	16 243	18 411
Domestic undertakings	10 349	11 651	12 472	12 644	13 825	15 363	16 243	18 411
Foreign controlled undertakings	3 054	3 564	27	18	26	39	36	42
Foreign companies (branches)	..	..	..	..	..	..	..	..
All undertakings	10 349	11 651	12 472	12 644	13 825	15 363	16 243	18 411
Non-life	11 849	12 985	13 358	11 949	13 819	15 465	15 636	17 051
Domestic undertakings	11 849	12 985	13 358	11 949	13 819	15 465	15 636	17 051
Foreign controlled undertakings	1 344	1 440	366	262	436	600	502	575
Foreign companies (branches)	..	..	..	..	..	..	..	..
All undertakings	11 849	12 985	13 358	11 949	13 819	15 465	15 636	17 051
Total								
Domestic undertakings	23 337	25 939	27 225	26 607	30 117	33 422	34 067	37 598
Foreign controlled undertakings	4 398	5 004	393	280	462	679	609	22
Foreign companies (branches)	..	..	..	..	..	..	..	..
All undertakings	23 337	25 939	27 225	26 607	30 117	33 422	34 067	37 598

ISRAEL

Table 1. Selected aggregates (cont.)

Million ILS

	2010	2011	2012	2013	2014	2015	2016	2017
1.3 Commissions								
Life								
Domestic undertakings	0	..	..	0	6	15	19	c
Foreign controlled undertakings	0	..	..	..	..	..	0	..
Foreign companies (branches)	..	..	..	..	..	..	..	..
All undertakings	0	..	..	0	6	15	19	c
Non-life								
Domestic undertakings	1 138	159	175	248	281	317	291	341
Foreign controlled undertakings	0	..	..	..	..	0	0	0
Foreign companies (branches)	..	..	..	..	..	..	..	..
All undertakings	1 138	159	175	248	281	317	291	341
Composite								
Domestic undertakings	4 783	5 070	5 512	5 688	5 940	6 296	6 709	7 109
Foreign controlled undertakings	897	947	41	39	..	42	40	..
Foreign companies (branches)	..	..	..	..	..	..	..	..
All undertakings	4 783	5 070	5 512	5 688	5 940	6 296	6 709	7 109
of which:								
Life	2 201	2 328	2 577	2 571	2 639	2 912	3 097	3 215
Domestic undertakings	2 201	2 328	2 577	2 571	2 639	2 912	3 097	3 215
Foreign controlled undertakings	614	635	1	1	1	1	1	1
Foreign companies (branches)	..	..	..	..	..	..	..	..
All undertakings	2 201	2 328	2 577	2 571	2 639	2 912	3 097	3 215
Non-life	2 583	2 742	2 936	3 118	3 300	3 384	3 612	3 893
Domestic undertakings	2 583	2 742	2 936	3 118	3 300	3 384	3 612	3 893
Foreign controlled undertakings	283	312	40	38	38	41	39	37
Foreign companies (branches)	..	..	..	..	..	..	..	..
All undertakings	2 583	2 742	2 936	3 118	3 300	3 384	3 612	3 893
Total								
Domestic undertakings	5 921	5 229	5 688	5 936	6 226	6 628	7 019	7 464
Foreign controlled undertakings	897	947	41	39	..	42	40	0
Foreign companies (branches)	..	..	..	..	..	..	..	..
All undertakings	5 921	5 229	5 688	5 936	6 226	6 628	7 019	7 464
1.4 Gross operating expenses								
Life								
Domestic undertakings	0	..	..	1	10	32	32	c
Foreign controlled undertakings	0	..	..	..	..	..	0	..
Foreign companies (branches)	..	..	..	..	..	..	..	..
All undertakings	0	..	..	1	10	32	32	c
Non-life								
Domestic undertakings	184	306	305	449	322	402	380	417
Foreign controlled undertakings	0	..	..	..	..	30	29	33
Foreign companies (branches)	..	..	..	..	..	..	..	..
All undertakings	184	306	305	449	322	402	380	417
Composite								
Domestic undertakings	4 136	5 198	5 270	5 285	5 169	5 719	6 033	6 504
Foreign controlled undertakings	881	1 158	260	272	276	282	275	278
Foreign companies (branches)	..	..	..	..	..	..	..	..
All undertakings	4 136	5 198	5 270	5 285	5 169	5 719	6 033	6 504
of which:								
Life	1 965	2 104	2 323	2 542	2 608	2 790	2 707	2 849
Domestic undertakings	1 965	2 104	2 323	2 542	2 608	2 790	2 707	2 849
Foreign controlled undertakings	521	565	53	61	56	54	55	51
Foreign companies (branches)	..	..	..	..	..	..	..	..
All undertakings	1 965	2 104	2 323	2 542	2 608	2 790	2 707	2 849
Non-life	2 172	2 445	2 373	2 502	2 561	2 721	2 785	3 002
Domestic undertakings	2 172	2 445	2 373	2 502	2 561	2 721	2 785	3 002
Foreign controlled undertakings	360	368	208	212	220	228	220	227
Foreign companies (branches)	..	..	..	..	..	..	..	..
All undertakings	2 172	2 445	2 373	2 502	2 561	2 721	2 785	3 002
Total								
Domestic undertakings	4 321	5 504	5 574	5 736	5 501	6 153	6 445	6 940
Foreign controlled undertakings	881	1 158	260	272	276	312	304	311
Foreign companies (branches)	..	..	..	..	..	..	..	..
All undertakings	4 321	5 504	5 574	5 736	5 501	6 153	6 445	6 940

Table 1. Selected aggregates (cont.)

Million ILS

	2010	2011	2012	2013	2014	2015	2016	2017
1.5 Insurance business written abroad by branches, gross premiums								
Life								
Branches and agencies	..	..	..	..	..	..	..	..
Subsidaries	..	..	..	..	..	..	..	..
Total	..	..	..	..	..	..	..	..
Non-life								
Branches and agencies	..	..	..	..	..	..	..	..
Subsidaries	..	..	..	..	..	..	..	..
Total	..	..	..	..	..	..	..	..
Composite								
Branches and agencies	..	..	..	..	..	..	..	..
Subsidaries	..	..	..	..	..	..	..	..
Total	..	..	..	..	..	..	..	..
of which:								
Life	..	..	..	..	..	..	..	..
Branches and agencies	..	..	..	..	..	..	..	..
Subsidaries	..	..	..	..	..	..	..	..
Total	..	..	..	..	..	..	..	..
Non-life	..	..	..	..	..	..	..	..
Branches and agencies	..	..	..	..	..	..	..	..
Subsidaries	..	..	..	..	..	..	..	..
Total	..	..	..	..	..	..	..	..
Total								
Branches and agencies	..	..	..	..	..	..	..	..
Subsidaries	..	..	..	..	..	..	..	..
Total	..	..	..	..	..	..	..	..

.. Not available; c Confidential data

Note: Detailed metadata at: *http://metalinks.oecd.org/ins/20190221/901a.*

The statistical data for Israel are supplied by and under the responsibility of the relevant Israeli authorities. The use of such data by the OECD is without prejudice to the status of the Golan Heights, East Jerusalem and Israeli settlements in the West Bank under the terms of international law.

Source: OECD Insurance Statistics (database)

ISRAEL

Table 2. Number of companies and employees

	2010	2011	2012	2013	2014	2015	2016	2017
2.1 Number of companies								
Life								
Domestic undertakings	..	..	..	1	1	2	2	1
Foreign controlled undertakings	..	..	..	..	..	0	..	..
Foreign companies (branches)	..	..	..	..	..	0	..	..
All undertakings	0	..	..	1	1	2	2	1
Non-life								
Domestic undertakings	11	10	10	12	12	10	10	10
Foreign controlled undertakings	..	..	..	..	..	1	1	1
Foreign companies (branches)	2	..	2	2	3	3	3	3
All undertakings	13	10	12	14	15	13	13	13
Composite								
Domestic undertakings	13	13	13	10	10	11	10	10
Foreign controlled undertakings	3	2	1	1	1	1	1	1
Foreign companies (branches)	..	2	..	..	..	0	..	..
All undertakings	13	15	13	10	10	11	10	10
Reinsurance								
Domestic undertakings	0	..	..	..	..	0	..	..
Foreign controlled undertakings	..	..	..	..	..	0	..	..
Foreign companies (branches)	..	..	..	..	..	0	..	..
All undertakings	0	..	..	..	0	0	0	..
Total								
Domestic undertakings	24	23	23	23	23	23	22	21
Foreign controlled undertakings	3	2	1	1	1	2	..	2
Foreign companies (branches)	2	2	2	2	3	3	3	3
All undertakings	26	25	25	25	26	26	25	24
2.2 Number of employees								
Insurance undertakings	..	..	..	..	..	..	..	..
Intermediaries	..	..	..	..	..	..	..	..
Total	..	..	..	..	..	..	..	..

.. Not available

Note: Detailed metadata at: *http://metalinks.oecd.org/ins/20190221/901a.*

The statistical data for Israel are supplied by and under the responsibility of the relevant Israeli authorities. The use of such data by the OECD is without prejudice to the status of the Golan Heights, East Jerusalem and Israeli settlements in the West Bank under the terms of international law.

Source: OECD Insurance Statistics (database)

ITALY

Table 1. Selected aggregates

Million EUR

	2010	2011	2012	2013	2014	2015	2016	2017
1.1 Insurance business written in the reporting country								
1.1.1 Insurance business, by ownership								
Gross premiums								
Domestic undertakings	127 810	112 362	107 192	120 973	145 244	149 011	136 278	132 924
Foreign controlled undertakings	37 340	32 577	29 138	34 302	44 419	45 694	44 287	41 990
Foreign companies (branches)	355	416	399	373	375	473	521	504
All undertakings	128 165	112 778	107 591	121 345	145 619	149 484	136 799	133 429
Premiums ceded								
Domestic undertakings	5 257	5 043	5 178	4 513	4 203	4 079	4 914	4 939
Foreign controlled undertakings	1 624	1 166	1 392	1 116	991	983	1 822	1 829
Foreign companies (branches)	52	57	45	49	58	53	62	57
All undertakings	5 308	5 099	5 223	4 563	4 262	4 132	4 976	4 996
Net written premiums								
Domestic undertakings	122 553	107 319	102 014	116 459	141 041	144 932	131 364	127 986
Foreign controlled undertakings	35 715	31 411	27 746	33 186	43 428	44 711	42 465	40 160
Foreign companies (branches)	304	359	354	323	317	420	459	447
All undertakings	122 857	107 678	102 368	116 782	141 358	145 352	131 823	128 433
1.1.2 Insurance business on foreign risks, gross premiums								
Life	6	1	0	1	1	1	1	1
Non-life	88	60	50	53	59	54	59	57
Composite	1 554	1 608	1 935	2 044	1 904	2 016	2 070	2 037
of which:								
Life	1 216	1 213	1 327	1 232	1 073	1 166	1 255	1 252
Non-life	339	395	607	811	831	849	814	784
Total	1 648	1 670	1 984	2 098	1 963	2 071	2 130	2 095
1.1.3 Life insurance payments, by class, gross premiums								
Annuities	1 077	1 309	1 243	1 012	956	737	710	716
Unit linked	15 409	12 496	13 800	15 497	21 829	31 884	23 848	31 305
Other life insurance	73 627	60 064	54 597	68 501	87 639	82 220	77 596	66 709
Total life insurance	90 114	73 869	69 639	85 010	110 424	114 842	102 154	98 730
***of which:** Pension contracts*	4 026	4 116	4 296	3 825	4 873	5 492	5 848	6 308
1.1.4 Non-life insurance payments, by class, gross premiums								
Motor vehicle insurance	19 886	20 815	20 247	18 661	17 468	16 590	16 260	16 097
Marine, aviation and other transport insurance	461	432	366	327	334	326	417	387
Freight insurance	225	234	227	208	212	204	198	202
Fire and other property damage insurance	5 090	5 127	5 056	5 269	5 611	5 544	5 863	5 851
Pecuniary loss insurance	1 319	1 223	961	967	1 018	1 034	1 119	1 204
General liability insurance	3 006	2 979	2 972	2 905	2 879	2 952	3 073	3 094
Accident and health	5 281	5 306	5 151	5 144	5 221	5 415	5 868	6 200
***of which:** Health*	2 210	2 229	2 150	2 114	2 149	2 323	2 655	2 909
Other non-life insurance	897	944	698	1 163	988	1 082	1 217	1 293
Treaty reinsurance	240	275	417	0	0	0	0	0
Total non-life insurance	36 405	37 333	36 095	34 646	33 730	33 147	34 015	34 326
1.2 Gross claims payments								
Life								
Domestic undertakings	28 862	31 179	29 764	23 754	22 852	22 955	21 169	21 166
Foreign controlled undertakings	9 213	14 849	14 078	11 058	10 413	12 229	10 866	10 142
Foreign companies (branches)	0	0	0	0	0	0	0	0
All undertakings	28 862	31 179	29 764	23 754	22 852	22 955	21 169	21 166
Non-life								
Domestic undertakings	5 907	5 191	5 084	5 061	5 016	4 931	4 776	5 209
Foreign controlled undertakings	1 767	1 748	1 802	1 758	1 853	2 005	2 008	2 021
Foreign companies (branches)	217	249	257	231	257	308	369	364
All undertakings	6 124	5 440	5 341	5 292	5 273	5 240	5 144	5 574
Composite								
Domestic undertakings	59 344	66 523	67 451	64 138	61 204	65 892	59 690	68 163
Foreign controlled undertakings	16 318	17 536	16 282	16 899	14 972	16 842	16 097	17 146
Foreign companies (branches)	0	0	0	0	0	0	0	0
All undertakings	59 344	66 523	67 451	64 138	61 204	65 892	59 690	68 163
of which:								
Life	37 621	45 192	47 143	44 754	43 279	48 546	43 755	52 096
Domestic undertakings	37 621	45 192	47 143	44 754	43 279	48 546	43 755	52 096
Foreign controlled undertakings	11 065	12 633	11 858	12 685	11 217	12 693	12 061	13 358
Foreign companies (branches)	0	0	0	0	0	0	0	0
All undertakings	37 621	45 192	47 143	44 754	43 279	48 546	43 755	52 096
Non-life	21 723	21 330	20 308	19 384	17 925	17 346	15 935	16 067
Domestic undertakings	21 723	21 330	20 308	19 384	17 925	17 346	15 935	16 067
Foreign controlled undertakings	217	4 903	4 424	4 215	3 754	4 149	4 037	3 788
Foreign companies (branches)	0	0	0	0	0	0	0	0
All undertakings	21 723	21 330	20 308	19 384	17 925	17 346	15 935	16 067
Total								
Domestic undertakings	94 113	102 893	102 298	92 953	89 071	93 778	85 635	94 539
Foreign controlled undertakings	27 298	34 132	32 162	29 715	27 238	31 075	28 972	29 309
Foreign companies (branches)	217	249	257	231	257	308	369	364
All undertakings	94 331	103 141	102 555	93 185	89 328	94 087	86 003	94 904

ITALY

Table 1. Selected aggregates (cont.)

Million EUR

	2010	2011	2012	2013	2014	2015	2016	2017
1.3 Commissions								
Life								
Domestic undertakings	988	727	601	576	650	641	626	620
Foreign controlled undertakings	607	532	405	384	430	436	449	434
Foreign companies (branches)	0	0	0	0	0	0	0	0
All undertakings	988	727	601	576	650	641	626	620
Non-life								
Domestic undertakings	1 932	1 721	1 620	1 576	1 656	1 706	1 748	1 829
Foreign controlled undertakings	655	629	560	548	608	734	767	752
Foreign companies (branches)	72	82	78	73	72	93	107	108
All undertakings	2 004	1 803	1 698	1 649	1 729	1 799	1 855	1 937
Composite								
Domestic undertakings	7 578	7 516	7 101	7 278	7 573	7 699	7 571	7 600
Foreign controlled undertakings	2 041	1 916	1 778	1 830	1 978	2 106	2 006	2 073
Foreign companies (branches)	0	0	0	0	0	0	0	0
All undertakings	7 578	7 516	7 101	7 278	7 573	7 699	7 571	7 600
of which:								
Life	2 384	2 187	1 868	2 088	2 273	2 447	2 306	2 317
Domestic undertakings	2 384	2 187	1 868	2 088	2 273	2 447	2 306	2 317
Foreign controlled undertakings	696	560	413	450	510	542	504	550
Foreign companies (branches)	0	0	0	0	0	0	0	0
All undertakings	2 384	2 187	1 868	2 088	2 273	2 447	2 306	2 317
Non-life	5 194	5 329	5 232	5 190	5 300	5 251	5 265	5 283
Domestic undertakings	5 194	5 329	5 232	5 190	5 300	5 251	5 265	5 283
Foreign controlled undertakings	1 346	1 356	1 366	1 380	1 468	1 564	1 502	1 523
Foreign companies (branches)	0	0	0	0	0	0	0	0
All undertakings	5 194	5 329	5 232	5 190	5 300	5 251	5 265	5 283
Total								
Domestic undertakings	10 498	9 964	9 322	9 431	9 879	10 046	9 945	10 049
Foreign controlled undertakings	3 304	3 078	2 743	2 763	3 015	3 277	3 222	3 259
Foreign companies (branches)	72	82	78	73	72	93	107	108
All undertakings	10 570	10 046	9 399	9 504	9 952	10 139	10 052	10 157
1.4 Gross operating expenses								
Life								
Domestic undertakings	1 310	1 033	912	876	953	948	963	970
Foreign controlled undertakings	778	734	600	570	622	634	673	658
Foreign companies (branches)	0	0	0	0	0	0	0	0
All undertakings	1 310	1 033	912	876	953	948	963	970
Non-life								
Domestic undertakings	2 443	2 324	2 168	2 154	2 252	2 332	2 390	2 501
Foreign controlled undertakings	884	873	750	794	818	968	1 012	992
Foreign companies (branches)	109	119	115	112	110	144	176	174
All undertakings	2 552	2 442	2 283	2 266	2 362	2 476	2 565	2 676
Composite								
Domestic undertakings	9 367	9 381	9 321	9 490	9 686	9 829	9 860	9 929
Foreign controlled undertakings	2 485	2 363	2 304	2 294	2 443	2 632	2 566	2 658
Foreign companies (branches)	0	0	0	0	0	0	0	0
All undertakings	9 367	9 381	9 321	9 490	9 686	9 829	9 860	9 929
of which:								
Life	3 069	2 867	2 788	2 970	3 109	3 292	3 196	3 223
Domestic undertakings	3 069	2 867	2 788	2 970	3 109	3 292	3 196	3 223
Foreign controlled undertakings	857	724	635	628	696	743	708	773
Foreign companies (branches)	0	0	0	0	0	0	0	0
All undertakings	3 069	2 867	2 788	2 970	3 109	3 292	3 196	3 223
Non-life	6 299	6 514	6 532	6 520	6 577	6 537	6 664	6 706
Domestic undertakings	6 299	6 514	6 532	6 520	6 577	6 537	6 664	6 706
Foreign controlled undertakings	1 628	1 639	1 669	1 667	1 747	1 889	1 858	1 885
Foreign companies (branches)	0	0	0	0	0	0	0	0
All undertakings	6 299	6 514	6 532	6 520	6 577	6 537	6 664	6 706
Total								
Domestic undertakings	13 121	12 737	12 401	12 520	12 891	13 109	13 213	13 400
Foreign controlled undertakings	4 147	3 971	3 653	3 658	3 883	4 234	4 251	4 307
Foreign companies (branches)	109	119	115	112	110	144	176	174
All undertakings	13 229	12 856	12 516	12 633	13 001	13 253	13 388	13 574

ITALY

Table 1. Selected aggregates (cont.)

Million EUR

	2010	2011	2012	2013	2014	2015	2016	2017
1.5 Insurance business written abroad by branches, gross premiums								
Life								
Branches and agencies	0	0	0	0	1	1	3	1
Subsidaries	1 327	1 938	2 813	3 333	3 469	4 224	1 339	1 712
Total	1 327	1 938	2 813	3 333	3 469	4 226	1 342	1 713
Non-life								
Branches and agencies	22	24	9	12	12	9	10	13
Subsidaries	29	0	0	0	0	0	0	0
Total	51	24	9	12	12	9	10	13
Composite								
Branches and agencies	667	717	762	823	892	868	1 376	1 114
Subsidaries	58 418	56 657	57 155	56 340	54 902	58 541	57 863	60 367
Total	59 085	57 375	57 917	57 163	55 795	59 409	59 239	61 482
of which:								
Life	41 238	38 781	39 265	39 445	39 878	42 059	41 554	43 469
Branches and agencies	88	106	127	154	175	235	477	215
Subsidaries	41 151	38 675	39 138	39 291	39 703	41 824	41 077	43 254
Total	41 238	38 781	39 265	39 445	39 878	42 059	41 554	43 469
Non-life	17 847	18 593	18 652	17 718	15 917	17 350	17 685	18 012
Branches and agencies	579	611	634	668	718	633	899	899
Subsidaries	17 268	17 982	18 018	17 049	15 199	16 717	16 785	17 113
Total	17 847	18 593	18 652	17 718	15 917	17 350	17 685	18 012
Total								
Branches and agencies	689	741	771	835	905	878	1 390	1 128
Subsidaries	59 775	58 596	59 968	59 673	58 371	62 765	59 202	62 079
Total	60 464	59 337	60 739	60 508	59 276	63 643	60 592	63 207

Note: Detailed metadata at: *http://metalinks.oecd.org/ins/20190221/99cd.*
Source: OECD Insurance Statistics (database)

ITALY

Table 2. Number of companies and employees

	2010	2011	2012	2013	2014	2015	2016	2017
2.1 Number of companies								
Life								
Domestic undertakings	45	43	41	41	38	35	32	30
Foreign controlled undertakings	23	24	23	23	20	19	17	13
Foreign companies (branches)	20	21	20	17	19	20	22	19
All undertakings	65	64	61	58	57	55	54	49
Non-life								
Domestic undertakings	76	71	69	67	63	58	54	50
Foreign controlled undertakings	25	24	21	20	18	19	18	16
Foreign companies (branches)	55	59	61	65	60	65	65	73
All undertakings	131	130	130	132	123	123	119	123
Composite								
Domestic undertakings	30	28	25	23	21	21	21	20
Foreign controlled undertakings	10	11	9	8	8	9	10	9
Foreign companies (branches)	9	9	12	13	14	14	13	14
All undertakings	39	37	37	36	35	35	34	34
Reinsurance								
Domestic undertakings	0	0	0	0	0	0	0	0
Foreign controlled undertakings	0	0	0	0	0	0	0	0
Foreign companies (branches)	7	8	7	7	7	7	7	7
All undertakings	7	8	7	7	7	7	7	7
Total								
Domestic undertakings	151	142	135	131	122	114	107	100
Foreign controlled undertakings	58	59	53	51	46	47	45	38
Foreign companies (branches)	91	97	100	102	100	106	107	113
All undertakings	242	239	235	233	222	220	214	213
2.2 Number of employees								
Insurance undertakings	41 234	40 817	40 798	39 887	40 259	40 588	40 872	40 386
Intermediaries	221 417	226 235	220 130	227 444	220 288	220 850	212 596	..
Total	262 651	267 052	260 928	267 331	260 547	261 438	253 468	..

.. Not available

Note: Detailed metadata at: *http://metalinks.oecd.org/ins/20190221/99cd.*

Source: OECD Insurance Statistics (database)

JAPAN

Table 1. Selected aggregates

Million JPY

	2010	2011	2012	2013	2014	2015	2016	2017
1.1 Insurance business written in the reporting country								
1.1.1 Insurance business, by ownership								
Gross premiums								
Domestic undertakings	40 592 027	41 906 428	44 184 695	42 971 395	46 031 579	46 908 456	42 615 488	41 452 663
Foreign controlled undertakings	3 937 600	4 089 357	6 746 278	6 184 716	6 724 592	7 046 820	6 617 836	6 432 494
Foreign companies (branches)	3 184 939	4 051 225	2 028 538	1 699 621	1 548 143	1 537 624	1 703 444	1 739 958
All undertakings	43 776 966	45 360 413	37 140 563	34 738 150	37 222 352	37 748 110	44 318 932	43 192 621
Premiums ceded								
Domestic undertakings	2 211 394	2 596 877	3 820 152	3 823 919	4 207 229	4 127 260	4 449 638	4 176 204
Foreign controlled undertakings	827 426	1 012 341	2 083 368	1 802 239	2 084 233	1 890 218	2 143 727	1 733 566
Foreign companies (branches)	381 244	554 339	20 507	38 391	47 768	75 917	214 477	239 041
All undertakings	2 592 633	3 041 779	2 188 965	1 780 848	2 129 106	2 022 086	4 664 115	4 415 245
Net written premiums								
Domestic undertakings	38 380 635	39 309 551	40 364 544	39 147 476	41 824 350	42 781 196	38 165 836	37 276 448
Foreign controlled undertakings	3 080 177	3 077 014	4 662 910	4 382 477	4 640 359	5 156 602	4 474 105	4 698 925
Foreign companies (branches)	2 804 409	3 500 605	2 008 031	1 661 230	1 500 375	1 461 707	1 488 976	1 499 865
All undertakings	41 185 044	42 322 354	34 951 598	32 957 302	35 093 246	35 726 024	39 654 812	38 776 313
1.1.2 Insurance business on foreign risks, gross premiums								
Life	..	..	..	..	..	..	..	..
Non-life	..	..	..	..	..	..	..	..
Composite total	..	..	..	..	..	..	..	..
Total	..	..	..	..	..	..	..	..
1.1.3 Life insurance payments, by class, gross premiums								
Annuities	..	..	4 374 166	4 312 468	5 154 122	4 729 892	4 340 846	3 607 407
Unit linked	..	..	..	..	..	..	..	..
Other life insurance	..	..	29 076 673	27 864 772	30 015 418	31 464 495	27 968 949	27 990 703
Total life insurance	34 454 319	35 863 385	33 450 839	32 177 240	35 169 540	36 194 387	32 309 795	31 598 110
***of which:** Pension contracts*	..	..	3 683 892	3 851 878	4 175 622	4 562 867	3 057 696	2 953 431
1.1.4 Non-life insurance payments, by class, gross premiums								
Motor vehicle insurance	3 541 931	3 650 671	5 268 338	5 632 807	5 786 949	5 916 489	6 026 253	5 814 388
Marine, aviation and other transport insurance	305 343	305 977	149 531	170 502	170 115	186 542	159 142	152 632
Freight insurance	64 556	67 288	217 090	242 939	248 817	242 488	230 397	239 546
Fire and other property damage insurance	1 619 666	1 762 054	1 787 943	1 983 049	2 104 111	2 228 178	..	..
Pecuniary loss insurance	..	..	216 797	266 835	299 082	342 570	..	..
General liability insurance	521 081	535 395	519 985	584 318	598 945	615 167	633 290	657 637
Accident and health	1 211 200	1 262 653	780 078	897 507	979 477	982 614	..	..
***of which:** Health*	..	..	-216	76	214	-152	..	..
Other non-life insurance	..	2 096 987	132 908	154 909	169 874	183 922	..	..
Treaty reinsurance	..	..	..	..	..	..	..	..
Total non-life insurance	7 263 777	9 730 581	9 072 670	9 932 866	10 357 370	10 697 970	10 859 799	10 750 127
1.2 Gross claims payments								
Life								
Domestic undertakings	30 677 277	29 178 265	31 012 138	33 069 327	34 214 304	31 685 988	28 227 418	28 115 903
Foreign controlled undertakings	2 821 726	2 738 842	5 218 820	6 584 738	6 428 288	5 559 928	5 107 453	5 198 975
Foreign companies (branches)	1 372 136	1 583 330	673 623	709 471	738 243	768 206	786 644	827 193
All undertakings	32 049 413	30 761 595	31 685 761	33 778 798	34 952 547	32 454 194	29 014 062	28 943 096
Non-life								
Domestic undertakings	4 243 987	9 249 885	6 215 207	5 904 278	5 953 809	5 917 050	6 694 135	5 856 017
Foreign controlled undertakings	218 720	400 264	251 245	341 353	373 601	366 795	383 518	237 359
Foreign companies (branches)	174 446	366 743	..	..	..	..	104 648	98 935
All undertakings	4 418 433	9 616 628	..	..	..	..	6 798 783	5 954 952
Composite, all undertakings	..	..	..	..	..	..	..	..
Total								
Domestic undertakings	34 921 264	38 428 150	37 227 345	38 973 605	40 168 113	37 603 038	34 921 553	33 971 920
Foreign controlled undertakings	3 040 446	3 139 106	5 470 065	6 926 091	6 801 889	5 926 723	5 490 971	5 436 334
Foreign companies (branches)	1 546 582	1 950 073	673 623	709 471	738 243	768 206	891 292	926 128
All undertakings	36 467 846	40 378 223	31 685 761	33 778 798	34 952 547	32 454 194	35 812 845	34 898 048
1.3 Commissions								
Life								
Domestic undertakings	..	..	..	..	..	..	..	..
Foreign controlled undertakings	..	..	..	..	..	..	..	..
Foreign companies (branches)	..	..	..	..	..	..	..	..
All undertakings	..	..	..	..	..	..	..	..
Non-life								
Domestic undertakings	1 190 122	1 241 891	1 141 653	1 149 357	1 229 205	1 273 631	1 240 454	1 221 324
Foreign controlled undertakings	70 683	71 775	48 003	25 883	33 975	37 223	20 067	-15 311
Foreign companies (branches)	64 395	67 079	..	..	..	..	-19 897	-29 330
All undertakings	1 254 517	1 308 970	..	..	..	..	1 220 557	1 191 994
Composite, all undertakings	..	..	..	..	..	..	..	..
Total								
Domestic undertakings	1 190 122	1 241 891	1 141 653	1 149 357	1 229 205	1 273 631	1 240 454	1 221 324
Foreign controlled undertakings	70 683	71 775	48 003	25 883	33 975	37 223	20 067	-15 311
Foreign companies (branches)	64 395	67 079	..	..	..	..	-19 897	-29 330
All undertakings	1 254 517	1 308 970	..	..	..	..	1 220 557	1 191 994

JAPAN

Table 1. Selected aggregates (cont.)

Million JPY

	2010	2011	2012	2013	2014	2015	2016	2017
1.4 Gross operating expenses								
Life								
Domestic undertakings	3 768 382	3 679 493	4 030 195	4 068 896	4 178 568	4 356 425	4 369 595	4 385 030
Foreign controlled undertakings	529 937	494 700	838 416	862 622	893 811	945 921	948 132	965 055
Foreign companies (branches)	537 616	565 754	319 261	320 576	320 518	349 858	357 069	366 406
All undertakings	4 305 998	4 245 247	4 349 456	4 389 472	4 499 086	4 706 283	4 726 664	4 751 436
Non-life								
Domestic undertakings	1 637 090	1 688 096	1 229 758	3 034 716	3 189 416	3 275 358	3 247 478	3 206 606
Foreign controlled undertakings	87 975	85 470	69 136	176 725	238 092	249 835	207 689	125 459
Foreign companies (branches)	114 656	124 057	..	..	..	..	34 405	37 023
All undertakings	1 751 746	1 812 153	..	..	..	..	3 281 883	3 243 629
Composite, all undertakings	..	..	..	..	..	..	..	..
Total								
Domestic undertakings	5 405 472	5 367 589	5 259 953	7 103 612	7 367 984	7 631 783	7 617 073	7 591 636
Foreign controlled undertakings	617 912	580 170	907 552	1 039 347	1 131 903	1 195 756	1 155 821	1 090 514
Foreign companies (branches)	652 272	689 811	319 261	320 576	320 518	349 858	391 474	403 429
All undertakings	6 057 744	6 057 400	4 349 456	4 389 472	4 499 086	4 706 283	8 008 547	7 995 065
1.5 Insurance business written abroad by branches, gross premiums								
Life								
Branches and agencies	..	..	..	..	..	..	..	..
Subsidaries	..	..	..	..	..	..	..	..
Total	..	..	..	..	..	..	..	..
Non-life								
Branches and agencies	..	..	..	..	..	..	..	..
Subsidaries	..	..	..	..	..	..	..	..
Total	..	..	..	..	..	..	..	..
Composite total	..	..	..	..	..	..	..	..
Total								
Branches and agencies	..	..	..	..	..	..	..	..
Subsidaries	..	..	..	..	..	..	..	..
Total	..	..	..	..	..	..	..	..

.. Not available

Note: Detailed metadata at: *http://metalinks.oecd.org/ins/20190221/d5a1*.

Source: OECD Insurance Statistics (database)

JAPAN

Table 2. Number of companies and employees

	2010	2011	2012	2013	2014	2015	2016	2017
2.1 Number of companies								
Life								
Domestic undertakings	43	39	40	40	39	38	38	38
Foreign controlled undertakings	15	14	15	15	13	13	13	13
Foreign companies (branches)	4	4	3	3	3	3	3	3
All undertakings	47	43	43	43	42	41	41	41
Non-life								
Domestic undertakings	28	29	30	30	30	30	30	29
Foreign controlled undertakings	5	5	5	6	7	7	7	6
Foreign companies (branches)	22	23	23	22	22	22	21	23
All undertakings	50	52	53	52	52	52	51	52
Composite, all undertakings	**0**	**0**	**0**	**0**	**0**	**0**	**0**	**..**
Reinsurance								
Domestic undertakings	..	2	..	..	..	..	..	..
Foreign controlled undertakings	..	0	..	..	..	..	..	..
Foreign companies (branches)	..	5	..	..	..	..	..	..
All undertakings	..	7	..	..	..	..	..	..
Total								
Domestic undertakings	..	..	..	..	..	68	68	67
Foreign controlled undertakings	..	..	..	..	..	20	20	19
Foreign companies (branches)	..	..	..	..	..	25	24	26
All undertakings	..	..	..	..	..	93	92	93
2.2 Number of employees								
Insurance undertakings	..	..	447 435	221 675	226 043	120 353	..	..
Intermediaries	..	..	..	2 283 335	2 293 863	2 059 743	..	..
Total	..	..	..	2 505 010	2 519 906	2 080 096	..	345 582

.. Not available

Note: Detailed metadata at: *http://metalinks.oecd.org/ins/20190221/d5a1.*

Source: OECD Insurance Statistics (database)

KOREA

Table 1. Selected aggregates

Million KRW

	2010	2011	2012	2013	2014	2015	2016	2017
1.1 Insurance business written in the reporting country								
1.1.1 Insurance business, by ownership								
Gross premiums								
Domestic undertakings	135 405 614	148 670 607	179 792 881	180 479 019	192 380 611	205 460 047	210 800 275	..
Foreign controlled undertakings	14 764 615	15 090 753	16 543 211	15 928 630	13 324 532	15 765 302	16 670 208	..
Foreign companies (branches)	4 250 510	4 083 506	3 894 692	4 755 050	4 594 745	2 267 929	4 629 847	..
All undertakings	139 656 124	152 754 113	183 687 573	185 234 069	196 975 356	207 727 976	215 430 122	..
Premiums ceded								
Domestic undertakings	8 248 307	7 618 035	8 770 133	9 411 425	9 694 294	10 255 858	10 505 959	..
Foreign controlled undertakings	529 774	322 429	581 696	538 227	478 174	638 961	599 183	..
Foreign companies (branches)	407 499	614 890	448 135	456 049	651 726	732 347	817 712	..
All undertakings	8 655 806	8 232 925	9 218 268	9 867 474	10 346 020	10 988 205	11 323 671	..
Net written premiums								
Domestic undertakings	127 157 307	141 052 572	171 022 748	171 067 594	182 686 317	195 204 189	200 294 316	..
Foreign controlled undertakings	14 234 841	14 768 324	15 961 515	15 390 403	12 846 358	15 126 341	16 071 025	..
Foreign companies (branches)	3 843 011	3 468 616	3 446 557	4 299 001	3 943 019	1 535 582	3 812 135	..
All undertakings	131 000 318	144 521 188	174 469 305	175 366 595	186 629 336	196 739 771	204 106 451	..
1.1.2 Insurance business on foreign risks, gross premiums								
Life	..	..	..	..	..	..	..	..
Non-life	1 393 220	..	..	..	..	..	..	..
Composite total	..	..	..	..	..	..	..	..
Total	1 393 220	..	..	..	..	..	..	..
1.1.3 Life insurance payments, by class, gross premiums								
Annuities	16 493 331	17 029 899	29 118 668	25 867 249	23 905 884	24 586 649	21 347 503	..
Unit linked	18 570 246	21 278 374	21 003 522	21 073 957	20 670 949	20 643 073	19 406 180	..
Other life insurance	45 875 642	48 349 089	57 004 710	61 618 265	65 998 453	71 983 930	79 057 566	..
Total life insurance	80 939 219	86 657 362	107 126 900	108 559 471	110 575 286	117 213 652	119 811 249	..
of which: *Pension contracts*	4 037 523	7 039 411	6 187 541	8 103 216	11 817 288	13 694 337	16 718 996	..
1.1.4 Non-life insurance payments, by class, gross premiums								
Motor vehicle insurance	12 712 741	13 714 894	13 667 642	13 692 186	14 188 378	15 635 198	16 975 333	..
Marine, aviation and other transport insurance	1 079 971	1 173 162	1 249 845	1 062 919	1 006 367	971 854	854 536	..
Freight insurance	..	..	..	0	0	..	..	..
Fire and other property damage insurance	343 250	433 977	509 590	515 217	484 799	472 624	471 017	..
Pecuniary loss insurance	1 367 999	1 551 994	1 697 064	1 637 782	1 601 517	1 672 799	1 693 861	..
General liability insurance	834 878	828 088	870 395	947 583	910 341	967 362	1 100 438	..
Accident and health	14 665 164	16 518 450	18 558 162	49 501 658	24 196 315	39 104 233	30 297 640	..
of which: *Health*	5 877 040	6 537 864	7 171 480	83 983	10 090 810	11 740 294	13 406 917	..
Other non-life insurance	25 457 371	30 630 990	38 774 054	8 105 434	32 685 216	30 357 048	42 702 138	..
Treaty reinsurance	..	..	..	0	0	..	..	..
Total non-life insurance	56 461 374	64 851 555	75 326 752	75 462 779	85 163 744	89 181 118	94 094 963	..
1.2 Gross claims payments								
Life								
Domestic undertakings	50 304 985	50 774 694	50 571 293	51 098 146	61 070 702	65 751 692	77 155 805	..
Foreign controlled undertakings	7 571 937	7 803 732	7 981 965	8 103 569	69 035 817	6 945 034	9 505 582	..
Foreign companies (branches)	1 268 464	1 295 108	1 251 467	1 252 924	1 292 842	1 333 124	1 410 493	..
All undertakings	51 573 449	52 069 802	51 822 760	52 351 070	62 363 544	67 084 816	78 566 298	..
Non-life								
Domestic undertakings	21 683 043	23 980 095	26 319 367	22 119 519	30 233 735	30 895 053	32 747 964	..
Foreign controlled undertakings	664 566	620 798	833 963	516 770	844 722	843 763	802 729	..
Foreign companies (branches)	1 043 797	919 952	914 946	7 033 799	1 098 087	1 264 227	1 282 459	..
All undertakings	22 726 840	24 900 047	27 234 313	29 153 318	31 331 823	32 159 280	34 030 423	..
Composite, all undertakings	..	..	..	..	..	..	..	..
Total								
Domestic undertakings	71 988 028	74 754 789	76 890 660	73 217 665	91 304 438	96 646 745	109 903 769	..
Foreign controlled undertakings	8 236 503	8 424 530	8 815 928	8 620 339	69 880 539	7 788 797	10 308 311	..
Foreign companies (branches)	2 312 261	2 215 060	2 166 413	8 286 723	2 390 929	2 597 351	2 692 952	..
All undertakings	74 300 289	76 969 849	79 057 073	81 504 388	93 695 367	99 244 096	112 596 721	..
1.3 Commissions								
Life								
Domestic undertakings	4 774 647	..	..	..	..	..	..	..
Foreign controlled undertakings	1 125 660	..	..	..	..	..	..	..
Foreign companies (branches)	43 548	..	..	..	..	..	..	..
All undertakings	4 818 195	..	..	..	..	..	..	..
Non-life								
Domestic undertakings	2 242 103	..	..	..	..	..	..	..
Foreign controlled undertakings	162 058	..	..	..	..	..	..	..
Foreign companies (branches)	68 803	..	..	..	..	..	..	..
All undertakings	2 310 906	..	..	..	..	..	..	..
Composite, all undertakings	..	..	..	..	..	..	..	..
Total								
Domestic undertakings	7 016 750	..	..	..	..	..	..	..
Foreign controlled undertakings	1 287 718	..	..	..	..	..	..	..
Foreign companies (branches)	112 351	..	..	..	..	..	..	..
All undertakings	7 129 101	..	..	..	..	..	..	..

KOREA

Table 1. Selected aggregates (cont.)

Million KRW

	2010	2011	2012	2013	2014	2015	2016	2017
1.4 Gross operating expenses								
Life								
Domestic undertakings	19 832 046	27 793 931	23 307 641	25 608 456	27 511 983	28 987 407	28 236 989	..
Foreign controlled undertakings	4 698 261	7 229 266	5 189 114	5 278 175	806 034	756 903	5 074 779	..
Foreign companies (branches)	845 704	1 024 103	734 416	770 753	4 595 483	5 009 714	760 976	..
All undertakings	20 677 750	28 818 034	24 042 057	26 379 209	32 107 466	33 997 121	28 997 965	..
Non-life								
Domestic undertakings	9 722 605	9 820 687	11 569 785	11 294 192	16 760 436	13 511 865	14 238 364	..
Foreign controlled undertakings	174 348	121 666	320 770	129 781	245 017	182 669	163 724	..
Foreign companies (branches)	479 237	428 369	331 833	1 592 503	1 116 586	405 386	411 714	..
All undertakings	10 201 842	10 249 056	11 901 618	12 886 695	17 877 022	13 917 251	14 650 078	..
Composite, all undertakings	..	..	..	..	..	..	..	..
Total								
Domestic undertakings	29 554 651	37 614 618	34 877 426	36 902 648	44 272 419	42 499 272	42 475 353	..
Foreign controlled undertakings	4 872 609	7 350 932	5 509 884	5 407 956	1 051 051	939 572	5 238 503	..
Foreign companies (branches)	1 324 941	1 452 472	1 066 249	2 363 256	5 712 069	5 415 100	1 172 690	..
All undertakings	30 879 592	39 067 090	35 943 675	39 265 904	49 984 488	47 914 372	43 648 043	..
1.5 Insurance business written abroad by branches, gross premiums								
Life								
Branches and agencies	..	..	..	..	..	..	..	..
Subsidaries	..	..	..	..	..	..	..	..
Total	..	..	..	..	..	..	..	..
Non-life								
Branches and agencies	..	..	..	..	..	..	..	..
Subsidaries	..	..	..	..	..	..	..	..
Total	1 393 220	..	..	..	..	..	..	..
Composite total	..	..	..	..	..	..	..	..
Total								
Branches and agencies	..	..	..	..	..	..	..	..
Subsidaries	..	..	..	..	..	..	..	..
Total	1 393 220	..	..	..	..	..	..	..

.. Not available

Note: Detailed metadata at: *http://metalinks.oecd.org/ins/20190221/ccc8.*

Source: OECD Insurance Statistics (database)

KOREA

Table 2. Number of companies and employees

	2010	2011	2012	2013	2014	2015	2016	2017
2.1 Number of companies								
Life								
Domestic undertakings	22	22	23	24	24	24	24	..
Foreign controlled undertakings	8	8	8	8	7	7	8	..
Foreign companies (branches)	1	1	1	1	1	1	1	..
All undertakings	23	23	24	25	25	25	25	..
Non-life								
Domestic undertakings	15	15	16	16	17	17	17	..
Foreign controlled undertakings	3	6	6	3	4	4	4	..
Foreign companies (branches)	8	8	8	8	5	5	5	..
All undertakings	23	23	24	24	22	22	22	..
Composite, all undertakings	**0**	**0**	**0**	**0**	**0**	**0**	**0**	..
Reinsurance								
Domestic undertakings	1	1	1	1	1	1	1	..
Foreign controlled undertakings	0	0	..	..	0	0	0	..
Foreign companies (branches)	6	6	6	6	8	8	9	..
All undertakings	7	7	7	7	9	9	10	..
Total								
Domestic undertakings	38	38	40	41	42	42	42	..
Foreign controlled undertakings	11	14	14	11	11	11	12	..
Foreign companies (branches)	15	15	15	15	14	14	15	..
All undertakings	53	53	55	56	56	56	57	..
2.2 Number of employees								
Insurance undertakings	55 927	57 861	62 155	63 859	61 158	59 685	58 833	..
Intermediaries	270 786	278 594	288 362	280 087	245 127	235 319	229 292	..
Total	326 713	336 455	350 517	343 946	306 285	295 004	288 125	..

.. Not available

Note: Detailed metadata at: *http://metalinks.oecd.org/ins/20190221/ccc8.*

Source: OECD Insurance Statistics (database)

LATVIA

Table 1. Selected aggregates

Million EUR

	2010	2011	2012	2013	2014	2015	2016	2017
1.1 Insurance business written in the reporting country								
1.1.1 Insurance business, by ownership								
Gross premiums								
Domestic undertakings	271	326	354	350	371	379	364	419
Foreign controlled undertakings	164	137	155	150	151	188	267	293
Foreign companies (branches)	57	73	93	121	146	152	168	227
All undertakings	328	399	447	471	517	531	532	646
Premiums ceded								
Domestic undertakings	23	24	26	17	19	22	25	44
Foreign controlled undertakings	9	6	5	4	4	7	18	27
Foreign companies (branches)	..	..	..	..	..	..	..	..
All undertakings	23	24	26	17	19	22	25	44
Net written premiums								
Domestic undertakings	248	302	328	333	352	357	339	375
Foreign controlled undertakings	155	131	150	146	147	182	249	266
Foreign companies (branches)	57	73	93	121	146	152	168	227
All undertakings	305	375	421	454	498	509	507	602
1.1.2 Insurance business on foreign risks, gross premiums								
Life	..	..	..	..	..	..	0	0
Non-life	..	..	..	..	..	..	160	204
Composite	..	..	..	..	..	..	0	0
of which:								
Life	..	..	..	..	..	..	0	0
Non-life	..	..	..	..	..	..	..	0
Total	..	..	..	..	..	..	160	204
1.1.3 Life insurance payments, by class, gross premiums								
Annuities	3	0	0	0	0	0	11	18
Unit linked	28	23	21	23	34	43	45	57
Other life insurance	44	50	57	66	73	72	68	70
Total life insurance	75	74	79	89	107	115	124	145
***of which:** Pension contracts*	0	0	0	0	0	0	..	..
1.1.4 Non-life insurance payments, by class, gross premiums								
Motor vehicle insurance	137	184	204	221	222	221	229	301
Marine, aviation and other transport insurance	2	3	3	2	2	2	2	5
Freight insurance	2	5	6	5	3	3	3	1
Fire and other property damage insurance	47	55	63	67	86	84	76	84
Pecuniary loss insurance	7	12	12	11	13	14	12	11
General liability insurance	10	15	21	17	21	21	19	19
Accident and health	36	41	50	46	52	58	55	63
***of which:** Health*	31	34	42	38	42	48	45	54
Other non-life insurance	11	9	10	12	12	13	13	16
Treaty reinsurance	0	0	0	0	0	0	0	0
Total non-life insurance	252	325	368	382	411	416	409	501
1.2 Gross claims payments								
Life								
Domestic undertakings	21	15	19	31	26	29	0	0
Foreign controlled undertakings	20	15	18	26	24	27	0	0
Foreign companies (branches)	11	26	27	31	31	34	0	0
All undertakings	32	41	46	62	57	63	0	0
Non-life								
Domestic undertakings	137	164	169	165	184	198	180	193
Foreign controlled undertakings	79	78	75	68	77	92	139	126
Foreign companies (branches)	15	18	25	38	43	50	60	78
All undertakings	152	182	194	204	226	248	240	271
Composite								
Domestic undertakings	..	..	..	..	..	..	33	43
Foreign controlled undertakings	..	..	..	..	..	..	27	31
Foreign companies (branches)	..	..	..	..	..	..	40	47
All undertakings	..	..	..	..	..	..	72	90
of which:								
Life	..	..	..	..	..	..	72	90
Domestic undertakings	..	..	..	..	..	..	33	43
Foreign controlled undertakings	..	..	..	..	..	..	27	31
Foreign companies (branches)	..	..	..	..	..	..	40	47
All undertakings	..	..	..	..	..	..	72	90
Non-life	..	..	..	..	..	..	..	0
Domestic undertakings	..	..	..	..	..	..	..	0
Foreign controlled undertakings	..	..	..	..	..	..	..	0
Foreign companies (branches)	..	..	..	..	..	..	..	0
All undertakings	..	..	..	..	..	..	..	0
Total								
Domestic undertakings	158	179	188	196	209	227	213	236
Foreign controlled undertakings	99	92	93	94	102	119	166	158
Foreign companies (branches)	26	44	52	69	73	83	99	125
All undertakings	184	223	240	265	283	311	312	361

LATVIA

Table 1. Selected aggregates (cont.)

Million EUR

	2010	2011	2012	2013	2014	2015	2016	2017
1.3 Commissions								
Life								
Domestic undertakings	2	0	1	1	1	0	0	0
Foreign controlled undertakings	2	0	1	1	1	1	0	0
Foreign companies (branches)	1	4	4	5	5	6	..	..
All undertakings	3	4	5	5	6	6	0	0
Non-life								
Domestic undertakings	19	33	38	32	45	34	32	40
Foreign controlled undertakings	5	2	5	..	7	11	16	13
Foreign companies (branches)	1	2	4	10	12	13	..	..
All undertakings	20	35	41	42	58	47	32	40
Composite								
Domestic undertakings	..	..	..	..	..	..	0	1
Foreign controlled undertakings	..	..	..	..	..	..	0	0
Foreign companies (branches)	..	..	..	..	..	..	..	..
All undertakings	..	..	..	..	..	..	0	1
of which:								
Life	..	..	..	..	..	..	0	1
Domestic undertakings	..	..	..	..	..	..	0	1
Foreign controlled undertakings	..	..	..	..	..	..	0	0
Foreign companies (branches)	..	..	..	..	..	..	..	..
All undertakings	..	..	..	..	..	..	0	1
Non-life	..	..	..	..	..	..	..	0
Domestic undertakings	..	..	..	..	..	..	..	0
Foreign controlled undertakings	..	..	..	..	..	..	..	0
Foreign companies (branches)	..	..	..	..	..	..	..	..
All undertakings	..	..	..	..	..	..	..	0
Total								
Domestic undertakings	21	33	38	33	46	34	33	41
Foreign controlled undertakings	6	2	6	1	8	11	16	14
Foreign companies (branches)	2	6	8	15	17	19	..	..
All undertakings	23	39	46	48	64	53	33	41
1.4 Gross operating expenses								
Life								
Domestic undertakings	7	5	4	4	4	4	0	0
Foreign controlled undertakings	6	4	4	4	4	4	0	0
Foreign companies (branches)	..	..	..	..	..	..	..	..
All undertakings	7	5	4	4	4	4	0	0
Non-life								
Domestic undertakings	88	100	110	102	108	109	56	87
Foreign controlled undertakings	48	43	45	40	40	51	30	51
Foreign companies (branches)	..	..	..	..	..	..	..	..
All undertakings	88	100	110	102	108	109	56	87
Composite								
Domestic undertakings	..	..	..	..	..	..	4	5
Foreign controlled undertakings	..	..	..	..	..	..	4	4
Foreign companies (branches)	..	..	..	..	..	..	..	..
All undertakings	..	..	..	..	..	..	4	5
of which:								
Life	..	..	..	..	..	..	4	5
Domestic undertakings	..	..	..	..	..	..	4	5
Foreign controlled undertakings	..	..	..	..	..	..	4	4
Foreign companies (branches)	..	..	..	..	..	..	..	..
All undertakings	..	..	..	..	..	..	4	5
Non-life	..	..	..	..	..	..	..	0
Domestic undertakings	..	..	..	..	..	..	..	0
Foreign controlled undertakings	..	..	..	..	..	..	..	0
Foreign companies (branches)	..	..	..	..	..	..	..	..
All undertakings	..	..	..	..	..	..	..	0
Total								
Domestic undertakings	95	104	115	106	112	113	60	92
Foreign controlled undertakings	54	47	49	44	44	55	34	55
Foreign companies (branches)	..	..	..	..	..	..	..	..
All undertakings	95	104	115	106	112	113	60	92

LATVIA

Table 1. Selected aggregates (cont.)

Million EUR

	2010	2011	2012	2013	2014	2015	2016	2017
1.5 Insurance business written abroad by branches, gross premiums								
Life								
Branches and agencies	0	0	0	0	0	0	0	0
Subsidaries	..	..	..	..	..	..	..	..
Total	0	0	0	0	0	0	0	0
Non-life								
Branches and agencies	56	126	143	158	168	157	158	203
Subsidaries	..	..	..	..	..	..	..	..
Total	56	126	143	158	168	157	158	203
Composite								
Branches and agencies	..	..	..	..	..	..	0	0
Subsidaries	..	..	..	..	..	..	..	..
Total	..	..	..	..	..	..	0	0
of which:								
Life	..	..	..	..	..	..	0	0
Branches and agencies	..	..	..	..	..	..	0	0
Subsidaries	..	..	..	..	..	..	..	..
Total	..	..	..	..	..	..	0	0
Non-life	..	..	..	..	..	..	..	0
Branches and agencies	..	..	..	..	..	..	..	0
Subsidaries	..	..	..	..	..	..	..	..
Total	..	..	..	..	..	..	..	0
Total								
Branches and agencies	56	126	143	158	168	157	158	203
Subsidaries	..	..	..	..	..	..	..	..
Total	56	126	143	158	168	157	158	203

.. Not available

Note: Detailed metadata at: *http://metalinks.oecd.org/ins/20190221/c7e9*.

Source: OECD Insurance Statistics (database)

LATVIA

Table 2. Number of companies and employees

	2010	2011	2012	2013	2014	2015	2016	2017
2.1 Number of companies								
Life								
Domestic undertakings	4	3	2	2	2	2	..	0
Foreign controlled undertakings	2	1	1	1	1	1	..	0
Foreign companies (branches)	5	5	5	5	5	4	..	0
All undertakings	9	8	7	7	7	6	..	0
Non-life								
Domestic undertakings	9	9	7	5	5	6	5	4
Foreign controlled undertakings	4	4	3	2	2	3	3	2
Foreign companies (branches)	6	5	8	7	9	10	8	7
All undertakings	15	14	15	12	14	16	13	11
Composite								
Domestic undertakings	0	0	0	0	0	0	2	2
Foreign controlled undertakings	0	0	0	0	0	0	1	1
Foreign companies (branches)	0	0	0	0	0	0	4	4
All undertakings	..	0	0	0	0	0	6	6
Reinsurance								
Domestic undertakings	0	0	0	0	0	0	..	0
Foreign controlled undertakings	0	0	0	0	0	0	..	0
Foreign companies (branches)	0	0	0	0	0	0	..	0
All undertakings	..	0	0	0	0	0	..	0
Total								
Domestic undertakings	13	12	9	7	7	8	7	6
Foreign controlled undertakings	6	5	4	3	3	4	4	3
Foreign companies (branches)	11	10	13	12	14	14	12	11
All undertakings	24	22	22	19	21	22	19	17
2.2 Number of employees								
Insurance undertakings	2 876	2 873	2 749	2 300	2 121	1 047	..	..
Intermediaries	1 254	1 195	1 168	846	773	905	..	..
Total	4 130	4 068	3 917	3 146	2 894	1 952	..	..

.. Not available

Note: Detailed metadata at: *http://metalinks.oecd.org/ins/20190221/c7e9*.

Source: OECD Insurance Statistics (database)

LITHUANIA

Table 1. Selected aggregates

Million EUR

	2010	2011	2012	2013	2014	2015	2016	2017
1.1 Insurance business written in the reporting country								
1.1.1 Insurance business, by ownership								
Gross premiums								
Domestic undertakings	317	283	309	288	303	326	393	425
Foreign controlled undertakings	300	272	299	278	294	316	383	416
Foreign companies (branches)	132	209	208	280	298	319	317	367
All undertakings	450	493	518	567	601	645	710	793
Premiums ceded								
Domestic undertakings	17	14	14	10	8	8	21	27
Foreign controlled undertakings	16	14	13	10	8	8	21	27
Foreign companies (branches)	..	..	..	..	21	24	15	40
All undertakings	..	..	..	..	29	32	36	68
Net written premiums								
Domestic undertakings	300	269	296	277	295	318	372	398
Foreign controlled undertakings	285	258	285	268	285	308	362	388
Foreign companies (branches)	..	..	..	..	277	295	302	327
All undertakings	..	..	..	..	572	613	674	725
1.1.2 Insurance business on foreign risks, gross premiums								
Life	..	..	..	..	..	..	..	..
Non-life	..	..	..	..	..	..	..	..
Composite	..	..	..	..	..	..	..	..
of which:								
Life	..	..	..	..	..	..	..	..
Non-life	..	..	..	..	..	..	..	..
Total	..	..	..	..	..	..	..	..
1.1.3 Life insurance payments, by class, gross premiums								
Annuities	2	2	3	3	4	5	6	7
Unit linked	110	114	115	126	152	170	157	137
Other life insurance	44	46	48	52	59	60	84	88
Total life insurance	156	162	166	181	215	236	247	231
of which: *Pension contracts*	..	..	..	..	..	..	1	..
1.1.4 Non-life insurance payments, by class, gross premiums								
Motor vehicle insurance	173	190	209	228	227	236	273	353
Marine, aviation and other transport insurance	2	1	2	2	2	2	2	2
Freight insurance	2	2	2	2	2	2	2	3
Fire and other property damage insurance	60	71	68	74	79	89	98	103
Pecuniary loss insurance	17	19	20	20	18	17	17	20
General liability insurance	14	15	16	19	20	20	20	21
Accident and health	25	31	34	40	37	42	49	56
of which: *Health*	14	18	21	25	21	24	30	35
Other non-life insurance	0	1	1	1	1	1	2	3
Treaty reinsurance	..	..	..	..	..	..	..	0
Total non-life insurance	294	330	352	386	386	409	463	561
1.2 Gross claims payments								
Life								
Domestic undertakings	6	10	10	15	13	15	26	29
Foreign controlled undertakings	6	10	10	15	13	15	23	26
Foreign companies (branches)	29	59	60	41	47	42	45	56
All undertakings	35	70	70	57	60	57	71	85
Non-life								
Domestic undertakings	162	121	126	105	105	116	134	169
Foreign controlled undertakings	137	104	106	85	92	102	134	169
Foreign companies (branches)	44	93	74	104	111	113	117	126
All undertakings	206	214	200	209	216	229	251	295
Composite								
Domestic undertakings	24	28	43	40	35	40	43	65
Foreign controlled undertakings	22	27	41	38	33	38	43	65
Foreign companies (branches)	1	2	3	4	4	6	8	11
All undertakings	24	30	46	44	40	46	51	75
of which:								
Life	20	24	41	39	35	40	43	66
Domestic undertakings	20	23	39	37	32	36	39	60
Foreign controlled undertakings	19	22	37	35	30	34	39	60
Foreign companies (branches)	1	1	2	2	2	3	4	6
All undertakings	20	24	41	39	35	40	43	66
Non-life	4	6	5	5	5	6	8	9
Domestic undertakings	4	5	4	3	3	4	4	4
Foreign controlled undertakings	4	5	4	3	3	4	4	4
Foreign companies (branches)	0	1	1	2	2	2	4	5
All undertakings	4	6	5	5	5	6	8	9
Total								
Domestic undertakings	192	159	179	161	154	171	203	263
Foreign controlled undertakings	166	141	157	138	138	155	200	260
Foreign companies (branches)	74	154	137	149	163	161	170	193
All undertakings	266	314	316	310	316	332	373	456

LITHUANIA

Table 1. Selected aggregates (cont.)

Million EUR

	2010	2011	2012	2013	2014	2015	2016	2017
1.3 Commissions								
Life								
Domestic undertakings	0	0	0	0	0	0	0	0
Foreign controlled undertakings	0	0	0	0	0	0	0	0
Foreign companies (branches)	..	..	..	..	0	0	0	0
All undertakings	..	..	..	..	0	0	0	0
Non-life								
Domestic undertakings	2	1	1	0	1	0	2	5
Foreign controlled undertakings	2	1	1	0	1	0	2	5
Foreign companies (branches)	..	..	..	..	3	3	2	7
All undertakings	..	..	..	..	3	3	4	12
Composite								
Domestic undertakings	0	2	2	3	1	1	0	0
Foreign controlled undertakings	0	2	2	3	1	1	0	0
Foreign companies (branches)	..	..	..	..	0	1	1	1
All undertakings	..	..	..	..	1	1	1	1
of which:								
Life	..	..	..	..	..	1	1	1
Domestic undertakings	0	1	1	1	..	1	0	0
Foreign controlled undertakings	0	1	1	1	..	1	0	0
Foreign companies (branches)	..	..	..	..	..	1	1	1
All undertakings	..	..	..	..	..	1	1	1
Non-life	..	..	..	..	..	0	0	0
Domestic undertakings	0	1	1	2	..	0	0	0
Foreign controlled undertakings	0	1	1	2	..	0	0	0
Foreign companies (branches)	..	..	..	..	..	0	0	0
All undertakings	..	..	..	..	..	0	0	0
Total								
Domestic undertakings	2	3	3	3	1	1	3	5
Foreign controlled undertakings	2	3	3	3	1	1	3	5
Foreign companies (branches)	..	..	..	..	3	4	3	8
All undertakings	..	..	..	..	4	5	6	13
1.4 Gross operating expenses								
Life								
Domestic undertakings	7	8	8	9	9	12	16	16
Foreign controlled undertakings	7	8	8	9	9	12	14	14
Foreign companies (branches)	..	..	..	..	8	6	7	6
All undertakings	..	..	..	..	17	18	22	21
Non-life								
Domestic undertakings	88	73	79	72	71	97	87	90
Foreign controlled undertakings	82	69	75	68	68	94	85	89
Foreign companies (branches)	..	..	..	..	63	95	63	65
All undertakings	..	..	..	..	134	192	150	155
Composite								
Domestic undertakings	14	18	20	22	17	28	9	14
Foreign controlled undertakings	12	16	18	21	16	25	9	14
Foreign companies (branches)	..	..	..	..	9	29	12	13
All undertakings	..	..	..	..	27	56	22	26
of which:								
Life	..	..	..	..	26	55	20	24
Domestic undertakings	13	15	17	19	17	27	8	13
Foreign controlled undertakings	11	13	15	17	15	24	8	13
Foreign companies (branches)	..	..	..	..	9	28	12	11
All undertakings	..	..	..	..	26	55	20	24
Non-life	..	..	..	..	1	2	2	2
Domestic undertakings	1	3	3	3	1	1	1	1
Foreign controlled undertakings	1	3	3	3	1	1	1	1
Foreign companies (branches)	..	..	..	..	0	1	1	1
All undertakings	..	..	..	..	1	2	2	2
Total								
Domestic undertakings	109	99	107	102	97	137	111	120
Foreign controlled undertakings	101	93	101	98	93	131	108	116
Foreign companies (branches)	..	..	..	..	81	130	82	83
All undertakings	..	..	..	..	178	267	194	203

LITHUANIA

Table 1. Selected aggregates (cont.)

Million EUR

	2010	2011	2012	2013	2014	2015	2016	2017
1.5 Insurance business written abroad by branches, gross premiums								
Life								
Branches and agencies	..	0	0	0	0	0	0	0
Subsidaries	..	..	..	..	..	..	..	..
Total	..	0	0	0	0	0	0	0
Non-life								
Branches and agencies	..	0	0	1	17	40	65	115
Subsidaries	..	..	..	..	..	..	..	..
Total	..	0	0	1	17	40	65	115
Composite								
Branches and agencies	..	20	22	26	31	37	40	46
Subsidaries	..	..	..	..	..	..	..	..
Total	..	20	22	26	31	37	40	46
of which:								
Life	..	9	10	11	14	18	19	22
Branches and agencies	..	9	10	11	14	18	19	22
Subsidaries	..	..	..	..	..	..	..	..
Total	..	9	10	11	14	18	19	22
Non-life	..	11	12	15	17	20	21	24
Branches and agencies	..	11	12	15	17	20	21	24
Subsidaries	..	..	..	..	..	..	..	..
Total	..	11	12	15	17	20	21	24
Total								
Branches and agencies	..	20	22	27	48	77	105	161
Subsidaries	..	..	..	..	..	..	..	..
Total	..	20	22	27	48	77	105	161

.. Not available

Note: Detailed metadata at: *http://metalinks.oecd.org/ins/20190221/f264.*

Source: OECD Insurance Statistics (database)

LITHUANIA

Table 2. Number of companies and employees

	2010	2011	2012	2013	2014	2015	2016	2017
2.1 Number of companies								
Life								
Domestic undertakings	1	1	1	1	1	1	3	3
Foreign controlled undertakings	1	1	1	1	1	1	2	2
Foreign companies (branches)	5	4	4	3	3	3	2	2
All undertakings	6	5	5	4	4	4	5	5
Non-life								
Domestic undertakings	8	6	6	5	5	5	4	4
Foreign controlled undertakings	5	3	3	2	2	3	3	3
Foreign companies (branches)	9	9	9	10	10	10	9	9
All undertakings	17	15	15	15	15	15	13	13
Composite								
Domestic undertakings	4	4	4	4	4	4	2	2
Foreign controlled undertakings	3	3	3	3	3	3	2	2
Foreign companies (branches)	1	1	1	1	1	1	1	1
All undertakings	5	5	5	5	5	5	3	3
Reinsurance								
Domestic undertakings	..	..	..	..	..	..	..	..
Foreign controlled undertakings	..	..	..	..	..	..	..	..
Foreign companies (branches)	..	..	..	..	..	..	..	..
All undertakings	..	..	..	..	..	..	..	..
Total								
Domestic undertakings	13	11	11	10	10	10	9	9
Foreign controlled undertakings	9	7	7	6	6	7	7	7
Foreign companies (branches)	15	14	14	14	14	14	12	12
All undertakings	28	25	25	24	24	24	21	21
2.2 Number of employees								
Insurance undertakings	4 398	3 875	4 390	4 519	4 414	4 482	4 562	4 599
Intermediaries	630	1 325	1 320	1 320	1 433	1 441	1 480	1 463
Total	5 028	5 200	5 710	5 839	5 847	5 923	6 042	6 062

.. Not available

Note: Detailed metadata at: *http://metalinks.oecd.org/ins/20190221/f264.*

Source: OECD Insurance Statistics (database)

LUXEMBOURG

Table 1. Selected aggregates

Million EUR

	2010	2011	2012	2013	2014	2015	2016	2017
1.1 Insurance business written in the reporting country								
1.1.1 Insurance business, by ownership								
Gross premiums								
Domestic undertakings	20 584	13 626	19 445	18 410	21 712	19 100	18 259	21 446
Foreign controlled undertakings	19 165	12 583	17 930	17 036	20 356	17 075	13 690	18 728
Foreign companies (branches)	133	150	144	191	76	78	70	77
All undertakings	20 717	13 776	19 589	18 601	21 788	19 178	18 329	21 523
Premiums ceded								
Domestic undertakings	5 362	2 935	6 109	4 624	6 122	3 030	3 235	3 026
Foreign controlled undertakings	5 220	2 737	5 892	4 246	5 863	2 770	2 943	2 657
Foreign companies (branches)	37	37	40	37	33	26	31	27
All undertakings	5 399	2 973	6 149	4 661	6 155	3 056	3 267	3 053
Net written premiums								
Domestic undertakings	15 222	10 691	13 336	13 787	15 590	16 070	15 024	18 421
Foreign controlled undertakings	13 945	9 846	12 037	12 790	14 493	14 305	10 747	16 070
Foreign companies (branches)	96	113	104	153	43	52	39	50
All undertakings	15 318	10 804	13 440	13 940	15 633	16 122	15 063	18 470
1.1.2 Insurance business on foreign risks, gross premiums								
Life	18 170	11 564	17 115	15 837	18 455	16 383	15 071	18 182
Non-life	426	547	476	572	438	587	621	784
Composite	0	0	..	0	0	0	0	0
of which:								
Life	0	0	..	0	0	0	0	0
Non-life	0	0	..	0	0	0	0	0
Total	18 596	12 112	17 591	16 408	18 893	16 969	15 692	18 967
1.1.3 Life insurance payments, by class, gross premiums								
Annuities	..	..	..	..	..	..	..	..
Unit linked	13 371	8 836	11 224	10 516	11 086	12 874	11 949	15 426
Other life insurance	..	3 382	6 826	6 413	9 103	4 685	4 767	4 283
Total life insurance	19 392	12 218	18 050	16 929	20 190	17 559	16 716	19 709
***of which:** Pension contracts*	19 392	..	..	..	..	..	..	..
1.1.4 Non-life insurance payments, by class, gross premiums								
Motor vehicle insurance	..	426	..	..	..	..	..	..
Marine, aviation and other transport insurance	..	0	..	..	..	..	..	..
Freight insurance	..	30	..	..	..	..	..	..
Fire and other property damage insurance	..	271	..	..	..	..	..	..
Pecuniary loss insurance	..	321	..	..	..	..	..	..
General liability insurance	..	106	..	..	..	..	..	..
Accident and health	..	90	..	..	..	..	..	..
***of which:** Health*	..	59	..	..	..	..	..	..
Other non-life insurance	..	53	..	..	..	..	..	..
Treaty reinsurance	..	27	..	..	..	..	..	..
Total non-life insurance	1 184	1 325	1 300	1 501	1 339	1 476	1 554	1 767
1.2 Gross claims payments								
Life								
Domestic undertakings	6 078	7 091	11 111	11 696	10 597	9 995	11 802	12 002
Foreign controlled undertakings	5 827	6 863	10 823	11 179	10 214	9 032	11 035	11 291
Foreign companies (branches)	9	34	10	25	25	27	28	27
All undertakings	6 087	7 125	11 122	11 721	10 622	10 023	11 829	12 029
Non-life								
Domestic undertakings	731	606	623	1 105	809	900	860	961
Foreign controlled undertakings	411	315	348	691	428	512	766	500
Foreign companies (branches)	27	31	27	39	36	18	31	37
All undertakings	758	637	650	1 143	845	918	891	999
Composite								
Domestic undertakings	0	0	..	0	0	0	0	0
Foreign controlled undertakings	0	0	..	0	0	0	0	0
Foreign companies (branches)	32	39	38	27	133	17	8	8
All undertakings	32	39	38	27	133	17	8	8
of which:								
Life	15	19	20	15	130	17	8	8
Domestic undertakings	0	0	..	0	0	0	0	0
Foreign controlled undertakings	0	0	..	0	0	0	0	0
Foreign companies (branches)	15	19	20	15	130	17	8	8
All undertakings	15	19	20	15	130	17	8	8
Non-life	17	20	18	12	3	0	0	0
Domestic undertakings	0	0	..	0	0	0	0	0
Foreign controlled undertakings	0	0	..	0	0	0	0	0
Foreign companies (branches)	17	20	18	12	3	0	0	0
All undertakings	17	20	18	12	3	0	0	0
Total								
Domestic undertakings	6 809	7 697	11 734	12 801	11 406	10 896	12 661	12 964
Foreign controlled undertakings	6 238	7 178	11 171	11 869	10 642	9 544	11 802	11 791
Foreign companies (branches)	68	104	76	90	195	62	66	72
All undertakings	6 878	7 800	11 810	12 891	11 600	10 958	12 728	13 036

LUXEMBOURG

Table 1. Selected aggregates (cont.)

Million EUR

	2010	2011	2012	2013	2014	2015	2016	2017
1.3 Commissions								
Life								
Domestic undertakings	367	353	328	327	317	326	291	320
Foreign controlled undertakings	351	..	328	309	297	289	186	283
Foreign companies (branches)	0	0	0	0	0	0	0	0
All undertakings	367	353	328	328	317	326	292	320
Non-life								
Domestic undertakings	206	217	205	217	211	237	251	284
Foreign controlled undertakings	126	..	205	119	109	122	143	151
Foreign companies (branches)	11	12	11	12	9	9	9	8
All undertakings	217	229	217	229	221	246	260	292
Composite								
Domestic undertakings	0	0	..	0	0	0	0	0
Foreign controlled undertakings	0	..	..	0	0	0	0	0
Foreign companies (branches)	12	11	12	12	3	4	4	3
All undertakings	12	11	12	12	3	4	4	3
of which:								
Life	4	5	5	5	3	4	4	3
Domestic undertakings	0	0	..	0	0	0	0	0
Foreign controlled undertakings	0	..	..	0	0	0	0	0
Foreign companies (branches)	4	5	5	5	3	4	4	3
All undertakings	4	5	5	5	3	4	4	3
Non-life	8	7	7	7	0	0	0	0
Domestic undertakings	0	0	..	0	0	0	0	0
Foreign controlled undertakings	0	..	..	0	0	0	0	0
Foreign companies (branches)	8	7	7	7	0	0	0	0
All undertakings	8	7	7	7	0	0	0	0
Total								
Domestic undertakings	573	570	533	544	528	563	542	604
Foreign controlled undertakings	477	..	533	428	406	411	329	435
Foreign companies (branches)	23	23	24	25	13	14	14	11
All undertakings	596	593	557	569	541	576	556	615
1.4 Gross operating expenses								
Life								
Domestic undertakings	243	288	656	362	376	406	417	433
Foreign controlled undertakings	231	274	622	347	358	374	352	392
Foreign companies (branches)	0	0	0	0	1	0	1	1
All undertakings	243	288	656	362	376	406	418	433
Non-life								
Domestic undertakings	54	53	270	66	72	82	81	96
Foreign controlled undertakings	30	27	270	34	41	46	78	58
Foreign companies (branches)	14	3	14	3	2	2	3	3
All undertakings	68	55	285	69	74	84	84	99
Composite								
Domestic undertakings	0	0	..	0	0	0	0	0
Foreign controlled undertakings	0	0	..	0	0	0	0	0
Foreign companies (branches)	17	6	18	7	1	1	1	1
All undertakings	17	6	18	7	1	1	1	1
of which:								
Life	6	2	7	3	1	1	1	1
Domestic undertakings	0	0	..	0	0	0	0	0
Foreign controlled undertakings	0	0	..	0	0	0	0	0
Foreign companies (branches)	6	2	7	3	1	1	1	1
All undertakings	6	2	7	3	1	1	1	1
Non-life	12	3	11	4	0	0	0	0
Domestic undertakings	0	0	..	0	0	0	0	0
Foreign controlled undertakings	0	0	..	0	0	0	0	0
Foreign companies (branches)	12	3	11	4	0	0	0	0
All undertakings	12	3	11	4	0	0	0	0
Total								
Domestic undertakings	297	341	926	429	448	488	498	529
Foreign controlled undertakings	261	302	892	381	399	421	430	450
Foreign companies (branches)	31	8	33	9	4	3	4	5
All undertakings	328	349	959	438	451	491	502	534

Table 1. Selected aggregates (cont.)

Million EUR

	2010	2011	2012	2013	2014	2015	2016	2017
1.5 Insurance business written abroad by branches, gross premiums								
Life								
Branches and agencies	2 830	2 161	2 619	2 648	3 250	3 552	4 622	3 492
Subsidaries	0	0	0	..	..	..	..	..
Total	2 830	2 161	2 619	2 648	3 250	3 552	4 622	3 492
Non-life								
Branches and agencies	1 122	1 088	1 417	1 546	1 831	1 965	2 022	1 957
Subsidaries	0	0	0	..	..	..	..	..
Total	1 122	1 088	1 417	1 546	1 831	1 965	2 022	1 957
Composite								
Branches and agencies	0	0	..	0	0	0	0	0
Subsidaries	0	0	..	..	..	..	..	..
Total	0	0	..	0	0	0	0	0
of which:								
Life	0	0	..	0	0	0	0	0
Branches and agencies	0	0	..	0	0	0	0	0
Subsidaries	0	0	..	..	..	..	..	..
Total	0	0	..	0	0	0	0	0
Non-life	0	0	..	0	0	0	0	0
Branches and agencies	0	0	..	0	0	0	0	0
Subsidaries	0	0	..	..	..	..	..	..
Total	0	0	..	0	0	0	0	0
Total								
Branches and agencies	3 952	3 250	4 036	4 194	5 082	5 516	6 644	5 449
Subsidaries	0	0	0	..	..	..	..	..
Total	3 952	3 250	4 036	4 194	5 082	5 516	6 644	5 449

.. Not available

Note: Detailed metadata at: *http://metalinks.oecd.org/ins/20190221/b3e1.*

Source: OECD Insurance Statistics (database)

LUXEMBOURG

Table 2. Number of companies and employees

	2010	2011	2012	2013	2014	2015	2016	2017
2.1 Number of companies								
Life								
Domestic undertakings	46	45	43	42	44	43	40	39
Foreign controlled undertakings	42	41	39	34	39	38	34	35
Foreign companies (branches)	2	2	1	2	2	2	3	3
All undertakings	48	47	44	44	46	45	43	42
Non-life								
Domestic undertakings	29	29	31	34	34	32	33	34
Foreign controlled undertakings	25	25	27	27	8	21	24	25
Foreign companies (branches)	11	10	11	10	10	10	10	9
All undertakings	40	39	42	44	44	42	43	43
Composite								
Domestic undertakings	0	0	0	0	0	0	0	0
Foreign controlled undertakings	0	0	0	0	0	0	0	0
Foreign companies (branches)	3	3	3	3	3	3	3	2
All undertakings	3	3	3	3	3	3	3	2
Reinsurance								
Domestic undertakings	244	242	238	226	224	217	208	204
Foreign controlled undertakings	225	222	219	207	205	204	191	187
Foreign companies (branches)	8	0	0	0	0	0	0	0
All undertakings	252	242	238	226	224	217	208	204
Total								
Domestic undertakings	319	316	312	302	302	292	281	277
Foreign controlled undertakings	292	288	285	268	252	263	249	247
Foreign companies (branches)	24	15	15	15	15	15	16	14
All undertakings	343	331	327	317	317	307	297	291
2.2 Number of employees								
Insurance undertakings	3 956	3 967	4 326	5 692	6 057	6 484	6 484	7 446
Intermediaries	9 859	9 375	9 659	10 030	550	561	522	586
Total	13 815	13 342	13 985	15 722	6 607	7 045	7 006	8 032

Note: Detailed metadata at: *http://metalinks.oecd.org/ins/20190221/b3e1*.

Source: OECD Insurance Statistics (database)

MEXICO

Table 1. Selected aggregates

Million MXN

	2010	2011	2012	2013	2014	2015	2016	2017
1.1 Insurance business written in the reporting country								
1.1.1 Insurance business, by ownership								
Gross premiums								
Domestic undertakings	247 010	281 792	310 747	347 196	363 530	395 083	450 740	502 856
Foreign controlled undertakings	153 858	167 708	189 698	207 890	220 225	242 872	265 159	290 985
Foreign companies (branches)	..	..	..	..	..	..	..	..
All undertakings	247 010	281 792	310 747	347 196	363 530	395 083	450 740	502 856
Premiums ceded								
Domestic undertakings	36 018	49 771	50 188	60 551	58 378	67 135	70 420	93 577
Foreign controlled undertakings	19 495	21 903	24 728	26 822	29 932	40 217	40 674	58 977
Foreign companies (branches)	..	..	..	..	..	..	..	..
All undertakings	36 018	49 771	50 188	60 551	58 378	67 135	70 420	93 577
Net written premiums								
Domestic undertakings	210 991	232 021	260 559	286 645	305 152	327 947	380 320	409 279
Foreign controlled undertakings	134 363	145 805	164 970	181 068	190 293	202 655	224 485	232 008
Foreign companies (branches)	..	..	..	..	..	..	..	..
All undertakings	210 991	232 021	260 559	286 645	305 152	327 947	380 320	409 279
1.1.2 Insurance business on foreign risks, gross premiums								
Life	..	..	..	..	..	..	..	..
Non-life	323	349	425	402	..	..	..	..
Composite	1 463	1 553	1 787	1 692	..	..	..	..
of which:								
Life	..	..	..	..	..	..	..	..
Non-life	..	..	..	..	..	..	..	..
Total	1 786	1 902	2 212	2 093	..	..	..	..
1.1.3 Life insurance payments, by class, gross premiums								
Annuities	15 849	15 749	17 633	20 099	20 521	19 719	19 286	21 310
Unit linked	0	..	..	..	..	..	..	..
Other life insurance	97 352	109 511	125 175	138 959	148 624	162 199	189 860	193 587
Total life insurance	113 201	125 260	142 808	159 058	169 145	181 918	209 146	214 897
***of which:** Pension contracts*	0	..	..	..	..	..	..	..
1.1.4 Non-life insurance payments, by class, gross premiums								
Motor vehicle insurance	50 357	56 099	62 944	66 562	68 735	75 858	91 375	103 014
Marine, aviation and other transport insurance	5 765	7 049	7 691	7 851	9 356	11 007	11 312	16 558
Freight insurance	..	..	..	..	..	..	..	..
Fire and other property damage insurance	8 026	14 010	9 980	16 520	12 232	13 815	14 497	18 115
Pecuniary loss insurance	636	686	749	5 210	501	947	1 131	12 278
General liability insurance	5 185	5 914	6 920	7 341	7 201	9 099	9 668	12 005
Accident and health	37 557	41 814	45 526	51 189	56 686	59 550	66 512	76 720
***of which:** Health*	1 626	1 835	1 918	2 682	2 719	2 622	3 218	3 518
Other non-life insurance	24 316	30 214	33 390	32 581	38 511	42 081	45 976	48 006
Treaty reinsurance	..	..	..	..	..	..	..	..
Total non-life insurance	131 842	155 785	167 200	187 253	193 221	212 357	240 470	286 696
1.2 Gross claims payments								
Life								
Domestic undertakings	9 487	9 566	10 279	11 800	12 325	13 760	14 829	16 234
Foreign controlled undertakings	4 314	4 663	..	..	5 875	6 443	6 971	7 390
Foreign companies (branches)	..	..	..	..	..	..	..	..
All undertakings	9 487	9 566	10 279	11 800	12 325	13 760	14 829	16 234
Non-life								
Domestic undertakings	14 463	14 750	14 874	21 716	17 912	19 552	23 827	32 868
Foreign controlled undertakings	5 042	4 751	..	..	4 093	4 923	5 515	7 449
Foreign companies (branches)	..	..	..	..	..	..	..	..
All undertakings	14 463	14 750	14 874	21 716	17 912	19 552	23 827	32 868
Composite								
Domestic undertakings	100 430	109 005	115 041	159 315	148 932	162 803	185 481	204 354
Foreign controlled undertakings	67 094	70 654	..	..	104 822	109 465	125 575	136 316
Foreign companies (branches)	..	..	..	..	..	..	..	..
All undertakings	100 430	109 005	115 041	159 315	148 932	162 803	185 481	204 354
of which:								
Life	48 676	50 966	55 436	76 467	81 643	88 136	101 700	115 199
Domestic undertakings	48 676	50 966	55 436	76 467	81 643	88 136	101 700	115 199
Foreign controlled undertakings	37 971	38 918	..	..	67 855	70 802	81 029	89 726
Foreign companies (branches)	..	..	..	..	..	..	..	..
All undertakings	48 676	50 966	55 436	76 467	81 643	88 136	101 700	115 199
Non-life	51 753	58 039	59 605	82 848	67 289	74 667	83 781	89 154
Domestic undertakings	51 753	58 039	59 605	82 848	67 289	74 667	83 781	89 154
Foreign controlled undertakings	29 122	31 736	..	..	36 968	38 662	44 546	46 591
Foreign companies (branches)	..	..	..	..	..	..	..	..
All undertakings	51 753	58 039	59 605	82 848	67 289	74 667	83 781	89 154
Total								
Domestic undertakings	124 380	133 321	140 195	192 832	179 169	196 115	224 138	253 455
Foreign controlled undertakings	76 449	80 068	..	..	114 791	120 830	138 061	151 155
Foreign companies (branches)	..	..	..	..	..	..	..	..
All undertakings	124 380	133 321	140 195	192 832	179 169	196 115	224 138	253 455

MEXICO

Table 1. Selected aggregates (cont.)

Million MXN

	2010	2011	2012	2013	2014	2015	2016	2017
1.3 Commissions								
Life								
Domestic undertakings	976	1 257	1 133	1 075	749	1 045	1 155	..
Foreign controlled undertakings	234	268	277	251	74	192	247	..
Foreign companies (branches)	..	..	..	..	..	..	..	..
All undertakings	976	1 257	1 133	1 075	749	1 045	1 155	..
Non-life								
Domestic undertakings	5 078	5 935	6 911	8 410	9 458	7 257	9 473	..
Foreign controlled undertakings	2 230	2 373	2 721	3 523	3 808	1 888	1 618	..
Foreign companies (branches)	..	..	..	..	..	..	..	..
All undertakings	5 078	5 935	6 911	8 410	9 458	7 257	9 473	..
Composite								
Domestic undertakings	34 055	38 671	44 178	46 777	49 973	48 713	56 225	..
Foreign controlled undertakings	21 885	24 611	28 060	29 464	31 616	30 146	33 073	..
Foreign companies (branches)	..	..	..	..	..	..	..	..
All undertakings	34 055	38 671	44 178	46 777	49 973	48 713	56 225	..
of which:								
Life	13 741	15 773	18 508	19 316	21 023	22 507	26 955	..
Domestic undertakings	13 741	15 773	18 508	19 316	21 023	22 507	26 955	..
Foreign controlled undertakings	9 518	10 807	12 501	12 940	17 514	14 838	17 151	..
Foreign companies (branches)	..	..	..	..	..	..	..	..
All undertakings	13 741	15 773	18 508	19 316	21 023	22 507	26 955	..
Non-life	20 315	22 898	25 670	27 462	28 950	26 206	29 270	..
Domestic undertakings	20 315	22 898	25 670	27 462	28 950	26 206	29 270	..
Foreign controlled undertakings	12 367	13 803	15 559	16 524	14 103	15 308	15 922	..
Foreign companies (branches)	..	..	..	..	..	..	..	..
All undertakings	20 315	22 898	25 670	27 462	28 950	26 206	29 270	..
Total								
Domestic undertakings	40 110	45 863	52 222	56 263	60 180	57 016	66 853	..
Foreign controlled undertakings	24 349	27 251	31 058	33 239	35 498	32 226	34 937	..
Foreign companies (branches)	..	..	..	..	..	..	..	..
All undertakings	40 110	45 863	52 222	56 263	60 180	57 016	66 853	..
1.4 Gross operating expenses								
Life								
Domestic undertakings	942	1 095	1 313	1 486	1 156	1 336	1 705	1 617
Foreign controlled undertakings	530	675	..	..	570	661	723	759
Foreign companies (branches)	..	..	..	..	..	..	..	..
All undertakings	942	1 095	1 313	1 486	1 156	1 336	1 705	1 617
Non-life								
Domestic undertakings	2 353	2 337	2 968	3 545	4 198	4 924	5 852	7 490
Foreign controlled undertakings	1 220	1 402	..	..	2 010	3 137	3 249	4 041
Foreign companies (branches)	..	..	..	..	..	..	..	..
All undertakings	2 353	2 337	2 968	3 545	4 198	4 924	5 852	7 490
Composite								
Domestic undertakings	14 102	14 115	14 382	16 389	16 621	18 736	21 447	23 147
Foreign controlled undertakings	9 018	8 627	..	..	10 470	12 270	13 297	13 037
Foreign companies (branches)	..	..	..	..	..	..	..	..
All undertakings	14 102	14 115	14 382	16 389	16 621	18 736	21 447	23 147
of which:								
Life	6 925	6 838	7 085	8 530	8 486	9 990	11 792	11 674
Domestic undertakings	6 925	6 838	7 085	8 530	8 486	9 990	11 792	11 674
Foreign controlled undertakings	5 339	5 052	..	..	6 273	7 388	8 480	7 981
Foreign companies (branches)	..	..	..	..	..	..	..	..
All undertakings	6 925	6 838	7 085	8 530	8 486	9 990	11 792	11 674
Non-life	7 178	7 277	7 298	7 859	8 135	8 746	9 655	11 473
Domestic undertakings	7 178	7 277	7 298	7 859	8 135	8 746	9 655	11 473
Foreign controlled undertakings	3 679	3 575	..	..	4 198	4 882	4 818	5 055
Foreign companies (branches)	..	..	..	..	..	..	..	..
All undertakings	7 178	7 277	7 298	7 859	8 135	8 746	9 655	11 473
Total								
Domestic undertakings	17 398	17 548	18 662	21 420	21 974	24 996	29 004	32 254
Foreign controlled undertakings	10 768	10 704	..	..	13 050	16 068	17 270	17 837
Foreign companies (branches)	..	..	..	..	..	..	..	..
All undertakings	17 398	17 548	18 662	21 420	21 974	24 996	29 004	32 254

MEXICO

Table 1. Selected aggregates (cont.)

Million MXN

	2010	2011	2012	2013	2014	2015	2016	2017
1.5 Insurance business written abroad by branches, gross premiums								
Life								
Branches and agencies	..	..	..	..	..	..	..	..
Subsidaries	..	..	..	..	..	..	..	..
Total	..	..	..	..	..	..	..	..
Non-life								
Branches and agencies	..	..	..	..	..	..	..	..
Subsidaries	..	..	..	..	..	..	..	..
Total	..	..	..	..	..	..	..	..
Composite								
Branches and agencies	..	..	..	..	..	..	..	..
Subsidaries	..	..	..	..	..	..	..	..
Total	..	..	..	..	..	..	..	..
of which:								
Life	..	..	..	..	..	..	..	..
Branches and agencies	..	..	..	..	..	..	..	..
Subsidaries	..	..	..	..	..	..	..	..
Total	..	..	..	..	..	..	..	..
Non-life	..	..	..	..	..	..	..	..
Branches and agencies	..	..	..	..	..	..	..	..
Subsidaries	..	..	..	..	..	..	..	..
Total	..	..	..	..	..	..	..	..
Total								
Branches and agencies	..	..	..	..	..	..	..	..
Subsidaries	..	..	..	..	..	..	..	..
Total	..	..	..	..	..	..	..	..

.. Not available

Note: Detailed metadata at: *http://metalinks.oecd.org/ins/20190221/3fb4*.

Source: *OECD Insurance Statistics (database)*

MEXICO

Table 2. Number of companies and employees

	2010	2011	2012	2013	2014	2015	2016	2017
2.1 Number of companies								
Life								
Domestic undertakings	21	21	20	20	16	16	17	15
Foreign controlled undertakings	12	12	11	11	9	9	10	8
Foreign companies (branches)	..	..	..	..	..	..	..	..
All undertakings	21	21	20	20	16	16	17	15
Non-life								
Domestic undertakings	42	44	47	45	49	46	44	60
Foreign controlled undertakings	25	27	27	27	26	23	22	31
Foreign companies (branches)	..	..	..	..	..	..	..	..
All undertakings	42	44	47	45	49	46	44	60
Composite								
Domestic undertakings	34	35	35	37	38	37	37	38
Foreign controlled undertakings	21	20	21	21	22	21	20	21
Foreign companies (branches)	..	..	..	..	..	..	..	..
All undertakings	34	35	35	37	38	37	37	38
Reinsurance								
Domestic undertakings	2	2	2	2	2	3	2	2
Foreign controlled undertakings	0	..	0	0	0	0	0	0
Foreign companies (branches)	..	..	..	..	..	..	..	..
All undertakings	2	2	2	2	2	3	2	2
Total								
Domestic undertakings	99	102	104	104	105	102	100	115
Foreign controlled undertakings	58	59	59	59	57	53	52	60
Foreign companies (branches)	..	..	..	..	..	..	..	..
All undertakings	99	102	104	104	105	102	100	115
2.2 Number of employees								
Insurance undertakings	14 133	14 487	14 491	14 500	14 799	19 168	..	..
Intermediaries	34 265	35 173	36 190	46 712	51 780	55 005	57 900	61 695
Total	48 398	49 660	50 681	61 212	66 579	74 173	57 900	61 695

.. Not available

Note: Detailed metadata at: *http://metalinks.oecd.org/ins/20190221/3fb4.*

Source: OECD Insurance Statistics (database)

NETHERLANDS

Table 1. Selected aggregates

Million EUR

	2010	2011	2012	2013	2014	2015	2016	2017
1.1 Insurance business written in the reporting country								
1.1.1 Insurance business, by ownership								
Gross premiums								
Domestic undertakings	38 602	41 183	39 012	38 077	36 523	33 708	69 887	71 228
Foreign controlled undertakings	7 430	9 625	9 255	7 674	2 969	5 812	4 102	4 371
Foreign companies (branches)	961	955	891	430	62	0	..	..
All undertakings	39 564	42 138	39 903	38 507	36 585	33 708	69 887	71 228
Premiums ceded								
Domestic undertakings	3 407	5 720	3 109	2 951	3 880	2 814	1 198	1 698
Foreign controlled undertakings	995	1 701	1 706	1 484	1 615	1 365	287	353
Foreign companies (branches)	42	116	79	20	0	0	..	..
All undertakings	3 449	5 836	3 188	2 971	3 880	2 814	1 198	1 698
Net written premiums								
Domestic undertakings	35 195	35 463	35 903	35 126	32 643	30 894	68 689	69 530
Foreign controlled undertakings	6 434	7 923	7 549	6 190	1 354	4 447	3 815	4 018
Foreign companies (branches)	919	839	812	410	62	0	..	..
All undertakings	36 115	36 302	36 715	35 536	32 705	30 894	68 689	69 530
1.1.2 Insurance business on foreign risks, gross premiums								
Life	..	..	..	..	..	..	269	273
Non-life	..	..	..	..	..	..	534	452
Composite total	..	..	..	..	..	..	..	252
Total	..	..	..	..	..	..	803	977
1.1.3 Life insurance payments, by class, gross premiums								
Annuities	12 058	12 001	10 892	10 998	10 806	9 035	0	0
Unit linked	7 758	9 332	7 836	7 086	6 504	5 533	5 262	4 553
Other life insurance	355	329	247	188	150	122	8 465	8 411
Total life insurance	20 171	21 662	18 975	18 272	17 460	14 690	13 727	12 964
of which: *Pension contracts*	6 941	6 887	6 034	5 810	5 552	5 208	334	157
1.1.4 Non-life insurance payments, by class, gross premiums								
Motor vehicle insurance	4 635	4 587	4 500	4 376	3 934	3 884	3 892	4 051
Marine, aviation and other transport insurance	543	563	596	525	435	404	361	283
Freight insurance	275	291	263	256	231	191	..	0
Fire and other property damage insurance	3 732	3 515	3 698	3 664	3 449	3 456	3 256	3 290
Pecuniary loss insurance	1 192	309	278	206	164	176	258	206
General liability insurance	1 140	1 045	1 116	1 125	1 064	1 033	882	883
Accident and health	8 285	8 585	8 560	8 167	7 867	7 851	46 459	47 499
of which: *Health*	..	..	..	..	..	..	45 064	46 044
Other non-life insurance	1 419	2 027	1 907	1 919	1 976	2 016	1 049	1 165
Treaty reinsurance	..	..	..	..	..	..	..	0
Total non-life insurance	21 221	20 923	20 918	20 238	19 120	19 011	56 157	57 377
1.2 Gross claims payments								
Life								
Domestic undertakings	21 020	23 689	25 331	24 085	25 487	22 576	20 919	25 124
Foreign controlled undertakings	3 870	3 206	3 538	3 205	1 136	4 504	4 203	4 286
Foreign companies (branches)	3 281	378	401	420	0	0	..	..
All undertakings	24 301	24 067	25 732	24 505	25 487	22 576	20 919	25 124
Non-life								
Domestic undertakings	13 434	13 957	13 999	14 304	13 666	13 806	50 966	51 936
Foreign controlled undertakings	2 046	2 840	2 870	2 915	867	1 937	1 053	844
Foreign companies (branches)	305	42	41	41	149	0	..	..
All undertakings	13 739	13 999	14 040	14 345	13 815	13 806	50 966	51 936
Composite, all undertakings	..	..	..	..	..	..	..	**473**
Total								
Domestic undertakings	34 454	37 646	39 330	38 389	39 153	36 382	71 885	77 533
Foreign controlled undertakings	5 916	6 046	6 408	6 120	2 003	6 441	5 256	5 130
Foreign companies (branches)	3 586	420	442	461	149	0	..	..
All undertakings	38 040	38 066	39 772	38 850	39 302	36 382	71 885	77 533
1.3 Commissions								
Life								
Domestic undertakings	605	614	473	243	190	158	..	..
Foreign controlled undertakings	342	325	196	64	17	49	..	..
Foreign companies (branches)	62	14	17	12	0	0	..	..
All undertakings	667	628	490	255	190	158	..	..
Non-life								
Domestic undertakings	2 999	3 070	3 197	2 891	2 713	2 663	..	..
Foreign controlled undertakings	682	851	833	734	282	464	..	..
Foreign companies (branches)	24	23	22	22	21	0	..	..
All undertakings	3 023	3 093	3 219	2 913	2 734	2 663	..	..
Composite, all undertakings	..	..	..	..	..	..	..	..
Total								
Domestic undertakings	3 604	3 684	3 670	3 134	2 903	2 821	..	..
Foreign controlled undertakings	1 024	1 176	1 029	798	299	513	..	..
Foreign companies (branches)	86	37	39	34	21	0	..	..
All undertakings	3 690	3 721	3 709	3 168	2 924	2 821	..	..

NETHERLANDS

Table 1. Selected aggregates (cont.)

Million EUR

	2010	2011	2012	2013	2014	2015	2016	2017
1.4 Gross operating expenses								
Life								
Domestic undertakings	2 642	2 768	2 827	2 266	2 497	2 072	2 183	2 002
Foreign controlled undertakings	646	349	342	297	113	378	417	356
Foreign companies (branches)	488	59	37	44	0	0	..	..
All undertakings	3 130	2 827	2 864	2 310	2 497	2 072	2 183	2 002
Non-life								
Domestic undertakings	4 775	4 863	4 933	4 809	4 635	4 485	6 219	6 156
Foreign controlled undertakings	845	1 244	1 181	1 136	373	771	525	550
Foreign companies (branches)	26	25	24	25	23	0	..	..
All undertakings	4 801	4 888	4 957	4 834	4 658	4 485	6 219	6 156
Composite, all undertakings	..	..	..	..	..	..	..	**115**
Total								
Domestic undertakings	7 417	7 631	7 759	7 075	7 132	6 557	8 402	8 273
Foreign controlled undertakings	1 491	1 593	1 523	1 433	486	1 149	942	906
Foreign companies (branches)	514	84	61	69	23	0	..	..
All undertakings	7 931	7 715	7 820	7 144	7 155	6 557	8 402	8 273
1.5 Insurance business written abroad by branches, gross premiums								
Life								
Branches and agencies	621	662	540	370	276	..	253	260
Subsidaries	..	..	..	..	..	..	..	..
Total	621	662	540	370	276	267	253	260
Non-life								
Branches and agencies	1 789	1 067	1 276	1 132	1 289	..	175	163
Subsidaries	..	..	..	..	..	..	..	..
Total	1 789	1 067	1 276	1 132	1 289	1 487	175	163
Composite total	..	..	..	..	..	..	..	**0**
Total								
Branches and agencies	2 410	1 729	1 816	1 502	1 565	..	428	423
Subsidaries	..	..	..	..	..	..	..	..
Total	2 410	1 729	1 816	1 502	1 565	1 754	428	423

.. Not available

Note: Detailed metadata at: *http://metalinks.oecd.org/ins/20190221/1e2e.*

Source: *OECD Insurance Statistics (database)*

NETHERLANDS

Table 2. Number of companies and employees

	2010	2011	2012	2013	2014	2015	2016	2017
2.1 Number of companies								
Life								
Domestic undertakings	49	52	41	36	38	..	31	30
Foreign controlled undertakings	8	8	6	6	7	..	11	10
Foreign companies (branches)	1	1	4	4	0	..	..	..
All undertakings	50	53	45	40	38	..	31	30
Non-life								
Domestic undertakings	193	174	158	316	136	..	107	101
Foreign controlled undertakings	14	5	15	14	8	..	9	8
Foreign companies (branches)	4	4	2	1	2	..	..	..
All undertakings	197	178	160	317	138	..	107	101
Composite, all undertakings	**0**	**0**	**0**	**0**	**0**	**0**	**0**	**0**
Reinsurance								
Domestic undertakings	14	16	15	11	10	..	9	9
Foreign controlled undertakings	2	1	1	0	0	..	0	0
Foreign companies (branches)	..	..	0	0	0	..	..	..
All undertakings	14	16	15	11	10	..	9	9
Total								
Domestic undertakings	256	242	214	363	184	..	147	140
Foreign controlled undertakings	24	14	22	20	15	..	20	18
Foreign companies (branches)	5	5	6	5	2	..	..	..
All undertakings	261	247	220	368	186	..	147	140
2.2 Number of employees								
Insurance undertakings	..	..	..	..	..	..	..	..
Intermediaries	..	..	..	..	..	..	..	..
Total	..	..	..	..	..	..	..	..

.. Not available

Note: Detailed metadata at: *http://metalinks.oecd.org/ins/20190221/1e2e.*

Source: OECD Insurance Statistics (database)

NEW ZEALAND

Table 1. Selected aggregates

Million NZD

	2010	2011	2012	2013	2014	2015	2016	2017
1.1 Insurance business written in the reporting country								
1.1.1 Insurance business, by ownership								
Gross premiums								
Domestic undertakings	..	..	..	..	..	..	..	..
Foreign controlled undertakings	..	..	..	..	..	..	..	..
Foreign companies (branches)	..	..	..	..	..	..	..	..
All undertakings	4 680	..	5 665	6 266	6 460	6 678	6 828	7 240
Premiums ceded								
Domestic undertakings	..	..	..	..	..	..	..	..
Foreign controlled undertakings	..	..	..	..	..	..	..	..
Foreign companies (branches)	..	..	..	..	..	..	..	..
All undertakings	610	..	1 207	1 412	1 292	1 305	1 789	1 852
Net written premiums								
Domestic undertakings	..	..	..	..	..	..	..	..
Foreign controlled undertakings	..	..	..	..	..	..	..	..
Foreign companies (branches)	..	..	..	..	..	..	..	..
All undertakings	5 730	..	6 365	6 758	7 186	7 523	7 303	7 729
1.1.2 Insurance business on foreign risks, gross premiums								
Life	..	..	..	..	..	..	..	..
Non-life	..	..	..	..	..	..	..	..
Composite	..	..	..	..	..	..	..	..
of which:								
Life	..	..	..	..	..	..	..	..
Non-life	..	..	..	..	..	..	..	..
Total	..	..	..	..	..	..	..	..
1.1.3 Life insurance payments, by class, gross premiums								
Annuities	..	..	..	..	..	..	..	..
Unit linked	..	..	..	..	..	..	..	..
Other life insurance	..	..	..	..	..	..	..	..
Total life insurance	..	..	..	..	..	..	..	..
of which: *Pension contracts*	..	..	..	..	..	..	..	..
1.1.4 Non-life insurance payments, by class, gross premiums								
Motor vehicle insurance	..	..	..	..	..	..	..	..
Marine, aviation and other transport insurance	..	..	..	..	..	..	..	..
Freight insurance	..	..	..	..	..	..	..	..
Fire and other property damage insurance	..	..	..	..	..	..	..	..
Pecuniary loss insurance	..	..	..	..	..	..	..	..
General liability insurance	..	..	..	..	..	..	..	..
Accident and health	..	..	..	..	..	..	..	..
of which: *Health*	..	..	..	..	..	..	..	..
Other non-life insurance	..	..	..	..	..	..	..	..
Treaty reinsurance	..	..	..	..	..	..	..	..
Total non-life insurance	4 680	..	5 665	6 266	6 460	6 678	6 828	7 240
1.2 Gross claims payments								
Life								
Domestic undertakings	..	..	..	..	..	..	..	..
Foreign controlled undertakings	..	..	..	..	..	..	..	..
Foreign companies (branches)	..	..	..	..	..	..	..	..
All undertakings	1 437	..	1 360	1 303	1 399	1 544	1 598	1 579
Non-life								
Domestic undertakings	..	..	..	..	..	..	..	..
Foreign controlled undertakings	..	..	..	..	..	..	..	..
Foreign companies (branches)	..	..	..	..	..	..	..	..
All undertakings	2 802	..	9 531	4 539	5 642	6 302	4 864	6 662
Composite								
Domestic undertakings	..	..	..	..	..	..	..	..
Foreign controlled undertakings	..	..	..	..	..	..	..	..
Foreign companies (branches)	..	..	..	..	..	..	..	..
All undertakings	..	..	..	..	..	..	..	..
of which:								
Life								
Domestic undertakings	..	..	..	..	..	..	..	..
Foreign controlled undertakings	..	..	..	..	..	..	..	..
Foreign companies (branches)	..	..	..	..	..	..	..	..
All undertakings	..	..	..	..	..	..	..	..
Non-life								
Domestic undertakings	..	..	..	..	..	..	..	..
Foreign controlled undertakings	..	..	..	..	..	..	..	..
Foreign companies (branches)	..	..	..	..	..	..	..	..
All undertakings	..	..	..	..	..	..	..	..
Total								
Domestic undertakings	..	..	..	..	..	..	..	..
Foreign controlled undertakings	..	..	..	..	..	..	..	..
Foreign companies (branches)	..	..	..	..	..	..	..	..
All undertakings	4 239	..	10 891	5 842	7 041	7 846	6 462	8 241

NEW ZEALAND

Table 1. Selected aggregates (cont.)

Million NZD

	2010	2011	2012	2013	2014	2015	2016	2017
1.3 Commissions								
Life								
Domestic undertakings	..	..	..	..	..	..	..	..
Foreign controlled undertakings	..	..	..	..	..	..	..	..
Foreign companies (branches)	..	..	..	..	..	..	..	..
All undertakings	..	..	..	..	..	..	..	..
Non-life								
Domestic undertakings	..	..	..	..	..	..	..	..
Foreign controlled undertakings	..	..	..	..	..	..	..	..
Foreign companies (branches)	..	..	..	..	..	..	..	..
All undertakings	..	..	..	..	..	..	..	..
Composite								
Domestic undertakings	..	..	..	..	..	..	..	..
Foreign controlled undertakings	..	..	..	..	..	..	..	..
Foreign companies (branches)	..	..	..	..	..	..	..	..
All undertakings	..	..	..	..	..	..	..	..
of which:								
Life	..	..	..	..	..	..	..	..
Domestic undertakings	..	..	..	..	..	..	..	..
Foreign controlled undertakings	..	..	..	..	..	..	..	..
Foreign companies (branches)	..	..	..	..	..	..	..	..
All undertakings	..	..	..	..	..	..	..	..
Non-life	..	..	..	..	..	..	..	..
Domestic undertakings	..	..	..	..	..	..	..	..
Foreign controlled undertakings	..	..	..	..	..	..	..	..
Foreign companies (branches)	..	..	..	..	..	..	..	..
All undertakings	..	..	..	..	..	..	..	..
Total								
Domestic undertakings	..	..	..	..	..	..	..	..
Foreign controlled undertakings	..	..	..	..	..	..	..	..
Foreign companies (branches)	..	..	..	..	..	..	..	..
All undertakings	..	..	..	..	..	..	..	..
1.4 Gross operating expenses								
Life								
Domestic undertakings	..	..	..	..	..	..	..	..
Foreign controlled undertakings	..	..	..	..	..	..	..	..
Foreign companies (branches)	..	..	..	..	..	..	..	..
All undertakings	2 403	..	2 169	2 151	2 384	2 323	2 489	2 476
Non-life								
Domestic undertakings	..	..	..	..	..	..	..	..
Foreign controlled undertakings	..	..	..	..	..	..	..	..
Foreign companies (branches)	..	..	..	..	..	..	..	..
All undertakings	4 213	..	12 070	6 102	7 490	8 472	6 875	8 884
Composite								
Domestic undertakings	..	..	..	..	..	..	..	..
Foreign controlled undertakings	..	..	..	..	..	..	..	..
Foreign companies (branches)	..	..	..	..	..	..	..	..
All undertakings	..	..	..	..	..	..	..	..
of which:								
Life	..	..	..	..	..	..	..	..
Domestic undertakings	..	..	..	..	..	..	..	..
Foreign controlled undertakings	..	..	..	..	..	..	..	..
Foreign companies (branches)	..	..	..	..	..	..	..	..
All undertakings	..	..	..	..	..	..	..	..
Non-life	..	..	..	..	..	..	..	..
Domestic undertakings	..	..	..	..	..	..	..	..
Foreign controlled undertakings	..	..	..	..	..	..	..	..
Foreign companies (branches)	..	..	..	..	..	..	..	..
All undertakings	..	..	..	..	..	..	..	..
Total								
Domestic undertakings	..	..	..	..	..	..	..	..
Foreign controlled undertakings	..	..	..	..	..	..	..	..
Foreign companies (branches)	..	..	..	..	..	..	..	..
All undertakings	6 616	..	14 239	8 253	9 874	10 795	9 364	11 360

NEW ZEALAND

Table 1. Selected aggregates (cont.)

Million NZD

	2010	2011	2012	2013	2014	2015	2016	2017
1.5 Insurance business written abroad by branches, gross premiums								
Life								
Branches and agencies	..	..	..	..	..	..	..	..
Subsidaries	..	..	..	..	..	..	..	..
Total	..	..	..	..	..	..	..	..
Non-life								
Branches and agencies	..	..	..	..	..	..	..	..
Subsidaries	..	..	..	..	..	..	..	..
Total	..	..	..	..	..	..	..	..
Composite								
Branches and agencies	..	..	..	..	..	..	..	..
Subsidaries	..	..	..	..	..	..	..	..
Total	..	..	..	..	..	..	..	..
of which:								
Life								
Branches and agencies	..	..	..	..	..	..	..	..
Subsidaries	..	..	..	..	..	..	..	..
Total	..	..	..	..	..	..	..	..
Non-life								
Branches and agencies	..	..	..	..	..	..	..	..
Subsidaries	..	..	..	..	..	..	..	..
Total	..	..	..	..	..	..	..	..
Total								
Branches and agencies	..	..	..	..	..	..	..	..
Subsidaries	..	..	..	..	..	..	..	..
Total	..	..	..	..	..	..	..	..

.. Not available

Note: Detailed metadata at: *http://metalinks.oecd.org/ins/20190221/d380.*

Source: *OECD Insurance Statistics (database)*

NEW ZEALAND

Table 2. Number of companies and employees

	2010	2011	2012	2013	2014	2015	2016	2017
2.1 Number of companies								
Life								
Domestic undertakings	..	..	..	..	..	..	..	..
Foreign controlled undertakings	..	..	..	..	..	..	..	..
Foreign companies (branches)	..	..	..	..	..	..	..	..
All undertakings	42	..	43	37	43	30	30	30
Non-life								
Domestic undertakings	..	..	..	..	..	..	..	..
Foreign controlled undertakings	..	..	..	..	..	..	..	..
Foreign companies (branches)	..	..	..	..	..	..	..	..
All undertakings	147	..	142	130	145	102	90	87
Composite								
Domestic undertakings	..	..	..	..	..	..	..	..
Foreign controlled undertakings	..	..	..	..	..	..	..	..
Foreign companies (branches)	..	..	..	..	..	..	..	..
All undertakings	..	..	..	..	..	..	..	..
Reinsurance								
Domestic undertakings	..	..	..	..	..	..	..	..
Foreign controlled undertakings	..	..	..	..	..	..	..	..
Foreign companies (branches)	..	..	..	..	..	..	..	..
All undertakings	..	..	..	..	..	..	..	..
Total								
Domestic undertakings	..	..	..	..	..	..	..	..
Foreign controlled undertakings	..	..	..	..	..	..	..	..
Foreign companies (branches)	..	..	..	..	..	..	..	..
All undertakings	189	..	185	167	188	132	120	117
2.2 Number of employees								
Insurance undertakings	..	..	..	10 780	10 720	10 680	..	..
Intermediaries	..	..	..	..	..	..	..	..
Total	9 650	..	10 640	10 780	..	..	..	..

.. Not available

Note: Detailed metadata at: *http://metalinks.oecd.org/ins/20190221/d380.*

Source: OECD Insurance Statistics (database)

NORWAY

Table 1. Selected aggregates

Million NOK

	2010	2011	2012	2013	2014	2015	2016	2017
1.1 Insurance business written in the reporting country								
1.1.1 Insurance business, by ownership								
Gross premiums								
Domestic undertakings	99 610	106 973	119 751	119 149	134 884	135 864	138 612	139 748
Foreign controlled undertakings	6 299	6 388	8 589	8 948	11 029	13 195	..	..
Foreign companies (branches)	24 719	26 383	30 039	30 872	31 867	30 638	31 150	29 049
All undertakings	124 329	133 356	149 790	150 021	166 751	166 502	169 762	168 797
Premiums ceded								
Domestic undertakings	..	..	6 252	6 396	6 891	7 973	7 053	7 061
Foreign controlled undertakings	..	..	316	173	198	218	..	..
Foreign companies (branches)	..	..	4 290	4 219	4 653	4 976	5 362	4 814
All undertakings	..	..	10 542	10 614	11 544	12 950	12 415	11 876
Net written premiums								
Domestic undertakings	..	..	113 499	112 754	127 993	127 890	131 559	132 686
Foreign controlled undertakings	..	..	8 273	8 775	10 832	12 978	..	..
Foreign companies (branches)	..	..	25 749	26 653	27 213	25 662	25 788	24 235
All undertakings	..	..	139 248	139 407	155 206	153 552	157 347	156 921
1.1.2 Insurance business on foreign risks, gross premiums								
Life	..	..	31	..	..	9	7	6
Non-life	2 779	1 556	7 352	6 202	11 468	11 250	10 855	10 417
Composite total	..	..	..	..	..	..	..	..
Total	2 779	1 556	7 383	6 202	11 468	11 260	10 862	10 422
1.1.3 Life insurance payments, by class, gross premiums								
Annuities	..	..	..	..	..	..	..	..
Unit linked	..	..	..	..	..	..	..	..
Other life insurance	..	..	..	..	..	..	..	..
Total life insurance	66 586	71 577	81 742	81 299	92 185	91 794	94 093	93 577
***of which:** Pension contracts*	..	..	69 652	66 873	..	..	..	..
1.1.4 Non-life insurance payments, by class, gross premiums								
Motor vehicle insurance	10 409	10 787	19 403	..	20 378	20 706	20 897	21 029
Marine, aviation and other transport insurance	3 974	4 009	9 581	..	6 574	5 201	15 291	5 292
Freight insurance	..	..	..	..	..	..	0	..
Fire and other property damage insurance	9 470	10 811	17 738	..	18 195	19 041	23 135	22 553
Pecuniary loss insurance	119	125	585	..	127	97	432	92
General liability insurance	647	686	1 755	..	1 695	1 637	2 000	1 774
Accident and health	3 205	3 229	6 111	..	5 608	5 553	10 526	10 288
***of which:** Health*	..	..	..	..	..	..	0	..
Other non-life insurance	5 993	5 967	12 875	..	21 989	13 048	7 085	6 088
Treaty reinsurance	..	..	..	..	..	..	0	..
Total non-life insurance	33 817	35 615	68 048	..	74 566	65 283	79 366	67 116
1.2 Gross claims payments								
Life								
Domestic undertakings	40 443	40 252	45 033	45 143	45 742	49 007	51 548	54 419
Foreign controlled undertakings	3 309	2 723	3 120	3 186	3 150	4 796	c	..
Foreign companies (branches)	405	494	482	692	476	235	288	281
All undertakings	40 848	40 746	45 515	45 835	46 218	49 242	51 836	54 700
Non-life								
Domestic undertakings	21 364	26 292	28 356	23 486	30 742	34 587	32 537	31 896
Foreign controlled undertakings	441	342	542	c	c	c	c	..
Foreign companies (branches)	16 445	17 552	24 549	20 026	22 287	21 584	21 146	20 655
All undertakings	37 809	43 844	52 905	43 512	53 030	56 170	53 683	52 550
Composite, all undertakings	..	..	..	..	..	..	..	..
Total								
Domestic undertakings	61 807	66 544	73 389	68 629	76 485	83 593	84 085	86 315
Foreign controlled undertakings	3 750	3 065	3 662	3 186	3 150	4 796	..	..
Foreign companies (branches)	16 850	18 046	25 031	20 718	22 763	21 819	21 434	20 935
All undertakings	78 657	84 590	98 420	89 347	99 248	105 413	105 519	107 250
1.3 Commissions								
Life								
Domestic undertakings	..	..	692	774	839	916	890	783
Foreign controlled undertakings	..	..	152	179	202	227	c	c
Foreign companies (branches)	..	..	0	0	0	..	..	..
All undertakings	..	..	692	774	839	916	890	783
Non-life								
Domestic undertakings	..	..	1 507	1 536	2 204	2 119	1 956	2 105
Foreign controlled undertakings	..	..	35	c	c	..	c	c
Foreign companies (branches)	..	..	1 101	1 084	1 099	1 107	950	915
All undertakings	..	..	2 608	2 619	3 303	3 226	2 906	3 020
Composite, all undertakings	..	..	..	..	..	..	..	..
Total								
Domestic undertakings	..	..	2 199	2 310	3 043	3 035	2 846	2 889
Foreign controlled undertakings	..	..	187	179	202	227	..	..
Foreign companies (branches)	..	..	1 101	1 084	1 099	1 107	950	915
All undertakings	..	..	3 300	3 393	4 142	4 142	3 797	3 804

NORWAY

Table 1. Selected aggregates (cont.)

Million NOK

	2010	2011	2012	2013	2014	2015	2016	2017
1.4 Gross operating expenses								
Life								
Domestic undertakings	6 839	5 818	7 019	6 688	7 205	7 383	7 750	7 380
Foreign controlled undertakings	646	688	692	185	807	765	c	..
Foreign companies (branches)	151	144	0	126	162	..	157	143
All undertakings	6 990	5 962	7 019	6 814	7 367	7 383	7 907	7 523
Non-life								
Domestic undertakings	5 703	6 155	5 527	5 925	6 585	6 138	6 139	6 956
Foreign controlled undertakings	141	76	48	c	c	c	c	..
Foreign companies (branches)	5 451	5 121	4 765	4 203	5 318	5 574	5 465	4 732
All undertakings	11 154	11 276	10 292	10 128	11 903	11 712	11 605	11 688
Composite, all undertakings	..	..	..	..	..	..	..	..
Total								
Domestic undertakings	12 542	11 973	12 546	12 613	13 790	13 521	13 889	14 336
Foreign controlled undertakings	787	764	740	185	807	765	..	..
Foreign companies (branches)	5 602	5 265	4 765	4 329	5 480	5 574	5 623	4 875
All undertakings	18 144	17 238	17 311	16 942	19 270	19 095	19 512	19 211
1.5 Insurance business written abroad by branches, gross premiums								
Life								
Branches and agencies	89	..	..	c	..	..	..	..
Subsidaries	..	..	..	..	..	..	..	..
Total	89	..	..	c	..	..	..	..
Non-life								
Branches and agencies	2 977	2 476	2 454	1 134	4 636	1 569	7 141	2 493
Subsidaries	..	..	..	c	c	..	..	..
Total	2 977	2 476	2 454	1 134	4 636	1 569	7 141	2 493
Composite total	..	..	..	..	..	..	..	..
Total								
Branches and agencies	3 066	2 476	2 454	1 134	4 636	1 569	7 141	2 493
Subsidaries	..	..	..	..	..	..	..	..
Total	3 066	2 476	2 454	1 134	4 636	1 569	7 141	2 493

.. Not available; c Confidential data

Note: Detailed metadata at: *http://metalinks.oecd.org/ins/20190221/79df.*

Source: OECD Insurance Statistics (database)

NORWAY

Table 2. Number of companies and employees

	2010	2011	2012	2013	2014	2015	2016	2017
2.1 Number of companies								
Life								
Domestic undertakings	12	12	10	12	10	10	10	13
Foreign controlled undertakings	2	2	2	2	2	2	2	3
Foreign companies (branches)	10	10	9	9	7	7	7	6
All undertakings	22	22	19	21	17	17	17	19
Non-life								
Domestic undertakings	77	76	63	59	59	58	59	58
Foreign controlled undertakings	1	1	1	1	1	2	2	2
Foreign companies (branches)	24	21	25	25	22	21	23	23
All undertakings	101	97	88	84	81	79	82	81
Composite, all undertakings	**0**	**0**	**0**	**0**	**0**	**0**	..	..
Reinsurance								
Domestic undertakings	..	..	..	..	..	..	..	..
Foreign controlled undertakings	..	..	..	..	..	..	..	..
Foreign companies (branches)	..	..	..	..	..	..	..	..
All undertakings	..	..	..	..	..	..	..	..
Total								
Domestic undertakings	89	88	73	71	69	68	69	71
Foreign controlled undertakings	3	3	3	3	3	4	4	5
Foreign companies (branches)	34	31	34	34	29	28	30	29
All undertakings	123	119	107	105	98	96	99	100
2.2 Number of employees								
Insurance undertakings	9 753	..	..	..	..	..	..	..
Intermediaries	..	..	..	..	..	..	..	..
Total	9 753	..	..	..	..	..	..	..

.. Not available

Note: Detailed metadata at: *http://metalinks.oecd.org/ins/20190221/79df.*

Source: OECD Insurance Statistics (database)

POLAND

Table 1. Selected aggregates

Million PLN

	2010	2011	2012	2013	2014	2015	2016	2017
1.1 Insurance business written in the reporting country								
1.1.1 Insurance business, by ownership								
Gross premiums								
Domestic undertakings	54 164	57 151	62 627	57 863	54 927	54 804	56 039	62 354
Foreign controlled undertakings	29 135	31 683	35 100	31 562	30 425	30 801	31 961	33 189
Foreign companies (branches)	..	..	..	..	..	..	..	..
All undertakings	54 164	57 151	62 627	57 863	54 927	54 804	56 039	62 354
Premiums ceded								
Domestic undertakings	3 393	3 852	4 598	4 214	4 170	5 197	6 765	7 203
Foreign controlled undertakings	2 043	4 647	4 224	3 664	3 533	4 355	4 798	4 664
Foreign companies (branches)	..	..	..	..	..	..	..	..
All undertakings	3 393	3 852	4 598	4 214	4 170	5 197	6 765	7 203
Net written premiums								
Domestic undertakings	50 771	53 299	58 029	53 649	50 757	49 606	49 274	55 151
Foreign controlled undertakings	27 092	27 036	30 876	27 898	26 892	26 446	27 163	28 524
Foreign companies (branches)	..	..	..	..	..	..	..	..
All undertakings	50 771	53 299	58 029	53 649	50 757	49 606	49 274	55 151
1.1.2 Insurance business on foreign risks, gross premiums								
Life	0	..	..	..	..	..	..	..
Non-life	202	..	..	..	..	..	..	..
Composite total	..	..	..	..	..	..	..	..
Total	203	..	..	..	..	..	..	..
1.1.3 Life insurance payments, by class, gross premiums								
Annuities	83	98	99	107	114	131	138	135
Unit linked	8 120	10 307	12 046	13 052	12 600	12 996	10 325	11 283
Other life insurance	23 150	21 415	24 203	18 082	15 933	14 377	13 370	13 120
Total life insurance	31 354	31 820	36 348	31 241	28 646	27 505	23 833	24 539
***of which:** Pension contracts*	329	376	371	396	356	356	..	..
1.1.4 Non-life insurance payments, by class, gross premiums								
Motor vehicle insurance	12 932	14 543	14 780	13 945	13 397	13 910	18 744	23 231
Marine, aviation and other transport insurance	163	232	256	267	275	210	185	195
Freight insurance	96	107	119	117	126	116	120	131
Fire and other property damage insurance	4 334	5 056	5 441	5 973	5 715	5 938	6 246	6 991
Pecuniary loss insurance	1 593	1 631	1 526	1 858	2 149	1 893	1 805	1 749
General liability insurance	1 302	1 459	1 773	1 891	1 964	2 134	1 915	2 076
Accident and health	1 621	1 688	1 801	1 926	2 007	2 273	2 222	2 348
***of which:** Health*	1 269	1 245	513	612	656	613	618	689
Other non-life insurance	698	575	554	622	627	804	947	1 071
Treaty reinsurance	0	..	..	..	..	..	..	..
Total non-life insurance	22 739	25 291	26 250	26 599	26 260	27 278	32 182	37 793
1.2 Gross claims payments								
Life								
Domestic undertakings	22 585	26 069	25 917	23 087	20 360	19 358	18 284	20 355
Foreign controlled undertakings	10 545	12 116	13 331	10 927	9 783	8 795	9 543	..
Foreign companies (branches)	..	..	..	..	..	..	..	..
All undertakings	22 585	26 069	25 917	23 087	20 360	19 358	18 284	20 355
Non-life								
Domestic undertakings	14 169	13 738	14 046	13 711	13 811	15 488	18 393	19 485
Foreign controlled undertakings	8 017	8 128	8 890	8 434	8 579	9 515	10 911	..
Foreign companies (branches)	..	..	..	..	..	..	..	..
All undertakings	14 169	13 738	14 046	13 711	13 811	15 488	18 393	19 485
Composite, all undertakings	..	..	..	..	..	..	..	..
Total								
Domestic undertakings	36 754	39 807	39 963	36 798	34 171	34 846	36 677	39 840
Foreign controlled undertakings	18 562	20 244	22 221	19 362	18 363	18 310	20 454	..
Foreign companies (branches)	..	..	..	..	..	..	..	..
All undertakings	36 754	39 807	39 963	36 798	34 171	34 846	36 677	39 840
1.3 Commissions								
Life								
Domestic undertakings	3 006	3 245	70	93	203	231	222	183
Foreign controlled undertakings	2 485	2 591	69	70	191	223	218	179
Foreign companies (branches)	..	..	..	..	..	..	..	..
All undertakings	3 006	3 245	70	93	203	231	222	183
Non-life								
Domestic undertakings	3 490	4 015	657	740	651	719	1 115	1 544
Foreign controlled undertakings	2 202	2 659	648	606	594	657	929	1 122
Foreign companies (branches)	..	..	..	..	..	..	..	..
All undertakings	3 490	4 015	657	740	651	719	1 115	1 544
Composite, all undertakings	..	..	..	..	..	..	..	..
Total								
Domestic undertakings	6 496	7 260	727	833	854	950	1 337	1 727
Foreign controlled undertakings	4 688	5 250	717	676	785	880	1 147	1 301
Foreign companies (branches)	..	..	..	..	..	..	..	..
All undertakings	6 496	7 260	727	833	854	950	1 337	1 727

POLAND

Table 1. Selected aggregates (cont.)

Million PLN

	2010	2011	2012	2013	2014	2015	2016	2017
1.4 Gross operating expenses								
Life								
Domestic undertakings	5 295	5 605	6 416	6 146	6 588	6 476	5 647	5 518
Foreign controlled undertakings	3 777	3 944	4 244	3 831	4 369	4 182	3 797	..
Foreign companies (branches)	..	..	..	..	..	..	..	..
All undertakings	5 295	5 605	6 416	6 146	6 588	6 476	5 647	5 518
Non-life								
Domestic undertakings	6 791	7 276	7 733	7 775	8 018	8 335	9 104	10 007
Foreign controlled undertakings	3 958	4 549	5 225	5 090	5 135	5 569	5 978	..
Foreign companies (branches)	..	..	..	..	..	..	..	..
All undertakings	6 791	7 276	7 733	7 775	8 018	8 335	9 104	10 007
Composite, all undertakings	..	..	..	..	..	..	..	..
Total								
Domestic undertakings	12 086	12 882	14 149	13 921	14 606	14 811	14 751	15 525
Foreign controlled undertakings	7 734	8 493	9 469	8 921	9 504	9 751	9 776	..
Foreign companies (branches)	..	..	..	..	..	..	..	..
All undertakings	12 086	12 882	14 149	13 921	14 606	14 811	14 751	15 525
1.5 Insurance business written abroad by branches, gross premiums								
Life								
Branches and agencies	14	19	26	..	79	92	..	95
Subsidaries	..	..	..	..	..	..	..	..
Total	14	19	26	..	79	92	..	95
Non-life								
Branches and agencies	14	62	53	..	98	116	..	..
Subsidaries	..	49	..	..	..	..	..	..
Total	14	111	53	..	98	116	..	..
Composite total	..	..	..	..	..	..	..	..
Total								
Branches and agencies	29	82	79	..	177	208	..	95
Subsidaries	..	49	..	..	..	..	..	..
Total	29	130	79	..	177	208	..	95

.. Not available

Note: Detailed metadata at: *http://metalinks.oecd.org/ins/20190221/ba21*.

Source: OECD Insurance Statistics (database)

POLAND

Table 2. Number of companies and employees

	2010	2011	2012	2013	2014	2015	2016	2017
2.1 Number of companies								
Life								
Domestic undertakings	30	28	28	27	26	28	27	27
Foreign controlled undertakings	23	22	23	21	19	21	21	20
Foreign companies (branches)	..	2	..	..	..	..	..	..
All undertakings	30	30	28	27	26	28	27	27
Non-life								
Domestic undertakings	32	32	30	30	30	32	33	33
Foreign controlled undertakings	21	22	21	19	19	22	20	19
Foreign companies (branches)	..	11	..	..	..	..	..	..
All undertakings	32	43	30	30	30	32	33	33
Composite, all undertakings	**0**	**0**	**0**	**0**	**0**	**0**	**0**	**..**
Reinsurance								
Domestic undertakings	1	1	1	1	1	1	1	1
Foreign controlled undertakings	1	1	1	1	1	1	1	1
Foreign companies (branches)	..	..	..	..	..	..	..	..
All undertakings	1	1	1	1	1	1	1	1
Total								
Domestic undertakings	63	61	59	58	57	61	61	61
Foreign controlled undertakings	45	45	45	41	39	44	42	40
Foreign companies (branches)	..	13	..	..	..	..	..	..
All undertakings	63	74	59	58	57	61	61	61
2.2 Number of employees								
Insurance undertakings	35 803	37 239	37 205	37 187	35 922	35 282	..	..
Intermediaries	62 347	68 168	58 879	69 621	58 004	49 126	..	..
Total	98 150	105 407	96 083	106 808	93 926	84 408	..	..

.. Not available

Note: Detailed metadata at: *http://metalinks.oecd.org/ins/20190221/ba21*.

Source: OECD Insurance Statistics (database)

PORTUGAL

Table 1. Selected aggregates

Million EUR

	2010	2011	2012	2013	2014	2015	2016	2017
1.1 Insurance business written in the reporting country								
1.1.1 Insurance business, by ownership								
Gross premiums								
Domestic undertakings	15 816	11 165	10 553	12 802	14 051	12 568	10 913	11 455
Foreign controlled undertakings	1 758	1 676	1 553	1 617	8 737	8 890	9 048	10 640
Foreign companies (branches)	75	73	0	0	0	0	0	0
All undertakings	15 891	11 238	10 553	12 802	14 051	12 568	10 913	11 455
Premiums ceded								
Domestic undertakings	1 013	982	1 096	1 144	1 118	1 194	1 214	1 307
Foreign controlled undertakings	80	153	130	140	836	924	992	1 180
Foreign companies (branches)	26	23	0	0	0	0	0	0
All undertakings	1 039	1 005	1 096	1 144	1 118	1 194	1 214	1 307
Net written premiums								
Domestic undertakings	14 802	10 183	9 457	11 658	12 933	11 374	9 698	10 148
Foreign controlled undertakings	1 678	1 523	1 423	1 477	7 902	7 966	8 056	9 460
Foreign companies (branches)	49	50	0	0	0	0	0	0
All undertakings	14 851	10 232	9 457	11 658	12 933	11 374	9 698	10 148
1.1.2 Insurance business on foreign risks, gross premiums								
Life	0	0	2	3	13	8	11	8
Non-life	1	2	15	14	13	13	4	7
Composite	0	0	54	64	92	107	127	129
of which:								
Life	0	0	27	27	53	63	70	74
Non-life	0	0	27	38	39	44	57	55
Total	1	2	72	81	118	129	142	144
1.1.3 Life insurance payments, by class, gross premiums								
Annuities	33	19	46	79	64	109	142	183
Unit linked	2 389	1 954	1 999	1 851	1 966	2 119	1 655	2 077
Other life insurance	9 414	5 240	4 633	7 094	8 220	6 254	4 708	4 450
Total life insurance	11 835	7 213	6 678	9 023	10 249	8 481	6 504	6 710
***of which:** Pension contracts*	..	..	..	..	..	..	..	..
1.1.4 Non-life insurance payments, by class, gross premiums								
Motor vehicle insurance	1 454	1 447	1 353	1 277	1 256	1 316	1 399	1 482
Marine, aviation and other transport insurance	37	35	35	33	29	28	25	27
Freight insurance	26	26	25	25	24	23	22	22
Fire and other property damage insurance	657	686	702	700	699	745	771	795
Pecuniary loss insurance	53	54	63	69	70	73	84	83
General liability insurance	93	90	89	84	87	94	99	102
Accident and health	1 504	1 480	1 430	1 413	1 452	1 602	1 783	1 999
***of which:** Health*	806	820	838	862	896	973	1 084	1 208
Other non-life insurance	165	170	177	178	183	205	225	235
Treaty reinsurance	0	0	0	0	0	0	0	0
Total non-life insurance	3 988	3 988	3 874	3 778	3 802	4 086	4 408	4 745
1.2 Gross claims payments								
Life								
Domestic undertakings	3 782	6 935	4 875	4 518	5 254	6 133	6 568	3 940
Foreign controlled undertakings	457	505	461	374	2 667	2 724	2 252	2 853
Foreign companies (branches)	0	0	0	0	0	0	0	0
All undertakings	3 782	6 935	4 875	4 518	5 254	6 133	6 568	3 940
Non-life								
Domestic undertakings	1 628	1 588	1 471	1 446	1 407	1 520	1 336	1 413
Foreign controlled undertakings	518	424	385	376	1 174	1 278	1 070	1 130
Foreign companies (branches)	0	0	0	0	0	0	0	0
All undertakings	1 628	1 588	1 471	1 446	1 407	1 520	1 336	1 413
Composite								
Domestic undertakings	7 074	7 987	5 927	5 427	5 201	5 128	4 554	4 230
Foreign controlled undertakings	474	517	541	562	3 991	3 922	4 501	4 180
Foreign companies (branches)	43	43	0	0	0	0	0	0
All undertakings	7 116	8 030	5 927	5 427	5 201	5 128	4 554	4 230
of which:								
Life	5 828	6 661	4 616	4 067	3 895	3 840	2 867	2 479
Domestic undertakings	5 787	6 621	4 616	4 067	3 895	3 840	2 867	2 479
Foreign controlled undertakings	151	173	184	167	2 904	2 839	2 815	2 431
Foreign companies (branches)	41	41	0	0	0	0	0	0
All undertakings	5 828	6 661	4 616	4 067	3 895	3 840	2 867	2 479
Non-life	1 288	1 369	1 311	1 360	1 306	1 288	1 687	1 751
Domestic undertakings	1 286	1 367	1 311	1 360	1 306	1 288	1 687	1 751
Foreign controlled undertakings	323	344	357	395	1 087	1 083	1 686	1 749
Foreign companies (branches)	2	2	0	0	0	0	0	0
All undertakings	1 288	1 369	1 311	1 360	1 306	1 288	1 687	1 751
Total								
Domestic undertakings	12 485	16 510	12 274	11 391	11 861	12 782	12 458	9 582
Foreign controlled undertakings	1 449	1 446	1 387	1 312	7 832	7 923	7 822	8 163
Foreign companies (branches)	43	43	0	0	0	0	0	0
All undertakings	12 527	16 553	12 274	11 391	11 861	12 782	12 458	9 582

PORTUGAL

Table 1. Selected aggregates (cont.)

Million EUR

	2010	2011	2012	2013	2014	2015	2016	2017
1.3 Commissions								
Life								
Domestic undertakings	69	38	47	144	40	77	105	103
Foreign controlled undertakings	9	9	7	7	15	41	42	85
Foreign companies (branches)	0	0	0	0	0	0	0	0
All undertakings	69	38	47	144	40	77	105	103
Non-life								
Domestic undertakings	179	155	157	156	153	178	164	183
Foreign controlled undertakings	58	44	40	38	117	133	98	115
Foreign companies (branches)	0	0	0	0	0	0	0	0
All undertakings	179	155	157	156	153	178	164	183
Composite								
Domestic undertakings	256	273	272	291	301	295	286	351
Foreign controlled undertakings	63	76	81	99	208	222	283	344
Foreign companies (branches)	22	20	0	0	0	0	0	0
All undertakings	277	293	272	291	301	295	286	351
of which:								
Life	119	114	87	98	100	82	49	58
Domestic undertakings	99	96	87	98	100	82	49	58
Foreign controlled undertakings	19	20	21	28	42	44	47	52
Foreign companies (branches)	20	18	0	0	0	0	0	0
All undertakings	119	114	87	98	100	82	49	58
Non-life	158	179	185	193	201	214	237	293
Domestic undertakings	157	177	185	193	201	214	237	293
Foreign controlled undertakings	44	56	60	71	165	178	236	291
Foreign companies (branches)	2	2	0	0	0	0	0	0
All undertakings	158	179	185	193	201	214	237	293
Total								
Domestic undertakings	504	466	476	591	493	550	554	637
Foreign controlled undertakings	131	130	128	144	339	396	423	543
Foreign companies (branches)	22	20	0	0	0	0	0	0
All undertakings	525	486	476	591	493	550	554	637
1.4 Gross operating expenses								
Life								
Domestic undertakings	234	202	206	314	212	244	300	298
Foreign controlled undertakings	37	37	36	33	136	163	168	248
Foreign companies (branches)	0	0	0	0	0	0	0	0
All undertakings	234	202	206	314	212	244	300	298
Non-life								
Domestic undertakings	555	528	511	496	495	550	467	494
Foreign controlled undertakings	179	155	144	133	398	441	357	388
Foreign companies (branches)	0	0	0	0	0	0	0	0
All undertakings	555	528	511	496	495	550	467	494
Composite								
Domestic undertakings	689	710	723	715	717	720	711	851
Foreign controlled undertakings	163	190	200	198	541	571	702	839
Foreign companies (branches)	38	39	0	0	0	0	0	0
All undertakings	727	750	723	715	717	720	711	851
of which:								
Life	270	258	221	234	230	222	148	173
Domestic undertakings	238	226	221	234	230	222	148	173
Foreign controlled undertakings	45	48	49	48	125	145	140	162
Foreign companies (branches)	32	32	0	0	0	0	0	0
All undertakings	270	258	221	234	230	222	148	173
Non-life	457	492	502	481	487	497	562	678
Domestic undertakings	451	484	502	481	487	497	562	678
Foreign controlled undertakings	118	142	151	151	416	427	562	677
Foreign companies (branches)	6	7	0	0	0	0	0	0
All undertakings	457	492	502	481	487	497	562	678
Total								
Domestic undertakings	1 478	1 440	1 440	1 525	1 425	1 513	1 478	1 643
Foreign controlled undertakings	379	381	380	364	1 076	1 176	1 227	1 474
Foreign companies (branches)	38	39	0	0	0	0	0	0
All undertakings	1 516	1 480	1 440	1 525	1 425	1 513	1 478	1 643

PORTUGAL

Table 1. Selected aggregates (cont.)

Million EUR

	2010	2011	2012	2013	2014	2015	2016	2017
1.5 Insurance business written abroad by branches, gross premiums								
Life								
Branches and agencies	4	6	2	3	13	8	11	8
Subsidaries	0	0	0	0	0	0	0	0
Total	4	6	2	3	13	8	11	8
Non-life								
Branches and agencies	7	8	14	12	12	12	1	3
Subsidaries	0	0	0	0	0	0	0	0
Total	7	8	14	12	12	12	1	3
Composite								
Branches and agencies	79	55	54	64	92	107	127	129
Subsidaries	0	0	0	0	0	0	0	0
Total	79	55	54	64	92	107	127	129
of which:								
Life	40	28	27	27	53	63	70	74
Branches and agencies	40	28	27	27	53	63	70	74
Subsidaries	0	0	0	0	0	0	0	0
Total	40	28	27	27	53	63	70	74
Non-life	39	27	27	38	39	44	57	55
Branches and agencies	39	27	27	38	39	44	57	55
Subsidaries	0	0	0	0	0	0	0	0
Total	39	27	27	38	39	44	57	55
Total								
Branches and agencies	89	69	70	79	117	128	138	140
Subsidaries	0	0	0	0	0	0	0	0
Total	89	69	70	79	117	128	138	140

.. Not available

Note: Detailed metadata at: *http://metalinks.oecd.org/ins/20190221/682c.*

Source: *OECD Insurance Statistics (database)*

PORTUGAL

Table 2. Number of companies and employees

	2010	2011	2012	2013	2014	2015	2016	2017
2.1 Number of companies								
Life								
Domestic undertakings	15	14	14	14	16	16	14	13
Foreign controlled undertakings	6	5	5	5	10	10	9	9
Foreign companies (branches)	6	6	6	5	5	5	4	4
All undertakings	21	20	20	19	21	21	18	17
Non-life								
Domestic undertakings	23	21	21	21	21	24	23	23
Foreign controlled undertakings	6	5	4	4	15	16	15	15
Foreign companies (branches)	26	24	25	24	23	21	19	19
All undertakings	49	45	46	45	44	45	42	42
Composite								
Domestic undertakings	7	7	6	6	5	5	5	6
Foreign controlled undertakings	2	2	2	2	3	3	4	4
Foreign companies (branches)	5	5	5	6	6	7	7	7
All undertakings	12	12	11	12	11	12	12	13
Reinsurance								
Domestic undertakings	1	1	1	1	1	1	1	1
Foreign controlled undertakings	0	0	0	0	1	1	1	1
Foreign companies (branches)	0	0	0	0	0	0	0	0
All undertakings	1	1	1	1	1	1	1	1
Total								
Domestic undertakings	46	43	42	42	43	46	43	43
Foreign controlled undertakings	14	12	11	11	29	30	29	29
Foreign companies (branches)	37	35	36	35	34	33	30	30
All undertakings	83	78	78	77	77	79	73	73
2.2 Number of employees								
Insurance undertakings	10 565	10 937	8 807	9 224	9 252	9 441	9 387	9 381
Intermediaries	25 897	25 397	24 624	24 207	23 465	22 738	21 426	20 258
Total	36 462	36 334	33 431	33 431	32 717	32 179	30 813	29 639

Note: Detailed metadata at: *http://metalinks.oecd.org/ins/20190221/682c.*
Source: OECD Insurance Statistics (database)

SLOVAK REPUBLIC

Table 1. Selected aggregates

Million EUR

	2010	2011	2012	2013	2014	2015	2016	2017
1.1 Insurance business written in the reporting country								
1.1.1 Insurance business, by ownership								
Gross premiums								
Domestic undertakings	2 015	2 040	2 036	2 082	2 106	2 020	..	4 186
Foreign controlled undertakings	1 861	1 875	1 863	1 901	1 918	1 827	..	..
Foreign companies (branches)	109	114	121	146	142	143	..	282
All undertakings	2 124	2 154	2 157	2 228	2 248	2 163	..	4 468
Premiums ceded								
Domestic undertakings	263	294	294	298	314	319	..	319
Foreign controlled undertakings	241	268	267	268	283	287	..	..
Foreign companies (branches)	16	17	17	19	17	17	..	31
All undertakings	279	312	311	316	331	336	..	350
Net written premiums								
Domestic undertakings	1 752	1 746	1 742	1 785	1 792	1 701	..	3 868
Foreign controlled undertakings	1 607	1 606	1 596	1 633	1 635	1 540	..	..
Foreign companies (branches)	93	96	104	127	126	126	..	250
All undertakings	1 845	1 842	1 846	1 912	1 917	1 827	..	4 118
1.1.2 Insurance business on foreign risks, gross premiums								
Life	..	..	..	..	..	..	..	..
Non-life	..	..	..	..	..	..	..	..
Composite	..	..	..	..	..	..	..	..
of which:								
Life	..	..	..	..	..	..	..	..
Non-life	..	..	..	..	..	..	..	..
Total	..	..	..	..	..	..	..	..
1.1.3 Life insurance payments, by class, gross premiums								
Annuities	637	619	607	649	623	586	..	2
Unit linked	315	338	409	423	417	351	..	166
Other life insurance	128	137	146	164	180	171	..	950
Total life insurance	1 079	1 094	1 162	1 236	1 220	1 108	..	1 119
***of which:** Pension contracts*	16	15	13	12	12	12	..	..
1.1.4 Non-life insurance payments, by class, gross premiums								
Motor vehicle insurance	579	568	548	528	532	547	..	309
Marine, aviation and other transport insurance	6	6	7	6	6	6	..	10
Freight insurance	8	8	8	8	8	8	..	..
Fire and other property damage insurance	235	248	247	250	257	257	..	276
Pecuniary loss insurance	23	25	24	27	33	34	..	11
General liability insurance	67	65	68	73	78	78	..	80
Accident and health	40	38	40	45	49	44	..	..
***of which:** Health*	2	2	2	2	2	3	..	..
Other non-life insurance	29	31	32	34	35	39	..	397
Treaty reinsurance	12	19	21	21	32	42	..	..
Total non-life insurance	997	1 009	996	992	1 028	1 055	..	1 083
1.2 Gross claims payments								
Life								
Domestic undertakings	84	97	93	91	107	98	186	76
Foreign controlled undertakings	84	97	93	91	107	98	..	73
Foreign companies (branches)	1	0	0	0	0	2	..	117
All undertakings	85	97	93	91	108	100	..	193
Non-life								
Domestic undertakings	5	5	1	0	0	0	..	..
Foreign controlled undertakings	5	5	1	0	0	0	..	..
Foreign companies (branches)	27	24	44	27	29	32	..	21
All undertakings	32	29	45	27	29	32	..	..
Composite								
Domestic undertakings	1 043	1 075	1 083	1 117	1 084	1 057	2 291	..
Foreign controlled undertakings	922	945	948	979	948	911	1 909	76
Foreign companies (branches)	3	5	12	14	16	16	..	21
All undertakings	1 046	1 079	1 094	1 131	1 099	1 073	..	..
of which:								
Life	528	566	640	658	646	575	..	..
Domestic undertakings	525	562	632	647	634	563	1 794	..
Foreign controlled undertakings	431	463	527	544	533	457	1 459	72
Foreign companies (branches)	3	4	8	11	12	12	..	17
All undertakings	528	566	640	658	646	575	..	..
Non-life	518	513	455	473	453	497	..	..
Domestic undertakings	518	513	451	470	450	494	497	..
Foreign controlled undertakings	490	483	421	435	415	454	450	4
Foreign companies (branches)	0	0	4	4	3	3	..	5
All undertakings	518	513	455	473	453	497	..	..
Total								
Domestic undertakings	1 132	1 177	1 176	1 208	1 191	1 155	2 477	76
Foreign controlled undertakings	1 010	1 047	1 042	1 070	1 055	1 010	1 909	149
Foreign companies (branches)	30	30	55	42	44	49	..	159
All undertakings	1 162	1 206	1 232	1 249	1 236	1 205	..	193

SLOVAK REPUBLIC

Table 1. Selected aggregates (cont.)

Million EUR

	2010	2011	2012	2013	2014	2015	2016	2017
1.3 Commissions								
Life								
Domestic undertakings	22	26	28	29	33	37	..	..
Foreign controlled undertakings	22	26	28	29	33	37	..	..
Foreign companies (branches)	0	1	1	1	1	2	..	23
All undertakings	22	27	29	30	34	39	..	..
Non-life								
Domestic undertakings	1	2	1	0	0	0	..	..
Foreign controlled undertakings	1	2	1	0	0	0	..	..
Foreign companies (branches)	9	9	11	13	15	18	..	21
All undertakings	10	11	12	13	15	18	..	..
Composite								
Domestic undertakings	221	230	238	251	259	250	..	..
Foreign controlled undertakings	210	219	225	238	244	233	..	..
Foreign companies (branches)	18	17	17	18	4	16	..	20
All undertakings	239	247	255	269	264	266	..	..
of which:								
Life	98	97	102	107	95	89	..	..
Domestic undertakings	80	82	86	93	95	77	..	..
Foreign controlled undertakings	77	79	81	90	91	73	..	..
Foreign companies (branches)	17	16	16	14	0	12	..	13
All undertakings	98	97	102	107	95	89	..	..
Non-life	141	149	154	162	168	177	..	..
Domestic undertakings	141	149	152	158	164	173	..	..
Foreign controlled undertakings	133	141	143	149	153	160	..	..
Foreign companies (branches)	1	1	2	4	4	5	..	7
All undertakings	141	149	154	162	168	177	..	..
Total								
Domestic undertakings	244	258	266	279	292	287	..	..
Foreign controlled undertakings	233	247	253	267	277	270	..	..
Foreign companies (branches)	27	27	30	32	21	36	..	64
All undertakings	271	285	296	311	313	323	..	..
1.4 Gross operating expenses								
Life								
Domestic undertakings	50	58	58	57	63	72	..	55
Foreign controlled undertakings	50	58	58	57	63	72	..	..
Foreign companies (branches)	1	2	3	2	2	3	..	51
All undertakings	51	60	60	59	65	75	..	105
Non-life								
Domestic undertakings	6	6	2	0	0	0	..	..
Foreign controlled undertakings	6	6	2	0	0	0	..	..
Foreign companies (branches)	20	23	26	30	31	32	..	41
All undertakings	26	29	28	30	31	32	..	41
Composite								
Domestic undertakings	488	492	510	522	529	505	..	502
Foreign controlled undertakings	463	465	481	492	498	472	..	..
Foreign companies (branches)	45	23	29	28	7	25	..	29
All undertakings	532	515	539	549	536	531	..	531
of which:								
Life	219	212	231	228	212	187	..	179
Domestic undertakings	196	190	207	207	212	170	..	161
Foreign controlled undertakings	184	180	195	197	202	160	..	..
Foreign companies (branches)	24	22	24	21	1	17	..	19
All undertakings	219	212	231	228	212	187	..	179
Non-life	313	302	308	321	324	344	..	351
Domestic undertakings	292	301	303	314	317	336	..	341
Foreign controlled undertakings	279	285	286	295	295	312	..	..
Foreign companies (branches)	21	1	5	7	6	8	..	10
All undertakings	313	302	308	321	324	344	..	351
Total								
Domestic undertakings	543	555	569	578	592	578	..	556
Foreign controlled undertakings	518	529	541	549	561	544	..	..
Foreign companies (branches)	66	48	57	60	40	60	..	121
All undertakings	610	603	627	639	632	638	..	677

SLOVAK REPUBLIC

Table 1. Selected aggregates (cont.)

Million EUR

	2010	2011	2012	2013	2014	2015	2016	2017
1.5 Insurance business written abroad by branches, gross premiums								
Life								
Branches and agencies	0	0	0	0	0	1	..	..
Subsidaries	0	0	0	0	1	5	..	..
Total	0	0	0	0	1	6	..	..
Non-life								
Branches and agencies	0	0	0	0	0	0	..	..
Subsidaries	0	0	0	0	0	0	..	..
Total	0	0	0	0	0	0	..	..
Composite								
Branches and agencies	0	0	1	1	2	2	..	..
Subsidaries	4	4	3	3	4	6	..	..
Total	4	4	4	5	6	8	..	..
of which:								
Life	0	0	0	0	0	0	..	..
Branches and agencies	0	0	0	0	0	0	..	..
Subsidaries	0	0	0	0	0	0	..	..
Total	0	0	0	0	0	0	..	..
Non-life	4	4	4	5	6	8	..	..
Branches and agencies	0	0	1	1	2	2	..	..
Subsidaries	4	4	3	3	4	6	..	..
Total	4	4	4	5	6	8	..	..
Total								
Branches and agencies	0	0	1	1	2	3	..	..
Subsidaries	4	4	3	3	5	10	..	..
Total	4	4	4	5	7	14	..	..

.. Not available

Note: Detailed metadata at: *http://metalinks.oecd.org/ins/20190221/6c9a.*

Source: OECD Insurance Statistics (database)

SLOVAK REPUBLIC

Table 2. Number of companies and employees

	2010	2011	2012	2013	2014	2015	2016	2017
2.1 Number of companies								
Life								
Domestic undertakings	6	6	5	5	5	5	3	3
Foreign controlled undertakings	6	6	5	5	5	5	3	2
Foreign companies (branches)	2	2	1	1	1	1	2	2
All undertakings	8	8	6	6	6	6	5	5
Non-life								
Domestic undertakings	2	2	1	0	0	0	0	0
Foreign controlled undertakings	2	2	1	0	0	0	0	0
Foreign companies (branches)	12	13	16	17	17	17	19	19
All undertakings	14	15	17	17	17	17	19	19
Composite								
Domestic undertakings	12	12	12	12	12	12	12	12
Foreign controlled undertakings	10	10	10	10	10	10	12	10
Foreign companies (branches)	1	2	2	2	2	2	18	2
All undertakings	13	14	14	14	14	14	30	14
Reinsurance								
Domestic undertakings	0	0	0	0	0	0	0	0
Foreign controlled undertakings	0	0	0	0	0	0	0	0
Foreign companies (branches)	1	1	1	1	1	1	0	0
All undertakings	1	1	1	1	1	1	0	0
Total								
Domestic undertakings	20	20	18	17	17	17	15	15
Foreign controlled undertakings	18	18	16	15	15	15	15	12
Foreign companies (branches)	16	18	20	21	21	21	39	23
All undertakings	36	38	38	38	38	38	54	38
2.2 Number of employees								
Insurance undertakings	6 213	6 087	5 878	5 778	5 937	..	..	..
Intermediaries	962	1 020	1 373	..	1 358	..	..	..
Total	7 175	7 107	7 251	..	7 295	..	..	..

.. Not available

Note: Detailed metadata at: *http://metalinks.oecd.org/ins/20190221/6c9a.*

Source: OECD Insurance Statistics (database)

SLOVENIA

Table 1. Selected aggregates

Million EUR

	2010	2011	2012	2013	2014	2015	2016	2017
1.1 Insurance business written in the reporting country								
1.1.1 Insurance business, by ownership								
Gross premiums								
Domestic undertakings	2 178	2 184	2 192	2 114	2 095	2 150	2 182	2 298
Foreign controlled undertakings	164	169	166	166	166	172	180	186
Foreign companies (branches)	..	..	..	..	..	..	..	..
All undertakings	2 178	2 184	2 192	2 114	2 095	2 150	2 182	2 298
Premiums ceded								
Domestic undertakings	277	279	283	258	274	256	269	310
Foreign controlled undertakings	41	40	27	27	28	33	39	42
Foreign companies (branches)	..	..	..	..	..	..	..	..
All undertakings	277	279	283	258	274	256	269	310
Net written premiums								
Domestic undertakings	1 901	1 905	1 909	1 856	1 821	1 894	1 914	1 988
Foreign controlled undertakings	123	128	139	140	137	139	141	144
Foreign companies (branches)	..	..	..	..	..	..	..	..
All undertakings	1 901	1 905	1 909	1 856	1 821	1 894	1 914	1 988
1.1.2 Insurance business on foreign risks, gross premiums								
Life	0	0	0	..	..	..	..	..
Non-life	..	..	..	0	0	0	..	..
Composite	0	0	2	2	1	1	..	..
of which:								
Life	..	..	..	0	0	1	..	..
Non-life	0	0	2	1	1	0	..	..
Total	1	0	2	2	2	2	..	..
1.1.3 Life insurance payments, by class, gross premiums								
Annuities	..	..	..	..	..	..	..	..
Unit linked	231	228	219	201	195	215	213	223
Other life insurance	254	252	266	273	284	283	279	293
Total life insurance	485	479	485	473	479	498	492	516
***of which:** Pension contracts*	52	51	65	45	37	37	39	41
1.1.4 Non-life insurance payments, by class, gross premiums								
Motor vehicle insurance	627	601	559	513	495	484	499	539
Marine, aviation and other transport insurance	14	15	18	15	16	18	18	19
Freight insurance	15	15	15	14	13	15	16	16
Fire and other property damage insurance	377	389	396	370	372	393	405	415
Pecuniary loss insurance	51	50	48	49	56	62	62	64
General liability insurance	54	58	61	63	65	64	72	73
Accident and health	528	544	580	585	574	591	591	623
***of which:** Health*	409	428	467	480	470	484	489	522
Other non-life insurance	25	32	30	31	24	25	28	33
Treaty reinsurance	0	0	0	..	0	0	0	0
Total non-life insurance	1 691	1 704	1 706	1 641	1 616	1 652	1 690	1 782
1.2 Gross claims payments								
Life								
Domestic undertakings	22	35	40	31	36	52	50	46
Foreign controlled undertakings	0	0	0	0	1	0	2	..
Foreign companies (branches)	..	..	..	..	..	..	..	..
All undertakings	22	35	40	31	36	52	50	46
Non-life								
Domestic undertakings	456	443	463	482	449	499	491	532
Foreign controlled undertakings	0	0	..	..	..	1	0	..
Foreign companies (branches)	..	..	..	..	..	..	..	..
All undertakings	456	443	463	482	449	499	491	532
Composite								
Domestic undertakings	889	878	902	951	941	911	903	995
Foreign controlled undertakings	72	77	84	93	90	91	95	104
Foreign companies (branches)	..	..	..	..	..	..	..	..
All undertakings	889	878	902	951	941	911	903	995
of which:								
Life	186	229	259	299	304	305	314	347
Domestic undertakings	186	229	259	299	304	305	314	347
Foreign controlled undertakings	35	41	47	51	50	51	50	50
Foreign companies (branches)	..	..	..	..	..	..	..	..
All undertakings	186	229	259	299	304	305	314	347
Non-life	704	649	642	651	637	606	590	648
Domestic undertakings	704	649	642	651	637	606	590	648
Foreign controlled undertakings	37	36	38	42	41	40	45	54
Foreign companies (branches)	..	..	..	..	..	..	..	..
All undertakings	704	649	642	651	637	606	590	648
Total								
Domestic undertakings	1 368	1 355	1 404	1 464	1 426	1 461	1 445	1 573
Foreign controlled undertakings	72	78	85	93	91	91	97	104
Foreign companies (branches)	..	..	..	..	..	..	..	..
All undertakings	1 368	1 355	1 404	1 464	1 426	1 461	1 445	1 573

SLOVENIA

Table 1. Selected aggregates (cont.)

Million EUR

	2010	2011	2012	2013	2014	2015	2016	2017
1.3 Commissions								
Life								
Domestic undertakings	8	7	6	3	3	3	3	4
Foreign controlled undertakings	0	0	0	0	0	0	0	..
Foreign companies (branches)	..	..	..	..	..	..	..	..
All undertakings	8	7	6	3	3	3	3	4
Non-life								
Domestic undertakings	2	2	2	4	7	8	7	8
Foreign controlled undertakings	0	0	..	..	..	0	0	..
Foreign companies (branches)	..	..	..	..	..	..	..	..
All undertakings	2	2	2	4	7	8	7	8
Composite								
Domestic undertakings	70	90	80	84	86	89	86	92
Foreign controlled undertakings	17	19	19	19	20	21	28	22
Foreign companies (branches)	..	..	..	..	..	..	..	..
All undertakings	70	90	80	84	86	89	86	92
of which:								
Life	26	36	27	32	32	34	32	32
Domestic undertakings	26	36	27	32	32	34	32	32
Foreign controlled undertakings	8	9	10	10	10	10	15	9
Foreign companies (branches)	..	..	..	..	..	..	..	..
All undertakings	26	36	27	32	32	34	32	32
Non-life	44	53	53	52	54	56	54	60
Domestic undertakings	44	53	53	52	54	56	54	60
Foreign controlled undertakings	9	9	9	9	10	11	13	13
Foreign companies (branches)	..	..	..	..	..	..	..	..
All undertakings	44	53	53	52	54	56	54	60
Total								
Domestic undertakings	80	99	89	91	96	100	96	104
Foreign controlled undertakings	17	19	20	19	20	21	28	22
Foreign companies (branches)	..	..	..	..	..	..	..	..
All undertakings	80	99	89	91	96	100	96	104
1.4 Gross operating expenses								
Life								
Domestic undertakings	27	26	28	14	15	16	12	15
Foreign controlled undertakings	2	1	2	2	1	1	1	..
Foreign companies (branches)	..	..	..	..	..	..	..	..
All undertakings	27	26	28	14	15	16	12	15
Non-life								
Domestic undertakings	80	74	80	81	86	90	97	97
Foreign controlled undertakings	1	1	..	..	..	0	1	..
Foreign companies (branches)	..	..	..	..	..	..	..	..
All undertakings	80	74	80	81	86	90	97	97
Composite								
Domestic undertakings	354	356	361	366	362	368	378	388
Foreign controlled undertakings	31	52	56	47	57	60	60	66
Foreign companies (branches)	..	..	..	..	..	..	..	..
All undertakings	354	356	361	366	362	368	378	388
of which:								
Life	86	91	93	104	99	100	99	102
Domestic undertakings	86	91	93	104	99	100	99	102
Foreign controlled undertakings	20	26	28	26	27	28	26	27
Foreign companies (branches)	..	..	..	..	..	..	..	..
All undertakings	86	91	93	104	99	100	99	102
Non-life	267	265	269	263	263	268	279	286
Domestic undertakings	267	265	269	263	263	268	279	286
Foreign controlled undertakings	11	26	28	21	30	32	33	39
Foreign companies (branches)	..	..	..	..	..	..	..	..
All undertakings	267	265	269	263	263	268	279	286
Total								
Domestic undertakings	460	456	469	461	462	474	487	500
Foreign controlled undertakings	34	55	57	49	59	62	62	66
Foreign companies (branches)	..	..	..	..	..	..	..	..
All undertakings	460	456	469	461	462	474	487	500

SLOVENIA

Table 1. Selected aggregates (cont.)

Million EUR

	2010	2011	2012	2013	2014	2015	2016	2017
1.5 Insurance business written abroad by branches, gross premiums								
Life								
Branches and agencies	0	0	..	..	..	..	..	..
Subsidaries	..	..	..	..	..	..	..	..
Total	0	0	..	..	..	..	..	..
Non-life								
Branches and agencies	..	..	..	..	..	..	..	1
Subsidaries	..	..	..	..	..	..	..	..
Total	..	..	..	..	..	..	..	1
Composite								
Branches and agencies	0	0	..	..	..	2	..	31
Subsidaries	..	..	..	..	..	..	..	..
Total	0	0	..	..	..	2	..	31
of which:								
Life	..	..	..	..	..	2	..	6
Branches and agencies	..	..	..	..	..	2	..	6
Subsidaries	..	..	..	..	..	..	..	..
Total	..	..	..	..	..	2	..	6
Non-life	0	0	..	..	..	0	..	25
Branches and agencies	0	0	..	..	..	0	..	25
Subsidaries	..	..	..	..	..	..	..	..
Total	0	0	..	..	..	0	..	25
Total								
Branches and agencies	0	0	..	..	..	2	..	32
Subsidaries	..	..	..	..	..	..	..	..
Total	0	0	..	..	..	2	..	32

.. Not available

Note: Detailed metadata at: *http://metalinks.oecd.org/ins/20190221/b317*.

Source: OECD Insurance Statistics (database)

SLOVENIA

Table 2. Number of companies and employees

	2010	2011	2012	2013	2014	2015	2016	2017
2.1 Number of companies								
Life								
Domestic undertakings	3	4	4	3	3	3	3	2
Foreign controlled undertakings	1	1	1	1	1	1	1	0
Foreign companies (branches)	0	0	0	0	0	0	0	0
All undertakings	3	4	4	3	3	3	3	2
Non-life								
Domestic undertakings	4	4	3	3	3	4	4	4
Foreign controlled undertakings	1	1	0	0	0	0	0	0
Foreign companies (branches)	1	1	3	4	4	4	4	4
All undertakings	5	5	6	7	7	8	8	8
Composite								
Domestic undertakings	8	8	8	8	8	8	7	7
Foreign controlled undertakings	3	3	3	3	3	3	3	3
Foreign companies (branches)	2	2	2	2	2	2	2	2
All undertakings	10	10	10	10	10	10	9	9
Reinsurance								
Domestic undertakings	2	2	2	2	2	2	2	2
Foreign controlled undertakings	0	0	0	0	0	0	0	0
Foreign companies (branches)	0	0	0	0	0	0	0	0
All undertakings	2	2	2	2	2	2	2	2
Total								
Domestic undertakings	17	18	17	16	16	17	16	15
Foreign controlled undertakings	5	5	4	4	4	4	4	3
Foreign companies (branches)	3	3	5	6	6	6	6	6
All undertakings	20	21	22	22	22	23	22	21
2.2 Number of employees								
Insurance undertakings	..	..	..	..	..	..	..	..
Intermediaries	..	..	..	..	..	..	..	..
Total	..	..	..	..	..	..	..	..

.. Not available

Note: Detailed metadata at: *http://metalinks.oecd.org/ins/20190221/b317.*

Source: OECD Insurance Statistics (database)

SPAIN

Table 1. Selected aggregates

Million EUR

	2010	2011	2012	2013	2014	2015	2016	2017
1.1 Insurance business written in the reporting country								
1.1.1 Insurance business, by ownership								
Gross premiums								
Domestic undertakings	57 485	61 922	56 608	58 110	57 662	59 048	66 541	65 719
Foreign controlled undertakings	8 322	8 045	14 689	12 578	12 542	11 038	..	..
Foreign companies (branches)	135	133	117	0	0	0	..	..
All undertakings	57 620	62 055	56 725	58 110	57 662	59 048	66 541	65 719
Premiums ceded								
Domestic undertakings	4 333	4 305	4 235	5 831	5 019	5 161	6 014	6 206
Foreign controlled undertakings	482	793	1 094	1 058	923	736	..	..
Foreign companies (branches)	44	44	42	0	0	0	..	..
All undertakings	4 377	4 349	4 277	5 831	5 019	5 161	6 014	6 206
Net written premiums								
Domestic undertakings	53 154	57 617	52 373	52 279	52 643	53 886	60 527	59 513
Foreign controlled undertakings	7 576	7 252	13 594	11 520	11 620	10 301	..	..
Foreign companies (branches)	91	89	75	0	0	0	..	..
All undertakings	53 245	57 706	52 448	52 279	52 643	53 886	60 527	59 513
1.1.2 Insurance business on foreign risks, gross premiums								
Life	..	1	16	22	7	11	13	9
Non-life	..	73	138	79	73	59	45	20
Composite	..	79	54	52	44	61	49	26
of which:								
Life	..	42	39	42	34	46	35	2
Non-life	..	36	16	10	9	15	14	24
Total	..	153	209	153	123	130	107	55
1.1.3 Life insurance payments, by class, gross premiums								
Annuities	6 097	8 992	7 052	7 946	6 406	5 881	8 746	8 318
Unit linked	4 760	4 077	3 748	3 062	2 816	2 721	2 981	4 431
Other life insurance	16 510	16 704	15 828	14 865	16 021	17 128	19 330	16 270
Total life insurance	27 367	29 773	26 629	25 873	25 244	25 730	31 056	29 019
***of which:** Pension contracts*	..	..	..	..	..	..	..	..
1.1.4 Non-life insurance payments, by class, gross premiums								
Motor vehicle insurance	10 731	10 698	9 961	9 610	9 445	9 695	10 451	10 918
Marine, aviation and other transport insurance	356	480	329	390	361	369	369	367
Freight insurance	194	268	194	294	268	261	270	281
Fire and other property damage insurance	1 147	2 701	913	2 246	2 315	2 610	2 895	2 770
Pecuniary loss insurance	298	359	311	175	178	208	283	247
General liability insurance	1 283	1 274	1 096	1 077	1 009	1 011	1 049	1 100
Accident and health	6 501	7 630	7 629	7 888	8 227	8 449	8 879	9 329
***of which:** Health*	5 611	6 650	6 777	7 031	7 356	7 536	7 902	8 224
Other non-life insurance	9 709	10 410	10 502	10 531	10 558	10 729	11 001	11 264
Treaty reinsurance	..	0	0	0	0	0	0	..
Total non-life insurance	30 219	33 820	30 933	32 211	32 362	33 332	35 197	36 275
1.2 Gross claims payments								
Life								
Domestic undertakings	6 082	12 763	15 189	14 147	16 777	18 872	3 070	3 685
Foreign controlled undertakings	1 414	1 996	2 127	1 814	1 688	1 582	..	..
Foreign companies (branches)	0	0	0	0	0	0	..	..
All undertakings	6 082	12 763	15 189	14 147	16 777	18 872	3 070	3 685
Non-life								
Domestic undertakings	7 982	9 573	9 489	9 463	9 250	9 593	9 453	10 280
Foreign controlled undertakings	1 406	4 025	3 926	3 947	3 890	2 592	..	..
Foreign companies (branches)	0	0	0	0	0	0	..	..
All undertakings	7 982	9 573	9 489	9 463	9 250	9 593	9 453	10 280
Composite								
Domestic undertakings	32 008	23 611	22 204	21 477	21 596	20 659	32 425	35 292
Foreign controlled undertakings	3 607	5 663	6 495	5 208	5 230	5 136	..	..
Foreign companies (branches)	55	63	49	0	0	0	..	..
All undertakings	32 063	23 674	22 252	21 477	21 596	20 659	32 425	35 292
of which:								
Life	19 737	11 327	11 547	9 702	9 986	8 948	20 670	22 722
Domestic undertakings	19 702	11 288	11 511	9 702	9 986	8 948	20 670	22 722
Foreign controlled undertakings	1 286	2 437	3 836	2 320	2 497	2 292	..	..
Foreign companies (branches)	35	38	36	0	0	0	..	..
All undertakings	19 737	11 327	11 547	9 702	9 986	8 948	20 670	22 722
Non-life	12 326	12 347	10 705	11 775	11 610	11 711	11 755	12 571
Domestic undertakings	12 306	12 323	10 693	11 775	11 610	11 711	11 755	12 571
Foreign controlled undertakings	1 321	3 226	2 659	2 888	2 733	2 843	..	..
Foreign companies (branches)	20	24	12	0	0	0	..	..
All undertakings	12 326	12 347	10 705	11 775	11 610	11 711	11 755	12 571
Total								
Domestic undertakings	46 072	45 947	46 882	45 088	47 622	49 125	44 947	49 258
Foreign controlled undertakings	6 427	11 684	12 548	10 968	10 809	9 310	..	..
Foreign companies (branches)	55	63	49	0	0	0	..	..
All undertakings	46 127	46 009	46 930	45 088	47 622	49 125	44 947	49 258

SPAIN

Table 1. Selected aggregates (cont.)

Million EUR

	2010	2011	2012	2013	2014	2015	2016	2017
1.3 Commissions								
Life								
Domestic undertakings	..	..	..	..	660	712	234	257
Foreign controlled undertakings	..	..	..	..	86	71	..	..
Foreign companies (branches)	..	..	..	..	0	0	..	..
All undertakings	..	..	..	..	660	712	234	257
Non-life								
Domestic undertakings	..	..	..	..	1 472	1 436	1 433	1 522
Foreign controlled undertakings	..	..	..	..	642	517	..	..
Foreign companies (branches)	..	..	..	..	0	0	..	..
All undertakings	..	..	..	..	1 472	1 436	1 433	1 522
Composite								
Domestic undertakings	..	..	..	..	2 270	2 635	3 328	4 629
Foreign controlled undertakings	..	..	..	..	669	710	..	..
Foreign companies (branches)	..	..	..	..	0	0	..	..
All undertakings	..	..	..	..	2 270	2 635	3 328	4 629
of which:								
Life	..	..	..	..	418	379	979	1 185
Domestic undertakings	..	..	..	..	418	379	979	1 185
Foreign controlled undertakings	..	..	..	..	94	103	..	..
Foreign companies (branches)	..	..	..	..	0	0	..	..
All undertakings	..	..	..	..	418	379	979	1 185
Non-life	..	..	..	..	1 852	2 255	2 349	3 444
Domestic undertakings	..	..	..	..	1 852	2 255	2 349	3 444
Foreign controlled undertakings	..	..	..	..	576	607	..	..
Foreign companies (branches)	..	..	..	..	0	0	..	..
All undertakings	..	..	..	..	1 852	2 255	2 349	3 444
Total								
Domestic undertakings	..	..	..	..	4 403	4 782	4 995	6 408
Foreign controlled undertakings	..	..	..	..	1 398	1 298	..	..
Foreign companies (branches)	..	..	..	..	0	0	..	..
All undertakings	..	..	..	..	4 403	4 782	4 995	6 408
1.4 Gross operating expenses								
Life								
Domestic undertakings	1 778	171	220	968	994	1 075	425	455
Foreign controlled undertakings	207	42	39	201	190	192	..	..
Foreign companies (branches)	31	0	0	0	..	..	..	..
All undertakings	1 809	171	220	968	994	1 075	425	455
Non-life								
Domestic undertakings	6 317	487	491	3 046	2 880	2 832	2 876	3 081
Foreign controlled undertakings	517	254	242	1 272	1 289	947	..	..
Foreign companies (branches)	41	0	0	0	..	..	..	..
All undertakings	6 358	487	491	3 046	2 880	2 832	2 876	3 081
Composite								
Domestic undertakings	..	622	564	5 322	5 034	5 250	6 332	6 550
Foreign controlled undertakings	..	140	120	1 152	1 070	1 100	..	..
Foreign companies (branches)	..	6	5	1	..	4	..	..
All undertakings	..	628	569	5 323	5 034	5 254	6 332	6 550
of which:								
Life	..	119	87	809	797	729	1 489	1 546
Domestic undertakings	..	117	85	809	797	729	1 489	1 546
Foreign controlled undertakings	..	25	26	162	178	186	..	..
Foreign companies (branches)	..	2	2	0	..	..	..	..
All undertakings	..	119	87	809	797	729	1 489	1 546
Non-life	..	509	482	4 515	4 237	4 525	4 843	5 004
Domestic undertakings	..	506	479	4 514	4 237	4 521	4 843	5 004
Foreign controlled undertakings	..	116	94	990	892	913	..	..
Foreign companies (branches)	..	4	3	1	0	4	..	..
All undertakings	..	509	482	4 515	4 237	4 525	4 843	5 004
Total								
Domestic undertakings	8 095	1 280	1 275	9 337	8 907	9 157	9 633	10 087
Foreign controlled undertakings	724	436	401	2 625	2 549	2 239	..	..
Foreign companies (branches)	72	6	5	1	..	4	..	..
All undertakings	8 167	1 286	1 280	9 338	8 907	9 161	9 633	10 087

SPAIN

Table 1. Selected aggregates (cont.)

Million EUR

	2010	2011	2012	2013	2014	2015	2016	2017
1.5 Insurance business written abroad by branches, gross premiums								
Life								
Branches and agencies	..	938	323	274	0	0	0	0
Subsidaries	..	..	..	..	..	..	..	..
Total	..	..	..	..	..	..	0	0
Non-life								
Branches and agencies	..	296	419	592	654	701	1 694	1 841
Subsidaries	..	..	..	..	..	..	..	..
Total	..	..	..	..	..	..	1 694	1 841
Composite								
Branches and agencies	..	759	135	885	1 286	1 361	1 262	1 385
Subsidaries	..	..	..	..	..	..	..	..
Total	..	..	..	..	..	..	1 262	1 385
of which:								
Life	..	..	..	..	..	..	518	574
Branches and agencies	..	157	23	212	559	694	518	574
Subsidaries	..	..	..	..	..	..	..	..
Total	..	..	..	..	..	..	518	574
Non-life	..	..	..	..	..	..	744	812
Branches and agencies	..	602	113	673	728	667	744	812
Subsidaries	..	..	..	..	..	..	..	..
Total	..	..	..	..	..	..	744	812
Total								
Branches and agencies	..	1 994	878	1 751	1 940	2 062	2 955	3 226
Subsidaries	..	..	..	..	..	..	..	..
Total	..	..	..	..	..	..	2 955	3 226

.. Not available

Note: Detailed metadata at: *http://metalinks.oecd.org/ins/20190221/c09d.*

Source: OECD *Insurance Statistics (database)*

SPAIN

Table 2. Number of companies and employees

	2010	2011	2012	2013	2014	2015	2016	2017
2.1 Number of companies								
Life								
Domestic undertakings	93	89	84	83	79	78	32	32
Foreign controlled undertakings	6	11	10	10	9	8	..	..
Foreign companies (branches)	0	0	0	0	0	0	..	..
All undertakings	93	89	84	83	79	78	32	32
Non-life								
Domestic undertakings	141	140	136	132	127	118	121	111
Foreign controlled undertakings	14	19	18	19	19	17	..	..
Foreign companies (branches)	1	0	0	0	0	1	..	..
All undertakings	142	140	136	132	127	119	121	111
Composite								
Domestic undertakings	51	47	46	47	45	41	75	74
Foreign controlled undertakings	8	10	10	8	8	8	..	..
Foreign companies (branches)	1	2	2	1	1	0	..	..
All undertakings	52	49	48	48	46	41	75	74
Reinsurance								
Domestic undertakings	0	2	2	2	3	3	3	3
Foreign controlled undertakings	0	..	0	0	0	0	..	..
Foreign companies (branches)	0	0	0	0	0	0	..	..
All undertakings	0	2	2	2	3	3	3	3
Total								
Domestic undertakings	285	278	268	264	254	240	231	220
Foreign controlled undertakings	28	40	38	37	36	33	..	..
Foreign companies (branches)	2	2	2	1	1	1	..	..
All undertakings	287	280	270	265	255	241	231	220
2.2 Number of employees								
Insurance undertakings	48 116	46 557	46 439	46 324	45 535	45 218	47 453	47 498
Intermediaries	3 006	..	..	121 427	129 549	..	..	..
Total	51 122	..	..	167 751	175 084	..	..	..

.. Not available

Note: Detailed metadata at: *http://metalinks.oecd.org/ins/20190221/c09d.*

Source: OECD Insurance Statistics (database)

SWEDEN

Table 1. Selected aggregates

Million SEK

	2010	2011	2012	2013	2014	2015	2016	2017
1.1 Insurance business written in the reporting country								
1.1.1 Insurance business, by ownership								
Gross premiums								
Domestic undertakings	184 684	182 225	167 132	177 197	332 028	339 533	334 834	379 418
Foreign controlled undertakings	65 344	63 298	65 752	66 854	66 041	62 537	67 208	78 911
Foreign companies (branches)	..	..	..	..	10 260	..	..	..
All undertakings	184 684	182 225	167 132	177 197	342 288	339 533	334 834	379 418
Premiums ceded								
Domestic undertakings	13 654	12 870	13 068	12 967	15 157	10 306	9 139	10 693
Foreign controlled undertakings	4 475	4 583	5 428	4 727	3 870	4 441	4 296	5 538
Foreign companies (branches)	..	..	..	..	..	..	..	..
All undertakings	13 654	12 870	13 068	12 967	15 157	10 306	9 139	10 693
Net written premiums								
Domestic undertakings	171 029	169 355	154 064	164 230	316 871	329 227	325 695	368 725
Foreign controlled undertakings	60 869	58 715	60 324	62 127	62 171	58 096	62 912	73 373
Foreign companies (branches)	..	..	..	..	10 260	..	..	..
All undertakings	171 029	169 355	154 064	164 230	327 131	329 227	325 695	368 725
1.1.2 Insurance business on foreign risks, gross premiums								
Life	..	..	..	..	581	667	60	58
Non-life	..	..	..	..	28 134	27 121	26 941	30 482
Composite total	..	..	..	..	..	..	..	..
Total	..	..	..	..	28 715	27 788	27 001	30 540
1.1.3 Life insurance payments, by class, gross premiums								
Annuities	70 960	72 263	73 378	73 377	205 927	169 626	94 037	107 773
Unit linked	5 742	3 790	1 708	1 188	2 366	75 221	85 696	97 951
Other life insurance	12 610	13 615	13 229	13 591	29 900	3 957	71 084	82 841
Total life insurance	89 312	89 668	88 315	88 156	238 192	248 804	250 817	288 565
of which: *Pension contracts*	..	..	..	..	..	..	..	..
1.1.4 Non-life insurance payments, by class, gross premiums								
Motor vehicle insurance	..	..	..	..	30 360	21 348	..	..
Marine, aviation and other transport insurance	..	..	..	..	2 627	749	..	..
Freight insurance	..	..	..	..	..	..	..	..
Fire and other property damage insurance	..	..	..	..	29 146	36 720	..	..
Pecuniary loss insurance	..	..	..	..	459	1 070	..	..
General liability insurance	..	..	..	..	4 045	4 119	..	..
Accident and health	..	..	..	..	5 674	5 155	..	..
of which: *Health*	..	..	..	..	..	..	..	..
Other non-life insurance	..	..	..	..	9 165	21 483	..	..
Treaty reinsurance	..	..	..	..	13 811	..	..	..
Total non-life insurance	94 518	91 819	76 947	84 766	95 287	90 644	83 954	90 800
1.2 Gross claims payments								
Life								
Domestic undertakings	50 681	53 464	58 780	64 657	60 930	64 815	76 869	76 390
Foreign controlled undertakings	7 837	7 533	3 499	6 337	6 055	5 719	5 852	5 784
Foreign companies (branches)	..	..	..	..	5 999	..	..	..
All undertakings	50 681	53 464	58 780	64 657	66 929	64 815	76 869	76 390
Non-life								
Domestic undertakings	67 685	68 400	69 882	69 100	75 805	64 537	65 941	66 635
Foreign controlled undertakings	31 815	31 370	31 639	31 398	31 024	23 701	22 495	25 544
Foreign companies (branches)	..	..	..	..	5 328	..	..	..
All undertakings	67 685	68 400	69 882	69 100	81 133	64 537	65 941	66 635
Composite, all undertakings	..	..	..	..	..	..	..	..
Total								
Domestic undertakings	118 366	121 864	128 662	133 757	136 735	129 352	142 810	143 025
Foreign controlled undertakings	39 652	38 903	35 138	37 735	37 079	29 420	28 347	31 328
Foreign companies (branches)	..	..	..	..	11 327	..	..	..
All undertakings	118 366	121 864	128 662	133 757	148 062	129 352	142 810	143 025
1.3 Commissions								
Life								
Domestic undertakings	..	..	..	..	4 167	3 782	3 063	3 545
Foreign controlled undertakings	..	..	..	..	1 302	610	274	589
Foreign companies (branches)	..	..	..	..	121	..	..	..
All undertakings	..	..	..	..	4 288	3 782	3 063	3 545
Non-life								
Domestic undertakings	..	..	..	..	4 168	4 264	3 848	3 953
Foreign controlled undertakings	..	..	..	..	2 049	2 589	2 362	2 482
Foreign companies (branches)	..	..	..	..	786	..	..	..
All undertakings	..	..	..	..	4 954	4 264	3 848	3 953
Composite, all undertakings	..	..	..	..	..	..	..	..
Total								
Domestic undertakings	..	..	..	..	8 335	8 046	6 911	7 498
Foreign controlled undertakings	..	..	..	..	3 351	3 199	2 636	3 071
Foreign companies (branches)	..	..	..	..	907	..	..	..
All undertakings	..	..	..	..	9 242	8 046	6 911	7 498

SWEDEN

Table 1. Selected aggregates (cont.)

Million SEK

	2010	2011	2012	2013	2014	2015	2016	2017
1.4 Gross operating expenses								
Life								
Domestic undertakings	10 514	10 785	11 509	12 115	12 738	13 573	12 617	13 248
Foreign controlled undertakings	3 264	3 488	3 557	3 630	3 639	2 122	1 297	1 918
Foreign companies (branches)	..	..	..	..	..	..	..	..
All undertakings	10 514	10 785	11 509	12 115	12 738	13 573	12 617	13 248
Non-life								
Domestic undertakings	15 117	14 468	14 989	15 004	16 878	16 854	15 781	15 863
Foreign controlled undertakings	8 189	7 262	7 138	7 248	8 238	7 704	7 205	7 691
Foreign companies (branches)	..	..	..	..	..	..	..	..
All undertakings	15 117	14 468	14 989	15 004	16 878	16 854	15 781	15 863
Composite, all undertakings	..	..	..	..	..	..	..	..
Total								
Domestic undertakings	25 631	25 253	26 498	27 119	29 616	30 427	28 398	29 111
Foreign controlled undertakings	11 453	10 750	10 695	10 878	11 877	9 826	8 502	9 609
Foreign companies (branches)	..	..	..	..	..	..	..	..
All undertakings	25 631	25 253	26 498	27 119	29 616	30 427	28 398	29 111
1.5 Insurance business written abroad by branches, gross premiums								
Life								
Branches and agencies	315	108	234	..	243	279	347	347
Subsidaries	..	..	..	..	..	..	..	..
Total	..	108	234	..	243	279	347	347
Non-life								
Branches and agencies	19 011	18 526	18 948	..	18 630	18 207	24 226	24 226
Subsidaries	..	..	..	..	..	..	..	..
Total	..	18 526	18 948	..	18 630	18 207	24 226	24 226
Composite total	..	..	..	..	..	..	..	..
Total								
Branches and agencies	19 326	18 634	19 182	..	18 873	18 486	24 573	24 573
Subsidaries	..	..	..	..	..	..	..	..
Total	..	18 634	19 182	..	18 873	18 486	24 573	24 573

.. Not available

Note: Detailed metadata at: *http://metalinks.oecd.org/ins/20190221/e96d.*

Source: OECD Insurance Statistics (database)

SWEDEN

Table 2. Number of companies and employees

	2010	2011	2012	2013	2014	2015	2016	2017
2.1 Number of companies								
Life								
Domestic undertakings	39	39	39	39	39	38	37	36
Foreign controlled undertakings	7	8	9	8	8	8	6	6
Foreign companies (branches)	9	5	5	5	6	8	6	4
All undertakings	48	44	44	44	45	46	43	46
Non-life								
Domestic undertakings	150	139	131	130	130	127	120	117
Foreign controlled undertakings	18	18	46	44	34	24	14	15
Foreign companies (branches)	39	31	32	32	28	33	31	25
All undertakings	189	170	163	162	158	160	151	157
Composite, all undertakings	**0**	**0**	**0**	**0**	**0**	**0**	**0**	..
Reinsurance								
Domestic undertakings	3	3	2	1	1	1	0	..
Foreign controlled undertakings	1	2	0	0	0	1	0	..
Foreign companies (branches)	..	..	0	..	0	0	..	..
All undertakings	3	3	2	1	1	1	..	..
Total								
Domestic undertakings	192	181	172	170	170	166	157	153
Foreign controlled undertakings	26	28	55	52	42	33	20	21
Foreign companies (branches)	48	36	37	37	34	41	37	29
All undertakings	240	217	209	207	204	207	194	203
2.2 Number of employees								
Insurance undertakings	19 017	18 848	19 158	19 059	19 573	18 792	20 600	21 900
Intermediaries	2 000	2 000	2 000	2 000	3 849	3 235	3 540	3 585
Total	21 017	20 848	21 158	21 059	23 422	22 027	..	25 485

.. Not available

Note: Detailed metadata at: *http://metalinks.oecd.org/ins/20190221/e96d.*

Source: OECD Insurance Statistics (database)

SWITZERLAND

Table 1. Selected aggregates

Million CHF

	2010	2011	2012	2013	2014	2015	2016	2017
1.1 Insurance business written in the reporting country								
1.1.1 Insurance business, by ownership								
Gross premiums								
Domestic undertakings	61 448	61 417	63 507	66 569	66 312	65 628	63 975	63 967
Foreign controlled undertakings	13 162	13 600	14 322	15 423	14 214	13 846	12 578	11 699
Foreign companies (branches)	2 834	2 062	2 331	2 267	1 923	2 091	2 522	2 768
All undertakings	64 282	63 479	65 838	68 836	68 235	67 720	66 497	66 735
Premiums ceded								
Domestic undertakings	4 802	4 000	4 479	4 536	4 346	4 141	3 363	4 085
Foreign controlled undertakings	1 289	1 024	1 219	963	831	731	506	502
Foreign companies (branches)	442	467	487	532	533	553	813	874
All undertakings	5 244	4 467	4 965	5 068	4 879	4 694	4 176	4 959
Net written premiums								
Domestic undertakings	56 646	57 417	59 028	62 033	61 966	61 487	60 612	59 882
Foreign controlled undertakings	11 873	12 577	13 102	14 460	13 383	13 115	12 072	11 197
Foreign companies (branches)	2 392	1 595	1 845	1 735	1 390	1 539	1 709	1 894
All undertakings	59 038	59 012	60 873	63 768	63 356	63 026	62 321	61 776
1.1.2 Insurance business on foreign risks, gross premiums								
Life	..	..	..	..	..	..	..	..
Non-life	..	..	..	..	..	..	..	..
Composite total	..	..	..	..	..	..	..	..
Total	..	..	..	..	..	..	..	..
1.1.3 Life insurance payments, by class, gross premiums								
Annuities	873	737	677	564	441	495	428	317
Unit linked	3 052	2 423	2 637	2 403	1 730	1 755	1 738	1 861
Other life insurance	26 239	27 397	27 841	29 707	30 478	30 359	28 518	27 445
Total life insurance	30 164	30 557	31 155	32 675	32 649	32 609	30 684	29 623
***of which:** Pension contracts*	..	..	..	..	..	..	..	..
1.1.4 Non-life insurance payments, by class, gross premiums								
Motor vehicle insurance	6 357	6 382	6 526	6 556	6 580	6 595	6 598	6 742
Marine, aviation and other transport insurance	964	804	968	1 060	876	732	657	681
Freight insurance	..	..	..	..	..	..	..	..
Fire and other property damage insurance	7 335	7 457	8 150	8 206	8 123	7 909	7 411	7 397
Pecuniary loss insurance	885	832	932	1 042	1 096	897	1 095	1 108
General liability insurance	3 550	3 243	3 514	3 558	3 658	3 562	3 293	3 447
Accident and health	12 540	12 551	13 093	13 889	13 414	13 387	14 585	15 626
***of which:** Health*	9 182	9 383	9 656	9 911	9 934	10 266	10 606	11 361
Other non-life insurance	1 073	1 036	1 151	1 351	1 378	1 525	1 649	1 715
Treaty reinsurance	..	..	..	..	..	..	..	..
Total non-life insurance	32 704	32 306	34 334	35 661	35 125	34 607	35 288	36 716
1.2 Gross claims payments								
Life								
Domestic undertakings	25 420	27 182	25 817	27 624	27 943	27 794	29 083	29 352
Foreign controlled undertakings	7 127	7 354	7 060	8 854	7 917	8 123	8 578	8 159
Foreign companies (branches)	44	104	186	306	3	3	3	3
All undertakings	25 464	27 286	26 003	27 930	27 946	27 797	29 086	29 355
Non-life								
Domestic undertakings	15 122	15 548	20 279	19 735	20 149	20 621	20 498	20 716
Foreign controlled undertakings	1 962	1 974	2 292	2 171	2 281	2 671	2 471	2 299
Foreign companies (branches)	85	404	667	798	874	902	1 105	1 164
All undertakings	15 207	15 952	20 946	20 533	21 023	21 523	21 603	21 880
Composite, all undertakings	..	..	..	..	..	..	..	..
Total								
Domestic undertakings	40 542	42 730	46 096	47 359	48 092	48 415	49 581	50 068
Foreign controlled undertakings	9 090	9 328	9 352	11 025	10 198	10 794	11 049	10 458
Foreign companies (branches)	129	509	853	1 104	877	905	1 108	1 167
All undertakings	40 671	43 238	46 949	48 463	48 969	49 320	50 689	51 235
1.3 Commissions								
Life								
Domestic undertakings	906	848	875	904	920	856	856	836
Foreign controlled undertakings	109	107	103	148	114	169	169	163
Foreign companies (branches)	9	8	8	11	0	0	1	1
All undertakings	915	856	883	915	920	856	857	837
Non-life								
Domestic undertakings	2 052	1 886	1 955	2 067	1 597	2 188	2 289	2 078
Foreign controlled undertakings	471	450	442	372	381	441	450	453
Foreign companies (branches)	76	85	88	95	91	78	65	24
All undertakings	2 128	1 970	2 043	2 162	1 688	2 266	2 354	2 102
Composite, all undertakings	..	..	..	..	..	..	..	..
Total								
Domestic undertakings	2 958	2 734	2 830	2 971	2 517	3 044	3 145	2 914
Foreign controlled undertakings	581	557	545	520	495	610	619	616
Foreign companies (branches)	85	92	96	106	91	78	66	25
All undertakings	3 043	2 826	2 926	3 077	2 608	3 122	3 211	2 939

SWITZERLAND

Table 1. Selected aggregates (cont.)

Million CHF

	2010	2011	2012	2013	2014	2015	2016	2017
1.4 Gross operating expenses								
Life								
Domestic undertakings	2 382	2 444	1 390	1 289	1 364	1 078	1 085	1 091
Foreign controlled undertakings	395	450	239	176	209	156	156	160
Foreign companies (branches)	12	11	4	4	2	1	1	2
All undertakings	2 394	2 455	1 394	1 293	1 366	1 079	1 086	1 093
Non-life								
Domestic undertakings	7 677	7 179	3 835	3 745	5 520	2 975	2 981	3 185
Foreign controlled undertakings	1 063	1 039	371	416	420	341	310	316
Foreign companies (branches)	459	408	80	100	108	103	215	195
All undertakings	8 136	7 588	3 915	3 845	5 628	3 078	3 196	3 380
Composite, all undertakings	..	..	..	..	..	..	..	..
Total								
Domestic undertakings	10 059	9 624	5 225	5 034	6 884	4 053	4 066	4 276
Foreign controlled undertakings	1 458	1 489	610	592	629	497	466	476
Foreign companies (branches)	471	419	84	104	110	104	216	197
All undertakings	10 530	10 043	5 309	5 138	6 994	4 157	4 282	4 473
1.5 Insurance business written abroad by branches, gross premiums								
Life								
Branches and agencies	2 219	2 036	2 006	1 967	1 794	1 604	1 567	1 613
Subsidaries	..	..	..	..	..	..	..	..
Total	2 219	2 036	2 006	1 967	1 794	1 604	1 567	1 613
Non-life								
Branches and agencies	16 881	13 446	15 417	15 563	15 331	14 100	12 578	12 689
Subsidaries	..	..	..	..	..	..	..	..
Total	16 881	13 446	15 417	15 563	15 331	14 100	12 578	12 689
Composite total	..	..	..	..	..	..	..	..
Total								
Branches and agencies	19 100	15 482	17 423	17 531	17 125	15 704	14 145	14 302
Subsidaries	..	..	..	..	..	..	..	..
Total	19 100	15 482	17 423	17 531	17 125	15 704	14 145	14 302

.. Not available

Note: Detailed metadata at: *http://metalinks.oecd.org/ins/20190221/e31b.*

Source: OECD Insurance Statistics (database)

SWITZERLAND

Table 2. Number of companies and employees

	2010	2011	2012	2013	2014	2015	2016	2017
2.1 Number of companies								
Life								
Domestic undertakings	21	20	19	19	18	17	16	16
Foreign controlled undertakings	1	1	1	1	1	1	1	1
Foreign companies (branches)	4	4	4	4	3	3	3	3
All undertakings	25	24	23	23	21	20	19	19
Non-life								
Domestic undertakings	79	79	81	80	79	76	74	73
Foreign controlled undertakings	6	6	6	6	6	6	5	5
Foreign companies (branches)	47	45	42	44	48	46	46	45
All undertakings	126	124	123	124	127	122	120	118
Composite, all undertakings	0	0	0	0	0	0	0	..
Reinsurance								
Domestic undertakings	62	62	61	62	62	59	55	55
Foreign controlled undertakings	8	7	7	7	7	7	7	6
Foreign companies (branches)	..	..	..	..	..	..	..	..
All undertakings	62	62	61	62	62	59	55	55
Total								
Domestic undertakings	162	161	161	161	159	152	145	144
Foreign controlled undertakings	15	14	14	14	14	14	13	12
Foreign companies (branches)	51	49	46	48	51	49	49	48
All undertakings	213	210	207	209	210	201	194	192
2.2 Number of employees								
Insurance undertakings	..	..	..	..	..	..	..	..
Intermediaries	..	..	..	..	..	..	..	..
Total	..	..	..	..	..	..	..	..

.. Not available

Note: Detailed metadata at: *http://metalinks.oecd.org/ins/20190221/e31b.*

Source: OECD Insurance Statistics (database)

TURKEY

Table 1. Selected aggregates

Million TRY

	2010	2011	2012	2013	2014	2015	2016	2017
1.1 Insurance business written in the reporting country								
1.1.1 Insurance business, by ownership								
Gross premiums								
Domestic undertakings	14 958	17 131	20 427	25 084	26 872	31 903	41 280	47 495
Foreign controlled undertakings	7 525	8 956	10 122	14 981	15 528	20 981	25 640	26 984
Foreign companies (branches)	27	32	46	68	77	126	152	201
All undertakings	14 985	17 164	20 473	25 152	26 949	32 029	41 431	47 696
Premiums ceded								
Domestic undertakings	3 443	4 287	4 483	6 077	6 686	7 984	9 816	13 268
Foreign controlled undertakings	1 834	2 229	2 192	3 458	3 510	4 773	5 482	6 672
Foreign companies (branches)	21	22	33	49	57	74	76	96
All undertakings	3 464	4 309	4 516	6 126	6 743	8 059	9 892	13 364
Net written premiums								
Domestic undertakings	11 515	12 845	15 944	19 006	20 186	23 919	31 464	34 227
Foreign controlled undertakings	5 691	6 728	7 931	11 522	12 018	16 208	20 158	20 312
Foreign companies (branches)	6	10	13	20	20	52	76	105
All undertakings	11 521	12 854	15 957	19 026	20 206	23 971	31 540	34 332
1.1.2 Insurance business on foreign risks, gross premiums								
Life	..	..	..	..	3 280	..	6 166	..
Non-life	..	..	..	..	22 711	..	34 322	..
Composite	..	..	..	..	958	..	943	..
of which:								
Life	..	..	..	..	24	..	19	..
Non-life	..	..	..	..	934	..	924	..
Total	..	..	..	..	26 948	..	41 431	..
1.1.3 Life insurance payments, by class, gross premiums								
Annuities	..	..	..	..	..	..	..	..
Unit linked	..	..	..	..	..	..	..	..
Other life insurance	..	..	..	..	..	..	..	..
Total life insurance	2 576	3 087	3 107	3 354	3 895	3 720	5 916	6 766
of which: *Pension contracts*	..	..	..	..	..	..	..	..
1.1.4 Non-life insurance payments, by class, gross premiums								
Motor vehicle insurance	5 867	6 761	8 091	10 411	10 648	13 102	19 156	19 981
Marine, aviation and other transport insurance	185	268	263	253	321	423	455	490
Freight insurance	327	359	378	416	530	580	585	652
Fire and other property damage insurance	3 401	3 783	4 390	5 512	6 992	8 105	9 032	10 101
Pecuniary loss insurance	135	204	228	302	318	443	439	549
General liability insurance	407	386	420	508	679	811	863	1 028
Accident and health	2 413	2 657	2 897	3 352	4 010	4 685	4 582	6 708
of which: *Health*	1 810	1 999	2 227	2 472	0	0	..	5 025
Other non-life insurance	44	77	61	74	147	99	134	226
Treaty reinsurance	..	..	..	..	..	0	..	..
Total non-life insurance	12 778	14 496	16 727	20 828	23 645	28 249	35 246	39 735
1.2 Gross claims payments								
Life								
Domestic undertakings	1 787	1 935	2 037	2 355	2 085	2 557	2 957	3 293
Foreign controlled undertakings	817	582	483	1 128	760	1 194	1 485	1 757
Foreign companies (branches)	0	..	..	..	..	..	0	..
All undertakings	1 787	1 935	2 037	2 355	2 085	2 557	2 957	3 293
Non-life								
Domestic undertakings	6 142	7 968	9 163	9 440	11 314	13 322	15 041	18 341
Foreign controlled undertakings	3 978	4 786	5 327	6 301	7 496	8 700	-9 940	11 648
Foreign companies (branches)	0	2	3	11	10	34	128	77
All undertakings	6 143	7 969	9 166	9 451	11 325	13 356	15 168	18 417
Composite								
Domestic undertakings	1 344	..	..	619	592	664	572	617
Foreign controlled undertakings	82	..	..	..	..	..	..	1
Foreign companies (branches)	0	..	..	..	..	..	..	..
All undertakings	1 344	0	721	619	592	664	572	617
of which:								
Life	10	0	6	7	11	6	9	15
Domestic undertakings	10	..	..	7	11	6	9	15
Foreign controlled undertakings	0	..	..	..	..	..	..	0
Foreign companies (branches)	0	..	..	..	..	..	..	..
All undertakings	10	0	6	7	11	6	9	15
Non-life	1 334	0	715	612	581	657	564	602
Domestic undertakings	1 334	..	..	612	581	657	564	602
Foreign controlled undertakings	82	..	..	..	..	..	..	1
Foreign companies (branches)	0	..	..	..	..	..	..	..
All undertakings	1 334	0	715	612	581	657	564	602
Total								
Domestic undertakings	9 273	9 903	11 200	12 413	13 991	16 543	18 570	22 251
Foreign controlled undertakings	4 877	5 369	5 810	7 429	8 256	9 894	-8 455	13 406
Foreign companies (branches)	0	2	3	11	10	34	128	77
All undertakings	9 273	9 905	11 924	12 425	14 001	16 578	18 698	22 328

TURKEY

Table 1. Selected aggregates (cont.)

Million TRY

	2010	2011	2012	2013	2014	2015	2016	2017
1.3 Commissions								
Life								
Domestic undertakings	..	..	..	..	..	..	..	..
Foreign controlled undertakings	..	..	..	..	..	..	..	..
Foreign companies (branches)	..	..	..	..	..	..	..	..
All undertakings	..	..	..	..	..	..	..	..
Non-life								
Domestic undertakings	..	..	..	..	..	..	..	..
Foreign controlled undertakings	..	..	..	..	..	..	..	..
Foreign companies (branches)	..	..	..	..	..	..	..	..
All undertakings	..	..	..	..	..	..	..	..
Composite								
Domestic undertakings	..	..	..	..	..	..	..	..
Foreign controlled undertakings	..	..	..	..	..	..	..	..
Foreign companies (branches)	..	..	..	..	..	..	..	..
All undertakings	..	..	..	..	..	..	..	..
of which:								
Life	..	..	..	..	..	..	..	..
Domestic undertakings	..	..	..	..	..	..	..	..
Foreign controlled undertakings	..	..	..	..	..	..	..	..
Foreign companies (branches)	..	..	..	..	..	..	..	..
All undertakings	..	..	..	..	..	..	..	..
Non-life	..	..	..	..	..	..	..	..
Domestic undertakings	..	..	..	..	..	..	..	..
Foreign controlled undertakings	..	..	..	..	..	..	..	..
Foreign companies (branches)	..	..	..	..	..	..	..	..
All undertakings	..	..	..	..	..	..	..	..
Total								
Domestic undertakings	..	..	..	..	..	..	..	..
Foreign controlled undertakings	..	..	..	..	..	..	..	..
Foreign companies (branches)	..	..	..	..	..	..	..	..
All undertakings	..	..	..	..	..	..	..	..
1.4 Gross operating expenses								
Life								
Domestic undertakings	717	836	978	2 009	1 198	1 595	1 970	2 644
Foreign controlled undertakings	287	361	422	1 242	765	1 033	1 241	1 724
Foreign companies (branches)	0	..	..	..	..	..	..	..
All undertakings	717	836	978	2 009	1 198	1 595	1 970	2 644
Non-life								
Domestic undertakings	2 336	2 859	3 230	3 726	4 309	4 648	5 579	6 263
Foreign controlled undertakings	1 585	1 827	1 976	2 564	2 944	3 110	3 847	4 170
Foreign companies (branches)	4	8	12	19	20	24	26	30
All undertakings	2 340	2 867	3 242	3 745	4 329	4 672	5 604	6 293
Composite								
Domestic undertakings	421	..	..	..	..	309	316	333
Foreign controlled undertakings	16	..	..	..	..	..	5	2
Foreign companies (branches)	0	..	..	..	..	..	..	..
All undertakings	421	0	285	294	289	309	316	333
of which:								
Life	7	0	8	10	8	10	10	5
Domestic undertakings	7	..	..	..	..	10	10	5
Foreign controlled undertakings	0	..	..	..	..	..	..	0
Foreign companies (branches)	0	..	..	..	..	..	..	..
All undertakings	7	0	8	10	8	10	10	5
Non-life	414	0	277	284	281	299	306	328
Domestic undertakings	414	..	..	..	..	299	306	328
Foreign controlled undertakings	16	..	..	..	..	..	5	2
Foreign companies (branches)	0	..	..	..	..	..	..	..
All undertakings	414	0	277	284	281	299	306	328
Total								
Domestic undertakings	3 473	3 694	4 209	5 735	5 507	6 552	7 865	9 240
Foreign controlled undertakings	1 888	2 188	2 399	3 806	3 708	4 143	5 092	5 895
Foreign companies (branches)	4	8	12	19	20	24	26	30
All undertakings	3 478	3 702	4 506	6 048	5 816	6 576	7 890	9 270

TURKEY

Table 1. Selected aggregates (cont.)

Million TRY

	2010	2011	2012	2013	2014	2015	2016	2017
1.5 Insurance business written abroad by branches, gross premiums								
Life								
Branches and agencies	..	..	..	..	..	..	..	..
Subsidaries	..	..	..	..	..	..	..	..
Total	..	..	..	..	..	..	..	..
Non-life								
Branches and agencies	..	..	..	..	..	..	..	..
Subsidaries	..	..	..	..	..	..	..	..
Total	..	..	..	..	..	..	..	..
Composite								
Branches and agencies	..	..	..	..	..	..	..	..
Subsidaries	..	..	..	..	..	..	..	..
Total	..	..	..	..	..	..	..	..
of which:								
Life								
Branches and agencies	..	..	..	..	..	..	..	..
Subsidaries	..	..	..	..	..	..	..	..
Total	..	..	..	..	..	..	..	..
Non-life								
Branches and agencies	..	..	..	..	..	..	..	..
Subsidaries	..	..	..	..	..	..	..	..
Total	..	..	..	..	..	..	..	..
Total								
Branches and agencies	..	..	..	..	..	..	..	..
Subsidaries	..	..	..	..	..	..	..	..
Total	..	..	..	..	..	..	..	..

.. Not available

Note: Detailed metadata at: *http://metalinks.oecd.org/ins/20190221/e635.*

Source: OECD Insurance Statistics (database)

TURKEY

Table 2. Number of companies and employees

	2010	2011	2012	2013	2014	2015	2016	2017
2.1 Number of companies								
Life								
Domestic undertakings	23	24	23	24	25	23	22	22
Foreign controlled undertakings	14	14	13	16	16	15	15	15
Foreign companies (branches)	0	..	0	..	0	..	0	0
All undertakings	23	24	23	24	25	23	22	22
Non-life								
Domestic undertakings	29	33	33	34	36	36	35	37
Foreign controlled undertakings	19	23	22	22	24	22	23	23
Foreign companies (branches)	2	2	2	2	2	2	2	2
All undertakings	31	35	35	36	38	38	37	39
Composite								
Domestic undertakings	3	..	0	..	0	..	0	0
Foreign controlled undertakings	1	..	0	..	0	..	0	0
Foreign companies (branches)	0	..	0	..	0	..	0	0
All undertakings	3	..	0	..	0	..	0	0
Reinsurance								
Domestic undertakings	1	2	1	1	1	1	2	2
Foreign controlled undertakings	0	..	0	..	0	..	1	1
Foreign companies (branches)	0	..	0	..	0	..	0	0
All undertakings	1	2	1	1	1	1	2	2
Total								
Domestic undertakings	56	59	57	59	62	60	59	61
Foreign controlled undertakings	34	37	35	38	40	37	39	39
Foreign companies (branches)	2	2	2	2	2	2	2	2
All undertakings	58	61	59	61	64	62	61	63
2.2 Number of employees								
Insurance undertakings	15 412	10 123	17 304	18 297	19 305	19 274	19 240	19 883
Intermediaries	16 282	16 706	16 994	15 603	15 587	18 931	35 992	40 231
Total	31 694	26 829	34 298	33 900	34 892	38 205	55 232	60 114

.. Not available

Note: Detailed metadata at: *http://metalinks.oecd.org/ins/20190221/e635.*

Source: OECD Insurance Statistics (database)

UNITED KINGDOM

Table 1. Selected aggregates

Million GBP

	2010	2011	2012	2013	2014	2015	2016	2017
1.1 Insurance business written in the reporting country								
1.1.1 Insurance business, by ownership								
Gross premiums								
Domestic undertakings	206 167	208 608	230 559	215 494	219 832	217 673	298 817	305 746
Foreign controlled undertakings	54 294	60 570	75 289	69 361	57 959	58 471	..	..
Foreign companies (branches)	4 258	3 204	2 735	2 237	2 407	2 741	247	471
All undertakings	210 425	211 811	233 294	217 731	222 239	220 414	299 064	306 217
Premiums ceded								
Domestic undertakings	21 397	24 305	28 545	27 456	33 780	24 299	68 763	36 758
Foreign controlled undertakings	7 143	7 946	8 285	9 270	11 048	10 801	0	..
Foreign companies (branches)	403	356	179	53	47	52	115	199
All undertakings	21 800	24 661	28 724	27 509	33 827	24 351	68 878	36 957
Net written premiums								
Domestic undertakings	184 770	184 303	202 014	188 038	186 052	193 374	230 054	268 988
Foreign controlled undertakings	47 151	52 623	67 004	60 091	46 911	47 670	..	..
Foreign companies (branches)	3 855	2 847	2 555	2 184	2 361	2 689	132	272
All undertakings	188 625	187 150	204 570	190 222	188 412	196 062	230 186	269 260
1.1.2 Insurance business on foreign risks, gross premiums								
Life	..	..	..	..	..	..	..	..
Non-life	..	..	..	..	..	..	..	..
Composite	..	..	..	..	..	..	..	..
of which:								
Life	..	..	..	..	..	..	..	..
Non-life	..	..	..	..	..	..	..	..
Total	..	..	..	..	..	..	..	..
1.1.3 Life insurance payments, by class, gross premiums								
Annuities	33 344	31 964	..	20 899	22 295	17 278	..	..
Unit linked	99 537	98 203	..	112 727	114 296	117 452	..	..
Other life insurance	16 864	14 777	..	9 393	11 834	10 622	..	..
Total life insurance	149 745	144 943	163 481	143 018	148 425	145 353	121 964	187 390
***of which:** Pension contracts*	126 173	125 482	143 813	104 333	132 542	128 601	..	..
1.1.4 Non-life insurance payments, by class, gross premiums								
Motor vehicle insurance	12 112	12 786	12 643	12 133	12 069	12 883	18 956	16 564
Marine, aviation and other transport insurance	3 351	3 513	3 634	3 805	3 098	2 604	9 395	9 610
Freight insurance	674	718	778	942	885	808	..	..
Fire and other property damage insurance	15 322	15 413	16 087	16 500	15 969	15 544	30 491	32 392
Pecuniary loss insurance	5 512	5 498	5 707	5 717	5 966	5 791	5 064	5 921
General liability insurance	8 747	8 561	8 750	10 218	10 593	10 308	16 201	16 585
Accident and health	7 244	6 907	7 287	7 895	7 662	7 821	10 872	13 590
***of which:** Health*	..	..	..	..	..	..	8 287	7 817
Other non-life insurance	2 486	2 815	2 442	2 859	2 962	3 177	2 407	2 341
Treaty reinsurance	..	..	..	..	..	..	..	..
Total non-life insurance	55 448	56 212	57 328	60 070	59 206	58 936	93 387	97 003
1.2 Gross claims payments								
Life								
Domestic undertakings	156 626	162 040	166 655	166 084	161 503	172 514	131 443	227 698
Foreign controlled undertakings	35 287	36 240	51 269	42 535	26 653	29 078	..	..
Foreign companies (branches)	3	5	4	-1	4	5	..	..
All undertakings	156 629	162 044	166 658	166 083	161 507	172 518	131 443	227 698
Non-life								
Domestic undertakings	30 795	31 223	30 566	33 152	32 079	30 897	30 260	32 185
Foreign controlled undertakings	14 747	15 499	16 160	17 593	17 062	16 387	..	..
Foreign companies (branches)	1 764	2 082	1 785	1 405	1 469	1 871	43	..
All undertakings	32 560	33 305	32 351	34 557	33 548	32 768	30 303	32 185
Composite								
Domestic undertakings	18 662	19 413	20 735	21 625	22 527	23 077	50 234	64 884
Foreign controlled undertakings	1 293	1 006	615	754	2 170	2 734	..	..
Foreign companies (branches)	2 272	880	1 729	0	0	0	..	..
All undertakings	20 934	20 293	22 464	21 625	22 527	23 077	50 234	64 884
of which:								
Life	19 734	19 063	21 386	20 366	21 254	21 794	23 337	30 083
Domestic undertakings	17 499	18 219	19 657	20 366	21 254	21 794	23 337	30 083
Foreign controlled undertakings	1 040	721	342	326	1 876	2 413	..	..
Foreign companies (branches)	2 235	845	1 729	0	0	0	..	..
All undertakings	19 734	19 063	21 386	20 366	21 254	21 794	23 337	30 083
Non-life	1 200	1 229	1 077	1 259	1 273	1 283	26 897	34 801
Domestic undertakings	1 164	1 194	1 077	1 259	1 273	1 283	26 897	34 801
Foreign controlled undertakings	253	284	273	428	294	321	..	..
Foreign companies (branches)	36	35	0	0	0	0	..	..
All undertakings	1 200	1 229	1 077	1 259	1 273	1 283	26 897	34 801
Total								
Domestic undertakings	206 083	212 675	217 956	220 861	216 108	226 488	211 938	324 767
Foreign controlled undertakings	51 327	52 744	68 043	60 882	45 885	48 198	..	..
Foreign companies (branches)	4 039	2 967	3 517	1 404	1 474	1 875	43	..
All undertakings	210 122	215 642	221 473	222 265	217 582	228 363	211 981	324 767

UNITED KINGDOM

Table 1. Selected aggregates (cont.)

Million GBP

	2010	2011	2012	2013	2014	2015	2016	2017
1.3 Commissions								
Life								
Domestic undertakings	..	..	..	..	..	..	..	..
Foreign controlled undertakings	..	..	..	..	..	..	..	..
Foreign companies (branches)	..	..	..	..	..	..	..	..
All undertakings	..	..	..	..	..	..	..	..
Non-life								
Domestic undertakings	..	..	..	..	..	..	..	..
Foreign controlled undertakings	..	..	..	..	..	..	..	..
Foreign companies (branches)	..	..	..	..	..	..	..	..
All undertakings	..	..	..	..	..	..	..	..
Composite								
Domestic undertakings	..	..	..	..	..	..	..	..
Foreign controlled undertakings	..	..	..	..	..	..	..	..
Foreign companies (branches)	..	..	..	..	..	..	..	..
All undertakings	..	..	..	..	..	..	..	..
of which:								
Life	..	..	..	..	..	..	..	..
Domestic undertakings	..	..	..	..	..	..	..	..
Foreign controlled undertakings	..	..	..	..	..	..	..	..
Foreign companies (branches)	..	..	..	..	..	..	..	..
All undertakings	..	..	..	..	..	..	..	..
Non-life	..	..	..	..	..	..	..	..
Domestic undertakings	..	..	..	..	..	..	..	..
Foreign controlled undertakings	..	..	..	..	..	..	..	..
Foreign companies (branches)	..	..	..	..	..	..	..	..
All undertakings	..	..	..	..	..	..	..	..
Total								
Domestic undertakings	..	..	..	..	..	..	..	..
Foreign controlled undertakings	..	..	..	..	..	..	..	..
Foreign companies (branches)	..	..	..	..	..	..	..	..
All undertakings	..	..	..	..	..	..	..	..
1.4 Gross operating expenses								
Life								
Domestic undertakings	6 464	6 488	6 511	6 453	6 694	6 794	8 085	3 332
Foreign controlled undertakings	740	989	961	976	929	850	..	..
Foreign companies (branches)	1	1	1	0	1	1	..	..
All undertakings	6 466	6 489	6 512	6 453	6 695	6 795	8 085	3 332
Non-life								
Domestic undertakings	5 985	6 110	6 843	7 125	6 782	6 639	15 414	14 910
Foreign controlled undertakings	2 892	2 921	3 168	3 589	3 549	3 562	..	..
Foreign companies (branches)	152	152	200	167	174	186	59	117
All undertakings	6 137	6 262	7 044	7 292	6 956	6 825	15 474	14 910
Composite								
Domestic undertakings	1 701	1 936	1 856	1 978	2 127	2 325	16 675	17 180
Foreign controlled undertakings	262	261	195	172	277	328	..	..
Foreign companies (branches)	77	79	22	0	0	0	..	..
All undertakings	1 778	2 015	1 877	1 978	2 127	2 325	16 675	17 180
of which:								
Life	1 542	1 751	1 637	1 736	1 874	2 038	3 140	2 572
Domestic undertakings	1 501	1 709	1 616	1 736	1 874	2 038	3 140	2 572
Foreign controlled undertakings	163	156	102	91	185	211	..	..
Foreign companies (branches)	41	42	22	0	0	0	..	..
All undertakings	1 542	1 751	1 637	1 736	1 874	2 038	3 140	2 572
Non-life	236	264	240	242	252	287	13 535	14 608
Domestic undertakings	200	227	240	242	252	287	13 535	14 608
Foreign controlled undertakings	98	105	94	82	92	117	..	..
Foreign companies (branches)	36	37	0	0	0	0	..	..
All undertakings	236	264	240	242	252	287	13 535	14 608
Total								
Domestic undertakings	14 150	14 534	15 209	15 556	15 602	15 759	40 174	35 422
Foreign controlled undertakings	3 893	4 171	4 324	4 737	4 754	4 740	..	..
Foreign companies (branches)	230	233	224	167	175	187	59	117
All undertakings	14 381	14 767	15 433	15 723	15 777	15 946	40 234	35 422

UNITED KINGDOM

Table 1. Selected aggregates (cont.)

Million GBP

	2010	2011	2012	2013	2014	2015	2016	2017
1.5 Insurance business written abroad by branches, gross premiums								
Life								
Branches and agencies	..	..	..	..	..	..	..	..
Subsidaries	..	..	..	..	..	..	..	..
Total	..	..	..	..	..	..	..	..
Non-life								
Branches and agencies	..	..	..	..	..	..	..	..
Subsidaries	..	..	..	..	..	..	..	..
Total	..	..	..	..	..	..	..	..
Composite								
Branches and agencies	..	..	..	..	..	..	..	..
Subsidaries	..	..	..	..	..	..	..	..
Total	..	..	..	..	..	..	..	..
of which:								
Life	..	..	..	..	..	..	..	..
Branches and agencies	..	..	..	..	..	..	..	..
Subsidaries	..	..	..	..	..	..	..	..
Total	..	..	..	..	..	..	..	..
Non-life	..	..	..	..	..	..	..	..
Branches and agencies	..	..	..	..	..	..	..	..
Subsidaries	..	..	..	..	..	..	..	..
Total	..	..	..	..	..	..	..	..
Total								
Branches and agencies	..	..	..	..	..	..	..	..
Subsidaries	..	..	..	..	..	..	..	..
Total	..	..	..	..	..	..	..	..

.. Not available

Note: Detailed metadata at: *http://metalinks.oecd.org/ins/20190221/571c.*

Source: OECD Insurance Statistics (database)

UNITED KINGDOM

Table 2. Number of companies and employees

	2010	2011	2012	2013	2014	2015	2016	2017
2.1 Number of companies								
Life								
Domestic undertakings	184	184	184	183	181	181	74	75
Foreign controlled undertakings	15	15	15	15	14	14	..	..
Foreign companies (branches)	1	1	1	1	1	1	1	1
All undertakings	185	185	185	184	182	182	75	76
Non-life								
Domestic undertakings	245	242	234	227	214	209	168	165
Foreign controlled undertakings	106	107	104	99	92	89	..	..
Foreign companies (branches)	16	16	15	10	12	7	13	11
All undertakings	261	258	249	237	226	216	181	176
Composite								
Domestic undertakings	21	21	21	21	25	25	21	22
Foreign controlled undertakings	7	7	7	7	8	8	..	..
Foreign companies (branches)	2	2	2	2	2	2	1	1
All undertakings	23	23	23	23	27	27	22	23
Reinsurance								
Domestic undertakings	32	31	31	30	29	26	16	19
Foreign controlled undertakings	20	20	19	18	16	13	..	..
Foreign companies (branches)	2	2	2	2	2	3	0	0
All undertakings	34	33	33	32	31	29	16	19
Total								
Domestic undertakings	482	478	470	461	449	441	279	281
Foreign controlled undertakings	148	149	145	139	130	124	..	..
Foreign companies (branches)	21	21	20	15	17	13	15	13
All undertakings	503	499	490	476	466	454	294	294
2.2 Number of employees								
Insurance undertakings	..	..	..	..	..	..	..	..
Intermediaries	..	..	..	..	..	..	..	..
Total	..	..	..	..	..	..	..	..

.. Not available

Note: Detailed metadata at: *http://metalinks.oecd.org/ins/20190221/571c.*

Source: OECD Insurance Statistics (database)

UNITED STATES

Table 1. Selected aggregates

Million USD

	2010	2011	2012	2013	2014	2015	2016	2017
1.1 Insurance business written in the reporting country								
1.1.1 Insurance business, by ownership								
Gross premiums								
Domestic undertakings	2 034 932	2 154 120	2 278 908	2 289 259	2 430 627	2 619 954	2 702 786	2 835 259
Foreign controlled undertakings	335 832	349 856	317 074	321 246	330 660	324 083	393 449	401 025
Foreign companies (branches)	629	731	909	662	696	1 129	1 007	1 034
All undertakings	2 035 562	2 154 851	2 279 817	2 289 921	2 431 323	2 621 083	2 703 793	2 836 293
Premiums ceded								
Domestic undertakings	531 114	560 386	601 133	657 662	609 531	713 961	743 307	810 265
Foreign controlled undertakings	163 993	170 330	140 316	175 424	134 223	139 675	195 708	226 256
Foreign companies (branches)	244	254	298	275	287	252	260	274
All undertakings	531 358	560 640	601 431	657 937	609 818	714 213	743 567	810 539
Net written premiums								
Domestic undertakings	1 503 818	1 593 733	1 677 776	1 631 597	1 821 096	1 905 993	1 959 479	2 024 995
Foreign controlled undertakings	171 839	179 526	176 758	145 822	196 437	184 408	197 742	174 769
Foreign companies (branches)	386	478	611	387	409	877	747	760
All undertakings	1 504 204	1 594 211	1 678 387	1 631 984	1 821 505	1 906 870	1 960 226	2 025 755
1.1.2 Insurance business on foreign risks, gross premiums								
Life	34 018	..	38 347	22 113	..	..	..	..
Non-life	..	..	..	..	..	..	..	..
Composite total	..	..	..	..	..	..	..	..
Total	34 018	..	38 347	22 113	..	..	..	..
1.1.3 Life insurance payments, by class, gross premiums								
Annuities	237 782	255 059	272 564	248 568	261 327	264 944	254 313	247 002
Unit linked	..	..	..	..	..	..	..	..
Other life insurance	762 172	811 561	557 259	533 515	527 280	561 674	581 948	612 083
Total life insurance	999 954	1 066 620	829 823	782 083	788 607	826 618	836 261	859 085
***of which:** Pension contracts*	..	..	..	..	..	..	..	..
1.1.4 Non-life insurance payments, by class, gross premiums								
Motor vehicle insurance	312 705	315 167	329 520	342 548	379 889	393 897	422 808	459 200
Marine, aviation and other transport insurance	3 452	3 337	3 545	3 245	3 070	2 911	4 815	2 732
Freight insurance	27 363	28 836	31 107	33 819	36 319	39 175	41 305	43 059
Fire and other property damage insurance	200 755	215 618	224 336	232 328	243 389	248 174	250 765	258 294
Pecuniary loss insurance	35 251	34 165	34 967	35 133	33 690	36 271	38 699	41 003
General liability insurance	170 571	172 997	183 263	191 562	204 069	208 722	211 362	218 298
Accident and health	482 830	516 841	550 291	566 173	646 938	714 394	761 509	799 804
***of which:** Health*	..	..	..	..	..	..	..	..
Other non-life insurance	3 532	3 018	3 179	3 505	3 780	3 728	3 921	4 493
Treaty reinsurance	..	0	..	..	0	0	0	..
Total non-life insurance	1 236 459	1 289 979	1 360 207	1 408 312	1 551 144	1 647 272	1 735 184	1 826 883
1.2 Gross claims payments								
Life								
Domestic undertakings	330 925	345 963	356 040	369 618	357 201	376 240	396 611	416 664
Foreign controlled undertakings	60 398	61 430	66 275	66 267	69 748	68 967	79 082	86 000
Foreign companies (branches)	2 293	0	0	0	0	0	0	0
All undertakings	333 218	345 963	356 040	369 618	357 201	376 240	396 611	416 664
Non-life								
Domestic undertakings	827 860	3 355 889	920 214	917 856	980 750	1 077 317	1 145 423	1 228 757
Foreign controlled undertakings	94 274	539 753	80 801	84 201	76 540	79 309	84 878	95 499
Foreign companies (branches)	309	2 253	723	234	240	359	504	609
All undertakings	828 168	3 358 142	920 937	918 090	980 990	1 077 676	1 145 927	1 229 366
Composite, all undertakings	..	..	..	..	..	..	..	..
Total								
Domestic undertakings	1 158 785	3 701 852	1 276 254	1 287 474	1 337 951	1 453 557	1 542 034	1 645 421
Foreign controlled undertakings	154 672	601 184	147 076	150 468	146 288	148 276	163 960	181 499
Foreign companies (branches)	2 602	2 253	723	234	240	359	504	609
All undertakings	1 161 386	3 704 105	1 276 977	1 287 708	1 338 191	1 453 916	1 542 538	1 646 030
1.3 Commissions								
Life								
Domestic undertakings	..	..	..	..	53 082	56 784	67 963	59 387
Foreign controlled undertakings	..	..	..	..	11 165	10 339	10 639	10 700
Foreign companies (branches)	..	..	..	..	0	0	0	0
All undertakings	..	..	..	..	53 082	56 784	67 963	59 387
Non-life								
Domestic undertakings	..	..	..	..	..	..	..	..
Foreign controlled undertakings	..	..	..	..	..	..	..	..
Foreign companies (branches)	..	..	..	..	..	..	..	..
All undertakings	..	..	..	..	..	..	..	..
Composite, all undertakings	..	..	..	..	..	..	..	..
Total								
Domestic undertakings	..	..	..	..	53 082	56 784	67 963	59 387
Foreign controlled undertakings	..	..	..	..	11 165	10 339	10 639	10 700
Foreign companies (branches)	..	..	..	..	0	0	0	0
All undertakings	..	..	..	..	53 082	56 784	67 963	59 387

UNITED STATES

Table 1. Selected aggregates (cont.)

Million USD

	2010	2011	2012	2013	2014	2015	2016	2017
1.4 Gross operating expenses								
Life								
Domestic undertakings	74 311	66 258	67 534	65 424	67 225	68 488	69 722	75 161
Foreign controlled undertakings	12 817	9 782	9 962	9 814	10 285	9 952	11 175	11 838
Foreign companies (branches)	565	0	0	0	0	0	..	..
All undertakings	74 876	66 258	67 534	65 424	67 225	68 488	69 722	75 161
Non-life								
Domestic undertakings	233 968	239 829	250 270	261 844	281 766	298 911	308 839	310 003
Foreign controlled undertakings	27 537	28 759	22 153	23 185	23 274	23 035	26 711	26 891
Foreign companies (branches)	238	283	312	165	194	410	354	360
All undertakings	234 207	240 112	250 582	262 009	281 960	299 321	309 193	310 363
Composite, all undertakings	..	..	..	..	..	..	..	..
Total								
Domestic undertakings	308 279	306 087	317 804	327 268	348 991	367 399	378 561	385 164
Foreign controlled undertakings	40 354	38 542	32 115	32 999	33 559	32 987	37 886	38 729
Foreign companies (branches)	803	283	312	165	194	410	354	360
All undertakings	309 083	306 370	318 116	327 433	349 185	367 809	378 915	385 524
1.5 Insurance business written abroad by branches, gross premiums								
Life								
Branches and agencies	0	..	..	..	..	..	..	..
Subsidaries	0	..	..	..	..	..	..	..
Total	0	..	..	..	..	..	..	..
Non-life								
Branches and agencies	..	..	..	..	..	..	..	..
Subsidaries	..	..	..	..	..	..	..	..
Total	..	..	..	..	..	..	..	..
Composite total	..	..	..	..	..	..	..	..
Total								
Branches and agencies	0	..	..	..	..	..	..	..
Subsidaries	0	..	..	..	..	..	..	..
Total	0	..	..	..	..	..	..	..

.. Not available

Note: Detailed metadata at: *http://metalinks.oecd.org/ins/20190221/fc9c.*

Source: OECD Insurance Statistics (database)

UNITED STATES

Table 2. Number of companies and employees

	2010	2011	2012	2013	2014	2015	2016	2017
2.1 Number of companies								
Life								
Domestic undertakings	902	904	904	995	1 031	1 030	738	735
Foreign controlled undertakings	166	168	162	156	158	158	168	157
Foreign companies (branches)	0	..	..	..	..	..	..	..
All undertakings	902	904	904	995	1 031	1 030	738	735
Non-life								
Domestic undertakings	3 441	3 426	3 428	3 425	3 404	3 185	3 205	3 419
Foreign controlled undertakings	373	388	407	403	404	390	418	405
Foreign companies (branches)	7	8	9	11	9	13	19	13
All undertakings	3 448	3 434	3 437	3 436	3 413	3 198	3 224	3 432
Composite, all undertakings	**0**	**0**	**0**	**0**	**0**	**0**	**0**	..
Reinsurance								
Domestic undertakings	257	251	250	247	234	354	221	228
Foreign controlled undertakings	84	73	62	65	64	76	52	44
Foreign companies (branches)	2	1	1	1	1	4	2	1
All undertakings	259	252	251	248	235	358	223	229
Total								
Domestic undertakings	4 600	4 581	4 582	4 667	4 669	4 569	4 164	4 382
Foreign controlled undertakings	623	629	631	624	626	624	638	606
Foreign companies (branches)	9	9	10	12	10	17	21	14
All undertakings	4 609	4 590	4 592	4 679	4 679	4 586	4 185	4 396
2.2 Number of employees								
Insurance undertakings	..	..	..	..	..	..	..	..
Intermediaries	..	..	..	..	..	..	..	..
Total	..	..	..	..	..	..	..	..

.. Not available

Note: Detailed metadata at: *http://metalinks.oecd.org/ins/20190221/fc9c.*

Source: OECD Insurance Statistics (database)

ORGANISATION FOR ECONOMIC CO-OPERATION AND DEVELOPMENT

The OECD is a unique forum where governments work together to address the economic, social and environmental challenges of globalisation. The OECD is also at the forefront of efforts to understand and to help governments respond to new developments and concerns, such as corporate governance, the information economy and the challenges of an ageing population. The Organisation provides a setting where governments can compare policy experiences, seek answers to common problems, identify good practice and work to co-ordinate domestic and international policies.

The OECD member countries are: Australia, Austria, Belgium, Canada, Chile, the Czech Republic, Denmark, Estonia, Finland, France, Germany, Greece, Hungary, Iceland, Ireland, Israel, Italy, Japan, Korea, Latvia, Lithuania, Luxembourg, Mexico, the Netherlands, New Zealand, Norway, Poland, Portugal, the Slovak Republic, Slovenia, Spain, Sweden, Switzerland, Turkey, the United Kingdom and the United States. The European Union takes part in the work of the OECD.

OECD Publishing disseminates widely the results of the Organisation's statistics gathering and research on economic, social and environmental issues, as well as the conventions, guidelines and standards agreed by its members.

OECD PUBLISHING, 2, rue André-Pascal, 75775 PARIS CEDEX 16
(21 2018 06 1 P) ISBN 978-92-64-09566-3 – 2019

www.ingramcontent.com/pod-product-compliance
Lightning Source LLC
Chambersburg PA
CBHW061214240926
51846CB00006B/1226